NetWare 5 Administration

The Cram Sheet

This Cram Sheet contains the distilled, key facts about the NetWare 5 Administration exam. Review this information last thing before you enter the test room, paying special attention to those areas where you feel you need the most review. You can transfer any of these facts onto a blank sheet of paper before beginning the exam.

NETWARE OVERVIEW

1. There are five different workstation types that are supported in NetWare 5:
   - DOS
   - Windows
   - OS/2
   - Macintosh
   - Unix

   Of these workstation types, only DOS and Windows-based workstations can be used to manage the NetWare network.

2. NDS is defined as a database in which all the network resources are stored. NDS also verifies that a client is authorized to access a resource and connects the client with that resource.

3. Networks, as defined by Novell, consist of five components:
   - Servers
   - Workstations
   - Peripherals
   - Network boards
   - Communication media

4. Regardless of the number of servers that exist on the network or where the User object is located, only a single logon is required for every NDS tree.

5. The NDS tree has three classes of objects:
   - **[Root]** The top most object in the Directory tree. It cannot be deleted, renamed, or moved. It can contain only Country, Organization, or Alias objects.
   - **Container** An object that contains other container or leaf objects within it. It can be a Country, Organization, or Organizational Unit object.
   - **Leaf** The lowest level of the NDS tree. It cannot contain other objects.

6. The NetWare Administrator program (occasionally called NWAdmin) is used to browse, view, and modify the NDS tree.

7. NDS does not search the entire Directory tree to find a specific object. To find an object that exists in another container, the Directory tree must know its exact context.

8. Context is defined as an object's location in the Directory tree. This allows two objects to have the same common name, as long as the objects are in different containers. The context makes each of these objects unique.

9. There are two types of naming conventions: distinguished name and relative distinguished name. The distinguished name is the combination of the common name and the context of an object. It lists all the objects that exist from the object to the [Root], and it's

WORKSTATION MANAGEMENT USING Z.E.N.WORKS

35. Z.E.N.works allows you to create Workstation Group objects and apply policies to them. This allows you to easily control the way a number of workstations are configured.

36. There are three situations in which workstation information should be updated in the NDS tree:
- When workstations are added, removed, or moved
- When workstations are not accounted for in the NDS tree
- When network boards are replaced in workstations

37. Before Workstation objects can be created in the NDS tree, a user must log in from the workstation. This registers the Workstation object in the NDS tree and allows you to import it.

38. There are three types of Policy Packages:
- Container Policy Package
- User Policy Package
- Workstation Policy Package

The User and Workstation Policy Packages each has three types:
- Windows 3.x
- Windows 95
- Windows NT Policy Packages

39. Z.E.N.works can be used to remotely control workstations using the Remote Control Policy in either the User or Workstation Policy Package.

40. The Help Requester Application can be used to either contact the help desk (if a MAPI-compliant messaging system is in place) or to supply the user with help desk contact information.

NETWARE 5 INSTALLATION

41. The NetWare operating system is composed of three main components:
- Kernel
- Server console
- NetWare Loadable Modules (NLMs)

42. Four types of NLMs are provided with NetWare:
- Disk drivers
- LAN drivers
- Name space modules
- NLM utilities

Certification Insider Press

- NETADMIN
- **NDIR**

Of these tools, only the NetWare Administrator program and NETADMIN can be used to control volume space usage by user. Only NetWare Administrator and FILER can be used to control volume space usage by directory.

23. The directory and file rights are:
    - Supervisor
    - Read
    - Write
    - Create
    - Erase
    - Modify
    - File Scan
    - Access Control

24. A trustee is defined as an object in the access control list (ACL) that has access to an object. There are five different objects that can be designated as a trustee:
    - User
    - Group
    - Organizational Role
    - Parent container
    - [Public]

25. There are two methods to blocking rights from being inherited from a higher level in the tree. First, you can use an Inherited Rights Filter (IRF). Second, you can create a new rights assignment at the lower level.

26. An object's effective rights are the rights that are granted to the object. These rights are calculated from the combination of all rights granted minus the rights blocked by the IRF.

LOGIN SCRIPTS

27. A login script is a set of instructions that the operating system executes during the login process.

28. There are four different types of login scripts. They are executed in the following order:
    - Container
    - Profile
    - User
    - Default

Under no circumstances will all four login scripts be executed at the same time.

29. Up to 16 search drives are supported by NetWare. When NetWare searches the drives, it checks for the files as defined by the **PATH** statement. The current directory is searched followed by the search drives in order.

NDS SECURITY

30. NDS has two sets of rights: object rights and property rights.

31. If the [Root] object is granted rights to the NDS, all users who are successfully logged in are automatically granted rights as well. For this reason, it's recommended that you do not assign the [Root] object as a trustee.

32. The six object rights are:
    - Supervisor
    - Browse
    - Create
    - Delete
    - Inheritable
    - Rename

    The six property rights are:
    - Supervisor
    - Compare
    - Read
    - Write
    - Add/Remove Self
    - Inheritable

33. Use the NetWare Administrator program to determine a user's effective rights.

THE APPLICATION LAUNCHER

34. Application Launcher allows an administrator to install applications to multiple desktops at the same time. It gives the administrator the following benefits:
    - A single-point to administer applications
    - Centralized maintenance and control of applications
    - Push-and-pull software distribution capabilities

unique for each object in the Directory. The relative distinguished name is the path from the current context to the object.

10. There are three different tools that can be used to create User objects in the NDS tree:
    - NetWare Administrator
    - ConsoleOne
    - UIMPORT

11. When creating a User object, two property values are mandatory. You need to enter both the username and the user's last name before you can create the object.

12. When you install NetWare 5, a single User object is created. This object is treated just like any other User object in the NDS tree. This means that you can rename it, move it, or even delete it.

LICENSING AND SECURITY

13. License container objects names are made up of three main attributes: publisher, product, and version. By default, the Admin user is granted ownership of all the licenses. Licenses can be assigned to User, Group, Organization, or Organizational Unit objects only.

14. NetWare has five different security systems:
    - Login
    - File-system
    - Server
    - Networking printing
    - NDS

PRINTING

15. NetWare 5 has replaced the queue-based printing of the previous versions of NetWare with Novell Distributed Printing Services (NDPS). This replaces the Print Queue, Print Server, and Printer objects in NDS. Under NDPS, these three objects are combined into a single entity, called the Printer Agent. Queue-based printing in NetWare 5 can still be used under NDPS because it's backwards compatible with earlier versions of NetWare.

16. NDPS is made up of four major components:
    - Printer Agent
    - NDPS Manager
    - NDPS Gateway
    - NDPS Broker

Of these four, only the NDPS Manager is represented as an object in NDS. Also, there can only be one NDPS Manager object per server. It manages all the Printer Agents.

17. Newer printers are NetWare-aware, meaning that they have a Printer Agent imbedded. If your printer does not have this capability, you'll need to install and configure a gateway. NetWare 5 ships with three different gateways:
    - HP gateway
    - Xerox gateway
    - Novell gateway

18. The NDPS Broker provides three different network services:
    - Service Registry Services (SRS)
    - Event Notification Services (ENS)
    - Resource Management Services (RMS)

    SRS allows public access printers to advertise themselves on the network. ENS allows for notifications to be sent to users or groups about the status of a printer. RMS allows resources to be centrally stored and down-loaded to the workstation when required.

19. There are two types of printers:
    - Public access printers
    - Controlled access printers

    A public access printer does not have an NDS object associated with it. Users located in the same container as a controlled access printer will gain access to it.

THE FILE SYSTEM

20. The NetWare file system is made up of five different components:
    - NetWare server
    - Volumes
    - Directories
    - Subdirectories
    - Files

21. Only the NetWare Administrator program and FILER can be used to salvage deleted files.

22. There are four tools that can be used to view volume space usage information:
    - NetWare Administrator
    - FILER

for
NetWare 5
Administration
CNE/CNA

Barry Shilmover
Doug Bamlett

The Coriolis Group, LLC
14455 N. Hayden Road, Suite 220
Scottsdale, Arizona 85260

480/483-0192
FAX 480/483-0193
http://www.coriolis.com

Library of Congress Cataloging-in-Publication Data
Shilmover, Barry
    Exam cram for NetWare 5 Administration CNE/CNA / by Barry
Shilmover and Doug Bamlett.
        p. cm.
    Includes index.
    ISBN 1-57610-350-1
    1. Electronic data processing personnel--Certification.   2. Microsoft
software--Examinations--Study guides.   3. NetWare (Computer
file)   I. Bamlett, Doug.   II. Title.
QA76.3.S54   1999
005.7'1369--dc21   99-17358
                                                        CIP

Printed in the United States of America
10 9 8 7 6 5 4 3 2 1

Publisher
Keith Weiskamp

Acquisitions Editor
Shari Jo Hehr

Marketing Specialist
Cynthia Caldwell

Project Editor
Jeff Kellum

Technical Reviewer
Todd Meadors

Production Coordinator
Meg E. Turecek

Cover Design
Jody Winkler

Layout Design
April Nielsen

14455 North Hayden Road, Suite 220 • Scottsdale, Arizona 85260

Coriolis: The Training And Certification Destination ™

Thank you for purchasing one of our innovative certification study guides, just one of the many members of the Coriolis family of certification products.

Certification Insider Press™ has long believed that achieving your IT certification is more of a road trip than anything else. This is why most of our readers consider us their *Training And Certification Destination*. By providing a one-stop shop for the most innovative and unique training materials, our readers know we are the first place to look when it comes to achieving their certification. As one reader put it, "I plan on using your books for all of the exams I take."

To help you reach your goals, we've listened to others like you, and we've designed our entire product line around you and the way you like to study, learn, and master challenging subjects. Our approach is *The Smartest Way To Get Certified™*.

In addition to our highly popular *Exam Cram* and *Exam Prep* guides, we have a number of new products. We recently launched Exam Cram Live!, two-day seminars based on *Exam Cram* material. We've also developed a new series of books and study aides—*Practice Tests Exam Crams* and *Exam Cram Flash Cards*—designed to make your studying fun as well as productive.

Our commitment to being the *Training And Certification Destination* does not stop there. We just introduced *Exam Cram Insider*, a biweekly newsletter containing the latest in certification news, study tips, and announcements from Certification Insider Press. (To subscribe, send an email to **eci@coriolis.com** and type "subscribe insider" in the body of the email.) We also recently announced the launch of the Certified Crammer Society and the Coriolis Help Center—two new additions to the Certification Insider Press family.

We'd like to hear from you. Help us continue to provide the very best certification study materials possible. Write us or email us at **cipq@coriolis.com** and let us know how our books have helped you study, or tell us about new features that you'd like us to add. If you send us a story about how we've helped you, and we use it in one of our books, we'll send you an official Coriolis shirt for your efforts.

Good luck with your certification exam and your career. Thank you for allowing us to help you achieve your goals.

Keith Weiskamp
Publisher, Certification Insider Press

About The Authors

Barry Shilmover graduated from the University of Calgary with a Bachelor of Science degree in Mechanical Engineering. The job market for Mechanical Engineers was virtually non-existent, so Barry left for Israel and took the Bio-Medical Engineering Masters program at the Technion Institute of Technology.

Upon returning to Canada, he decided to get into the computer industry. His first "paying" computer job was working for the Calgary Board of Education developing software and evaluating both hardware and software. Shortly after, his department was abolished and he was moved into the networking group.

After about a year of running a 325-node, 8 NetWare-server network at a local high school, Barry helped design and implement the CBEnet project, which used one network to connect all 200 schools.

After leaving the school board, Barry worked for a small Internet service company and a small system integration company. After completing his MCSE, Barry decided that it was time to go off on his own and formed a small consulting company. He holds the MSCE+I, MCT, A+, and CNA certifications as well as instructs at the Southern Alberta Institute of Technology.

Barry currently lives in Calgary, Alberta, with his wife, Shawna, and 14-month-old son, Jory.

Doug Bamlett began his career in Network Engineering in 1987 with his first installation of NetWare version ELS level II. From there, he furthered his studies by obtaining his CNE and taking a variety of digital communications courses at Southern Alberta Institute of Technology and University of Calgary.

He currently operates his company, Common Sense Consulting, which markets, designs, services, and supports local and wide area networks in Alberta and British Columbia.

Doug is currently working on his MCNE and also intends on obtaining his CNI. When he is not bending his brain on digital endeavors, he likes to fly hang-gliders, skiing, surfing, SCUBA diving, and participating in a variety of other sports. He is an avid reader and appreciates fine dining and theater.

Acknowledgments

. . . .

For me, writing this part of the book has always been the toughest part. Most of my thanks have to go to my wife, Shawna. Shawna, without you, none of this would have been possible. You kept me on track when I was ready to quit and put up with my late nights (and there were many) and missed outings. To my son, Jory, what can I say? You make everything worthwhile. Your smile, your laugh, your love means more than you can ever know. During this book we (Shawna, Jory, and I) sold a house, bought a new one, moved, and got very sick (Jory, you had us really worried for a while there). To my family, thanks for putting up with all the lost visits. Yes, I am still alive and hope to see you soon (even though you live in the same city as us). You are the best.

To my co-author, Doug, all that needs to be said is "thanks." It has been a pleasure. To the LANWrights staff, a huge thanks. "Y'all" are the best. Especially to Ed Tittel and Mary Burmeister: Thank you for your support and understanding during the "curse"-mas season. If not for you support and flexibility, I would not have finished this book. Ed, thanks again for allowing me to work with you, it has been (once again) a pleasure. Mary, thanks a million, you are the best editor I have ever worked with.

—*Barry Shilmover*

Thanks to Barry Shilmover, my co-author, for your encouragement and support in writing this book. You're a great team player and always go beyond what is expected of you. Mary Burmeister, you did a fantastic job of keeping me on track, getting the work done, in spite of the hurdles. Ed Tittel, your timely emails were a great source of inspiration to me to stay motivated and produce results. You coach an excellent team!

To my long time customers and now good friends, Bob Keast, Randy Hicks, Joanne Leskow, Wayne Robertson, Diana Wilson, Dave Watkins, Vik Banerjee, Lenny Ansel, and Ron Leech, your friendship and support has contributed a great deal to my success in business.

Acknowledgments

To Pastors Ron Leech, Dave and Gordie Lagore, and Kenneth Copeland: Thanks for your endless spiritual input. My life is substantially richer for the contributions you have made to me. Last, but most importantly, thanks to my parents, Joseph and Lea, for making this possible.

—*Doug Bamlett*

Contents At A Glance

Table Of Contents

Chapter 16
Sample Test **345**

Chapter 17
Answer Key **379**

Glossary **393**

Index **407**

Introduction

Welcome to *Exam Cram for NetWare 5 Administration CNE/CNA*! This book aims to help you get ready to take—and pass—Novell certification Test 050-639, titled "NetWare 5 Administration." This Introduction explains Novell's certification programs in general and talks about how the *Exam Cram* series can help you prepare for Novell's certification tests.

Exam Cram books help you understand and appreciate the subjects and materials you need to pass Novell certification tests. *Exam Cram* books are aimed strictly at test preparation and review. They do not teach you everything you need to know about a topic (such as the ins and outs of designing a Novell Directory Services tree or everything there is to know about Z.E.N.works). Instead, we (the authors) present and dissect the questions and problems we've found that you're likely to encounter on a test. We've worked from Novell's own training materials, preparation guides, and tests, and from a battery of third-party test preparation tools. Our aim is to bring together as much information as possible about Novell certification tests.

Nevertheless, to completely prepare yourself for any Novell test, we recommend that you begin by taking the Self-Assessment included in this book immediately following this Introduction. This tool will help you evaluate your knowledge base against the requirements for a CNE under both ideal and real circumstances.

Based on what you learn from that exercise, you might decide to begin your studies with some classroom training or by reading one of the many study guides available.

> *Note:* When this book was written, there were no study guides on the "NetWare 5 Administration" test.

We also strongly recommend that you install, configure, and fool around with any software that you'll be tested on—especially NetWare 5 itself—because nothing beats hands-on experience and familiarity when it comes to understanding questions you're likely to encounter on a certification test. Book learning is essential, but hands-on experience is the best teacher of all!

Novell Professional Certifications

Novell's various certifications currently encompass six separate programs, each of which boasts its own special acronym (as a would-be certificant, you need to have a high tolerance for alphabet soup of all kinds):

➤ **CNA (Certified Novell Administrator)** This is the least prestigious of all the certification tracks from Novell. Candidates can demonstrate their skills in any of a number of areas of expertise. This certification requires passing one test in any of five tracks. (Three of the tracks are specific to NetWare versions 3.x, 4.x, and 5; two are specific to GroupWise versions. For the purposes of this book, we assume the NetWare 5 track is the one for you.) Table 1 shows the required test for the CNA certification. For more information about this program and its requirements, visit **http://education.novell.com/cna/**.

➤ **CNE (Certified Novell Engineer)** This is the primary target for most people who seek a Novell certification of one kind or another. Candidates who wish to demonstrate their skills in installing and managing NetWare networks make up its primary audience. This certification is obtained by passing six or seven tests, including five or six required core

Table 1   Novell CNA And CNE Requirements*

CNA

Only 1 test required	
Test 050-639	NetWare 5 Administration

CNE

All 5 of these tests are required	
Test 050-639	NetWare 5 Administration
Test 050-632	Networking Technologies
Test 050-640	NetWare 5 Advanced Administration
Test 050-634	NDS Design and Implementation
Test 050-635	Service and Support
Choose 1 elective from this group	
Test 050-629	Securing Intranets with BorderManager
Test 050-628	Network Management Using ManageWise 2.1
Test 050-641	Network Management Using ManageWise 2.6
Test 050-636	intraNetWare: Integrating Windows NT
Test 050-618	GroupWise 5 Administration
Test 050-633	GroupWise 5.5 System Administration

* This is not a complete listing. We have included only those tests needed for the NetWare 5 track. If you are currently a CNE certified in NetWare 4, you need only take the CNE NetWare 4.11 to NetWare 5 Update test (Test 050-638) to be certified in NetWare 5.

tests (depending on which track you pursue) and a single elective. Table 1 shows the required and elective tests for CNE certification in the NetWare 5 track. For more information about this program and its requirements, visit **http://education.novell.com/cne/**.

➤ **MCNE (Master CNE)** Candidates for this certification program must first prove their basic expertise by obtaining CNE certification. To obtain MCNE status, candidates must pass four to six additional tests in any of seven specialized areas. This is Novell's most elite certification. For more information about this program and its requirements, visit **http://education.novell.com/mcne/**.

➤ **CIP (Certified Internet Professional)** This certification program is designed for individuals who seek to step into one or more of a variety of professional Internet roles. These roles include that of Certified Internet Business Strategist, Certified Web Designer, Certified Web Developer, Certified Internet Manager, and Certified Internet Architect. To qualify, candidates must pass anywhere from one to five required tests, depending on which role they seek to fill. For more information about this program and its requirements, visit **http://www.netboss.com/**.

➤ **CNI (Certified Novell Instructor)** Candidates who wish to teach any elements of the Novell official curriculum (and there is usually an official class tied to each of the Novell certification tests) must meet several requirements to obtain CNI certification. They must take a special instructor training class, demonstrate their proficiency in a classroom setting, and take a special version of the test for each certification topic they wish to teach, to show a higher level of knowledge and understanding of the topics involved. For more information about this program and its requirements, visit **http://education.novell.com/cni/**.

Novell also offers a Master CNI (MCNI) credential to exceptional instructors who have two years of CNI teaching experience, and who possess an MCNE certification as well.

➤ **CNS (Certified Novell Salesperson)** This is a newer Novell certification and focuses on the knowledge that sales professionals need to master to present and position Novell's various networking products accurately and professionally. To obtain this certification, an individual must pass a self-study class on sales skills and Novell products, as well as take regular product update training when it becomes available. This level of certification is intended to demonstrate a salesperson's ability to position and represent Novell's many products accurately and fairly. For more information about this program and its requirements, visit **http:// education.novell.com/powersell/**.

Certification is an ongoing activity. Once a Novell product becomes obsolete, Novell certified professionals typically have 12 to 18 months during which they may recertify on new product versions. If individuals do not recertify within the specified period, their certifications become invalid. Because technology keeps changing and new products continually supplant old ones, this should come as no surprise to anyone. Certification is not a one-time achievement, but rather a commitment to a set of evolving tools and technologies.

The best place to keep tabs on Novell's certification program and its various certifications is on the Novell Web site. The current root URL for all Novell certification programs is **http://education.novell.com/certinfo/**. If this URL doesn't work, try searching for "certification" or "certification programs" from Novell's home page (**www.novell.com**). You will then find the latest, most up-to-date information about Novell's certification programs.

Taking A Certification Exam

Alas, testing is not free. Each computer-based Novell test costs $95, and if you don't pass, you may retest for an additional $95 for each additional try. In the United States and Canada, tests are administered by Sylvan Prometric and Virtual University Enterprises (VUE). Here's how you can contact them:

➤ **Sylvan Prometric** Sign up for a test through the company's Web site at **www.slspro.com**. In the United States or Canada, call 800-233-3382; outside that area, call 612-820-5706.

➤ **Virtual University Enterprises** Sign up for a test or get the phone numbers for local testing centers through the Web page at **www.vue.com**. In the United States or Canada, call 800-511-8123 or 888-834-8378; outside North America, call 612-897-7370.

To sign up for a test, you need a valid credit card, or contact either company for mailing instructions to send them a check (in the U.S.). Only when payment is verified, or a check has cleared, can you actually register for a test.

To schedule a test, call the number or visit either of the Web pages at least one day in advance. To cancel or reschedule a test, you must call before 7 P.M. Pacific Standard Time the day before the scheduled test time (or you may be charged, even if you don't show up for the test). When you want to schedule a test, have the following information ready:

➤ Your name, organization, and mailing address.

➤ Your Novell Test ID. (Inside the U.S., this means your Social Security number; citizens of other nations should call ahead to find out what type of identification number is required to register for a test.)

➤ The name and number of the test you wish to take.

➤ A method of payment. (As we've already mentioned, a credit card is the most convenient method, but alternate means can be arranged in advance, if necessary.)

Once you sign up for a test, you'll be informed as to when and where the test is scheduled. Try to arrive at least 15 minutes early. You must supply two forms of identification—one of which must be a photo ID—to be admitted into the testing room.

All tests are completely closed-book. In fact, you will not be allowed to take anything with you into the testing area, but you will be furnished with a blank sheet of paper and a pen or, in some cases, an erasable plastic sheet and an erasable pen. We suggest that you immediately write down on that sheet of paper all the information you've memorized for the test. In *Exam Cram* books, this information appears on a tear-out sheet inside the front cover of each book. You'll have some time to compose yourself, to record this information, and even to take a sample orientation test before you begin the real thing. We suggest you take the orientation test before taking your first test, but because they're all more or less identical in layout, behavior, and controls, you probably won't need to do this more than once.

When you complete a Novell certification test, the software will tell you whether you've passed or failed. Results are broken into topical areas that map to the test's specific test objectives. Even if you fail, we suggest you ask for—and keep—the detailed report that the test administrator should print for you. You should use this report to help you prepare for another go-round, if needed.

If you need to retake a test, you'll have to schedule a new test with Sylvan Prometric or VUE and pay another $95.

 The first time you fail a test, you can retake the test the next day. However, if you fail a second time, you must wait 14 days before retaking that test. The 14-day waiting period remains in effect for all retakes after the first failure.

Tracking Novell Certification Status

As soon as you pass one of the applicable Novell tests, you'll attain Certified NetWare Administrator (CNA) status. Novell also generates transcripts that indicate which tests you have passed and your certification status. You can check (or print) your transcript at any time by visiting the official Novell site for certified professionals through its login page at **http://certification. novell.com/pinlogin.htm**. As the name of the Web page (pinlogin) is meant to suggest, you need an account name and a Personal Identification Number (PIN) to access this page. You'll receive this information by email about two weeks after you pass any exam that might qualify you for CNA or CNE status.

At the Novell certification site, you can also update your personal profile, including your name, address, phone and fax numbers, email address, and other contact information. You can view a list of all certifications that you've received so far and check a complete list of all exams you've taken.

Benefits Of Novell Certification

Once you pass the necessary set of tests (one for CNA, six or seven for CNE, four to six more for the MCNE), you'll become certified (or obtain an additional certification). Official certification normally takes anywhere from four to six weeks, so don't expect to get your credentials overnight. When the package for a qualified certification arrives, it includes a set of materials that contain several important elements:

➤ A certificate, suitable for framing, along with an official membership card.

➤ A license to use the appropriate Novell certified professional logo, which allows you to use that logo in advertisements, promotions, and documents, and on letterhead, business cards, and so on. As part of your certification packet, you'll get a logo sheet, which includes camera-ready artwork. (Note: Before using any artwork, individuals must sign and return a licensing agreement that indicates they'll abide by its terms and conditions.)

➤ A subscription to the *NetWare Connection* magazine, which provides ongoing data about testing and certification activities, requirements, and changes to the program.

➤ Access to a special Web site, commensurate with your current level of certification, through the **http://certification.novell.com/pinlogin.htm** login page. You'll find more than your own personal records here—you'll also find reports of new certification programs, special downloads, practice test information, and other goodies not available to the general public.

Many people believe that the benefits of Novell CNA or CNE certification go well beyond the perks that Novell provides to newly anointed members of these elite groups. For years, job listings have included requirements for CNA, CNE, and so on, and many individuals who complete the program can qualify for increases in pay and/or responsibility. As an official recognition of hard work and broad knowledge, any of the Novell certifications is a badge of honor in many IT organizations, and a requirement for employment in many others.

How To Prepare For An Exam

Preparing for any NetWare-related test (including "NetWare 5 Administration") requires that you obtain and study materials designed to provide comprehensive information about the product and its capabilities that will appear on the specific test for which you are preparing. The following list of materials will help you study and prepare:

➤ The objectives for the course that relates to Test 050-639 appear in the information that Novell provides for Course 560: NetWare 5 Administration. You can read these objectives on the Novell Web site at **http://education.novell.com/testinfo/objectives/560tobj.htm**. These will also define the feedback topics when you take the test, so this document should be an essential part of your planning and preparation for the exam. You might even want to print a copy and use it along with your other study materials.

➤ General information about Novell tests is also available, including what type of test will be delivered for each topic, how many questions you'll see on any given test, the minimum passing score (which Novell calls a "Cut Score") for each test, and the maximum amount of time allotted for each test. All this information is compiled in a table called "Test Data" that you can read at **http://education.novell.com/testinfo/testdata.htm**.

In addition, you'll probably find any or all of the following materials useful as you prepare for the "NetWare 5 Administration" test:

➤ **Novell Course 560: NetWare 5 Administration** Novell Education offers a 5-day, in-depth class that covers the materials for this test at a level intended to permit experienced IT professionals to learn how to install, configure, and manage NetWare 5 with little or no prior experience.

➤ **The Novell Support Connection CD** This monthly CD-based publication delivers numerous electronic titles on topics relevant to NetWare and other key Novell products and topics, primarily, "Monthly Update" CDs (there are two at the time of this writing). Offerings on these CDs include product facts, technical articles and white papers, tools and utilities, and other information.

A subscription to the Novell Support Connection costs $495 per year (a $100 discount is available to all CNEs and MCNEs as one of the benefits of certification), but it is well worth the cost. Visit **http://support.novell.com/** and check out the information under the "Support Connection CD" menu entry for more details.

➤ **Classroom Training** Although you'll find Novell Authorized Education Centers worldwide that teach the official Novell curriculum, unlicensed third-party training companies (such as Wave Technologies, American Research Group, Learning Tree, Data-Tech, and others) offer classroom training on NetWare 5 Administration as well. These companies aim to help you prepare to pass Test 050-639. Although such training runs upwards of $350 per day, most of the individuals lucky enough to partake (including your humble authors, who've even taught such courses) find them to be quite worthwhile.

➤ **Other Publications** You'll find direct references to other resources in this book, but there's no shortage of information available about NetWare 5 Administration. To help you sift through the various offerings available, we end each chapter with a "Need To Know More?" section that provides pointers to more complete and exhaustive resources covering the chapter's subjects. This should give you some idea of where we think you should look for further discussion and more details, if you feel like you need them.

By far, this set of required and recommended materials represents a nonpareil collection of sources and resources for NetWare 5 Administration and related topics. We anticipate that you'll find that this book belongs in this company. In the next section, we explain how this book works, and we give you some good reasons why this book counts as a member of the required and recommended materials list.

About This Book

Each topical *Exam Cram* chapter follows a regular structure, along with graphical cues about important or useful information. Here's the structure of a typical chapter:

➤ **Opening Hotlists** Each chapter begins with a list of the terms, tools, and techniques that you must learn and understand before you can be fully conversant with that chapter's subject matter. We follow the hotlists with one or two introductory paragraphs to set the stage for the rest of the chapter.

➤ **Topical Coverage** After the opening hotlists, each chapter covers a series of topics related to the chapter's subject title. Throughout this section, we highlight topics or concepts likely to appear on a test using a special Exam Alert layout, like this:

This is what an Exam Alert looks like. Normally, an Exam Alert stresses concepts, terms, software, or activities that are likely to relate to one or more certification test questions. For that reason, we think any information found offset in Exam Alert format is worthy of unusual attentiveness on your part. Indeed, most of the information that appears on The Cram Sheet appears as Exam Alerts within the text as well.

Pay close attention to any material flagged as an Exam Alert. Although all the information in this book pertains to what you need to know to pass the exam, we flag certain items that are especially important. You'll find what appears in the meat of each chapter to be worth knowing, too, when preparing for the test. Because this book's material is highly condensed, we recommend that you use this book along with other resources to achieve the maximum benefit.

In addition to the Exam Alerts, we have provided tips that will help you build a better foundation for NetWare 5 Administration knowledge. Although the information may not be on the exam, it's certainly related and will help you become a better test-taker.

 This is how tips are formatted. Keep your eyes open for these, and you'll become a NetWare 5 Administration expert in no time!

➤ **Practice Questions** Although we talk about test questions and topics throughout each chapter, this section presents a series of mock test questions and explanations for both correct and incorrect answers. We also try to point out especially tricky questions by using a special icon, like this:

Ordinarily, this icon flags the presence of a particularly devious inquiry, if not an outright trick question. Trick questions are calculated to be answered incorrectly if not read more than once, and carefully, at that. Although they're not ubiquitous, such questions make occasional appearances on the Novell tests. That's why we say test questions are as much about reading comprehension as they are about knowing your material inside out and backwards.

➤ **Details And Resources** Every chapter ends with a "Need To Know More?" section, which provides direct pointers to Novell and third-party resources offering more details on the chapter's subject. In addition, this section tries to rank or at least rate the quality and thoroughness of the topic's coverage by each resource.

If you find a resource you like in this collection, use it, but don't feel compelled to use all the resources we cite. On the other hand, we recommend only resources we use on a regular basis, so none of our recommendations will be a waste of your time or money. But purchasing them all at once probably represents an expense that many network administrators and would-be CNAs and CNEs might find hard to justify.

The bulk of the book follows this chapter structure slavishly, but there are a few other elements that we'd like to point out. Chapter 16 includes a Sample Test that provides a good review of the material presented throughout the book to ensure you're ready for the exam. Chapter 17 is an Answer Key to the Sample Test that appears in Chapter 16. We suggest you take the sample test when you think you're ready for the "real thing," and that you seek out other practice tests to work on if you don't get at least 77 percent of the questions correct. In addition, you'll find a Glossary, which explains terms, and an index that you can use to track down terms as they appear in the text.

Finally, the tear-out Cram Sheet attached next to the inside front cover of this *Exam Cram* book represents a condensed and compiled collection of facts and tips that we think you should memorize before taking the test. Because you can dump this information out of your head onto a piece of paper before taking the exam, you can master this information by brute force—you need to remember it only long enough to write it down when you walk into the test room. You might even want to look at it in the car or in the lobby of the testing center just before you walk in to take the test.

Novell Terms

While studying for your "NetWare 5 Administration" test, you may come across terms that we represent a certain way in our material, but that are represented differently in other resources. Some of these are as follows:

➤ **NetWare Administrator** You may see this referred to as NWAdmin in some resources; however, NWAdmin is not acknowledged by Novell as a copyrighted term. Try not to confuse NetWare Administrator with NETADMIN, which is the text-based version of NetWare Administrator.

➤ **Network board** A network board is also called a network interface card (NIC), network adapter, network card, and network interface board. Novell uses the term *network board* most often. However, the network board vendors usually refer to network boards as NICs.

➤ **Novell Directory Services (NDS)** You may also see this service referred to as NetWare Directory Services (it even appears as such on Novell's own Web site, www.novell.com). However, the official trademark name is Novell Directory Services.

➤ **NDS tree** The NDS tree is also called the Directory tree and sometime it's simply referred to as the Directory (with a capital D).

➤ **Object Trustees property** This is also called the ACL, and you'll sometimes see it referred to as the Object Trustees (ACL) property.

One general source of confusion (as is the case with NDS) is that sometimes an "N" in an acronym is thought to stand for "NetWare" when it really stands for "Novell." As long as you know the specifics of the utility itself, you should be okay—the name isn't going to be a huge issue.

How To Use This Book

If you're prepping for a first-time test, we've structured the topics in this book to build on one another. Therefore, some topics in later chapters make more sense after you've read earlier chapters. That's why we suggest you read this book from front to back for your initial test preparation. If you need to brush up on a topic or you have to bone up for a second try, use the index or table of contents to go straight to the topics and questions that you need to study. Beyond helping you prepare for the test, we think you'll find this book useful as a tightly focused reference to some of the most important aspects of the "NetWare 5 Administration" test.

Given all the book's elements and its specialized focus, we've tried to create a tool that will help you prepare for—and pass—Novell Test 050-639, "NetWare 5 Administration." Please share your feedback on the book with us, especially if you have ideas about how we can improve it for future test-takers. We'll consider everything you say carefully, and we'll respond to all suggestions.

Send your questions or comments to us at **cipq@coriolis.com** or to our series editor, Ed Tittel, at **etittel@lanw.com**. He coordinates our efforts and ensures that all questions get answered. Please remember to include the title of the book in your message; otherwise, we'll be forced to guess which book you're writing about. And we don't like to guess—we want to *know*! Also, be sure to check out the Web pages at **www.certificationinsider.com** and **www.lanw.com/examcram,** where you'll find information updates, commentary, and certification information.

Thanks, and enjoy the book!

Self-Assessment

Based on recent statistics from Novell, as many as 400,000 individuals are at some stage of the certification process but haven't yet received a CNA, CNE, or other Novell certification. We also know that easily twice that number may be considering whether to obtain a Novell certification of some kind. That's a huge audience!

The reason we included a Self-Assessment in this *Exam Cram* book is to help you evaluate your readiness to tackle CNE (and even the MCNE) certification. It should also help you understand what you need to master the topic of this book—namely, Test 050-639, "NetWare 5 Administration." But before you tackle this Self-Assessment, let's talk about concerns you may face when pursuing a CNE, and what an ideal CNE candidate might look like.

CNEs In The Real World

In the following section, we describe an ideal CNE candidate, knowing full well that only a few real candidates will meet this ideal. In fact, our description of that ideal candidate might seem downright scary. But take heart: Although the requirements to obtain a CNE may seem pretty formidable, they are by no means impossible to meet. However, you should be keenly aware that it does take time, requires some expense, and consumes substantial effort to get through the process.

More than 150,000 CNEs are already certified, so it's obviously an attainable goal. You can get all the real-world motivation you need from knowing that many others have gone before, so you'll be able to follow in their footsteps. If you're willing to tackle the process seriously and do what it takes to obtain the necessary experience and knowledge, you can take—and pass—all the certification tests involved in obtaining a CNE. In fact, we've designed these *Exam Crams* to make it as easy on you as possible to prepare for these exams. But prepare you must!

The same, of course, is true for other Novell certifications, including:

➤ **MCNE (Master CNE)** This certification is like the CNE certification but requires a CNE, plus four to six additional exams, across eight different tracks that cover topics such as network management, connectivity, messaging, Internet solutions, plus a variety of hybrid network environments.

➤ **CNA (Certified Novell Administrator)** This entry-level certification requires passing a single core exam in any one of the five possible NetWare tracks, which include NetWare 3, NetWare 4/intraNetWare, and NetWare 5, plus GroupWise 4 and GroupWise 5. ("NetWare 5 Administration" is the only required test to pass for the NetWare 5 CNA certification.)

➤ **Other Novell certifications** The requirements for these certifications range from two or more tests (Certified Novell Instructor, or CNI) to many tests, plus a requirement for minimum time spent as an instructor (Master CNI).

The Ideal CNE Candidate

Just to give you some idea of what an ideal CNE candidate is like, here are some relevant statistics about the background and experience such an individual might have. Don't worry if you don't meet these qualifications, or don't come that close—this is a far from ideal world, and where you fall short is simply where you'll have more work to do:

➤ Academic or professional training in network theory, concepts, and operations. This includes everything from networking media and transmission techniques through network operating systems, services, protocols, routing algorithms, and applications.

➤ Four-plus years of professional networking experience, including experience with Ethernet, token ring, modems, and other networking media. This must include installation, configuration, upgrade, and troubleshooting experience, plus some experience in working with and supporting users in a networked environment.

➤ Two-plus years in a networked environment that includes hands-on experience with NetWare 4.x and, hopefully, some training on and exposure to NetWare 5 (which only started shipping in August, 1998, so nobody outside Novell has years of experience with it—yet). Some knowledge of NetWare 3.x is also advisable, especially on networks where this product remains in use. Individuals must also acquire a solid understanding of each system's architecture, installation, configuration, maintenance, and troubleshooting techniques. An ability to run down and research information about software, hardware components, systems, and technologies on the Internet and elsewhere is also becoming an essential job skill.

➤ A thorough understanding of key networking protocols, addressing, and name resolution, including Transmission Control Protocol/Internet Protocol (TCP/IP) and Internetwork Packet Exchange/Sequenced Packet Exchange (IPX/SPX). Also, some knowledge of Systems Network Architecture (SNA), Digital Equipment Corporation Network (DECnet), Xerox Network System (XNS), Open Systems Interconnection (OSI), and NetBEUI is strongly recommended.

➤ A thorough understanding of Novell's naming, directory services, and file and print services is absolutely essential.

➤ Familiarity with key NetWare-based TCP/IP-based services, including Hypertext Transfer Protocol (HTTP) Web servers, Dynamic Host Configuration Protocol (DHCP), Domain Name System (DNS), plus familiarity with one or more of the following: BorderManager, NetWare MultiProtocol Router (MPR), ManageWise, and other supporting Novell products and partner offerings.

➤ Working knowledge of Windows NT is an excellent accessory to this collection of facts and skills, including familiarity with Windows NT Server, Windows NT Workstation, and Microsoft implementation of key technologies, such as Internet Information Server (IIS), Internet Explorer, DHCP, Windows Internet Name Service (WINS), and Domain Name Service (DNS).

Fundamentally, this boils down to a bachelor's degree in computer science, plus three or more years of work experience in a technical position involving network design, installation, configuration, and maintenance. We believe that less than half of all CNE candidates meet these requirements, and that, in fact, most meet less than half of these requirements—at least, when they begin the certification process. But because all 150,000 people who already have been certified have survived this ordeal, you can survive it too—especially if you heed what our Self-Assessment can tell you about what you already know and what you need to learn.

Put Yourself To The Test

The following series of questions and observations is designed to help you figure out how much work you must do to pursue Novell certification and what types of resources you may consult on your quest. Be absolutely honest in your answers, or you'll end up wasting money on exams you're not yet ready to take. There are no right or wrong answers, only steps along the path to certification. Only you can decide where you really belong in the broad spectrum of aspiring candidates.

Two things should be clear from the outset, however:

➤ Even a modest background in computer science will be helpful.

➤ Hands-on experience with Novell products and technologies is an essential ingredient to certification success. If you don't already have it, you'll need to get some along the way; if you do already have it, you still need to get more along the way!

Educational Background

1. Have you ever taken any computer-related classes? [Yes or No]

   If Yes, proceed to question 2; if No, proceed to question 4.

2. Have you taken any classes on computer operating systems? [Yes or No]

   If Yes, you'll probably be able to handle Novell's architecture and system component discussions. If you're rusty, brush up on basic operating system concepts, especially virtual memory, multitasking regimens, program load and unload behaviors, and general computer security topics.

   If No, consider some basic reading in this area. We strongly recommend a good general operating systems book, such as *Operating System Concepts*, by Abraham Silberschatz and Peter Baer Galvin (Addison-Wesley, 1997, ISBN 0-201-59113-8). If this title doesn't appeal to you, check out reviews for other, similar titles at your favorite online bookstore.

3. Have you taken any networking concepts or technologies classes? [Yes or No]

   If Yes, you'll probably be able to handle Novell's networking terminology, concepts, and technologies (brace yourself for occasional departures from normal usage). If you're rusty, brush up on basic networking concepts and terminology, especially networking media, transmission types, the OSI reference model, networking protocols and services, and networking technologies, such as Ethernet, token ring, Fiber Distributed Data Interface (FDDI), and wide area network (WAN) links.

   If No, you might want to read several books in this topic area. The two best books that we know of are *Computer Networks, 3rd Edition*, by Andrew S. Tanenbaum (Prentice-Hall, 1996, ISBN 0-13-349945-6) and *Computer Networks and Internets*, by Douglas E. Comer (Prentice-Hall, 1997, ISBN 0-13-239070-1). We also strongly recommend the Laura

Chappell book, *Novell's Guide to LAN/WAN Analysis* (IDG/Novell Press, 1998, ISBN 0-7645-4508-6), for its outstanding coverage of NetWare-related protocols and network behavior. In addition, Sandy Stevens and J.D. Marymee's *Novell's Guide to Bordermanager* (IDG/Novell Press, 1998, ISBN 0-7645-4540-X) is also worth a once-over for those who wish to be well-prepared for CNE topics and concepts.

Skip to the next section, "Hands-On Experience."

4. Have you done any reading on operating systems or networks? [Yes or No]

   If Yes, review the requirements stated in the first paragraphs after questions 2 and 3. If you meet those requirements, move on to the next section, "Hands-On Experience." If No, consult the recommended reading for both topics. A strong background will help you prepare for the Novell exams better than just about anything else.

Hands-On Experience

The most important key to success on all of the Novell tests is hands-on experience, especially with NetWare 4.x, intraNetWare, and NetWare 5, plus the many system services and other software components that cluster around NetWare—such as GroupWise, Novell Directory Services (NDS), and the Netscape FastTrack Server—which appear on many of the Novell certification tests. If we leave you with only one realization after taking this Self-Assessment, it should be that there's no substitute for time spent installing, configuring, and using the various Novell and ancillary products upon which you'll be tested repeatedly and in depth.

5. Have you installed, configured, and worked with:

   ➤ NetWare 3.x? NetWare 4.x? NetWare 5? [Yes or No]

   The more times you answer Yes, the better off you are. Please make sure you understand basic concepts as covered in Test 050-639 and advanced concepts as covered in Test 050-640.

   You should also study the NDS interfaces, utilities, and services for Test 050-634, and plan to take Course 580: Service and Support to prepare yourself for Test 050-635. To succeed on this last exam, you must know how to use the Micro House Support Source product, which costs more than $1,000 for a yearly subscription, but to which you'll have a week's exposure and after-hours access in Course 580.

You can download objectives, practice exams, and other information about Novell exams from the company's education pages on the Web at **http://education.novell.com**. Use the "Test info" link to find specific test information, including objectives, related courses, and so forth.

If you haven't worked with NetWare, NDS, and whatever product or technology you choose for your elective subject, you must obtain one or two machines and a copy of NetWare 5. Then, you must learn the operating system and IPX, TCP/IP, and whatever other software components on which you'll be tested.

In fact, we recommend that you obtain two computers, each with a network board, and set up a two-node network on which to practice. With decent NetWare-capable computers selling for under $600 apiece these days, this shouldn't be too much of a financial hardship. You can download limited use and duration evaluation copies of most Novell products, including NetWare 5, from the company's Web page at **www.novell.com/catalog/evals.html**.

For any and all of these Novell exams, check to see if Novell Press (an imprint of IDG Books Worldwide) offers related titles. Also, David James Clarke IV is working on NetWare 5 upgrades to his outstanding *CNE Study Guide* series. When they become available, they should become essential items in your test preparation toolkit.

6. For any specific Novell product that is not itself an operating system (for example, GroupWise, BorderManager, and so forth), have you installed, configured, used, and upgraded this software? [Yes or No]

If the answer is Yes, skip to the next section, "Testing Your Exam-Readiness." If it's No, you must get some experience. Read on for suggestions on how to do this.

Experience is a must with any Novell product test, be it something as simple as Web Server Management or as challenging as NDS installation and configuration. Here again, you can look for downloadable evaluation copies of whatever software you're studying at **www.novell.com/catalog/evals.html**.

If you have the funds, or your employer will pay your way, consider checking out one or more of the many training options that Novell offers. This could be something as expensive as taking a class at a Novell Authorized Education Center (NAEC), to cheaper options that include Novell's Self-Study Training programs, their video and computer based training options, and even classes that are now available online. Be sure to check out the many training options that Novell itself offers, and that it authorizes third parties to deliver, at **http:// education.novell.com/general/trainopt.htm**.

Before you even think about taking any Novell test, make sure you've spent enough time with the related software to understand how it may be installed and configured, how to maintain such an installation, and how to troubleshoot that software when things go wrong. This will help you in the exam, and in real life!

Testing Your Exam-Readiness

Whether you attend a formal class on a specific topic to get ready for an exam or use written materials to study on your own, some preparation for the Novell certification exams is essential. At $95 a try, pass or fail, you want to do everything you can to pass on your first try. That's where studying comes in.

We have included a practice test in this book, so if you don't score that well on the first test, you need to study more and then locate and tackle a second practice test. If you still don't hit a score of at least 77 percent after two or more tests, keep at it until you get there.

For any given subject, consider taking a class if you've tackled self-study materials, taken the test, and failed anyway. The opportunity to interact with an instructor and fellow students can make all the difference in the world, if you can afford that privilege. For information about Novell courses, visit Novell Education at **http://education.novell.com** and follow the "Training options" link.

If you can't afford to take a class, visit the Novell Education page anyway, because it also includes pointers to a CD that includes free practice exams (it's called the Guide CD, and you can read more about it at **http://education. novell.com/theguide/**). Even if you can't afford to spend much at all, you should still invest in some low-cost practice exams from commercial vendors, because they can help you assess your readiness to pass a test better than any other tool. The following Web sites offer practice exams online for less than $100 apiece (some for significantly less than that):

➤ **www.bfq.com** Beachfront Quizzer

➤ **www.certify.com** CyberPass

➤ **www.stsware.com** Self Test Software

➤ **www.syngress.com** Syngress Software

7. Have you taken a practice exam on your chosen test subject? [Yes or No]

   If Yes, and your score meets or beats the Cut Score for the related Novell test, you're probably ready to tackle the real thing. If your score isn't above that crucial threshold, keep at it until you break that barrier.

   If No, obtain all the free and low-budget practice tests you can find (see the previous list) and get to work. Keep at it until you can break the passing threshold comfortably.

Taking a good-quality practice exam and beating Novell's minimum passing grade, known as the Cut Score, is the best way to assess your test readiness. When we're preparing ourselves, we shoot for 10 percent over the Cut Score—just to leave room for the "weirdness factor" that sometimes shows up on Novell exams.

Assessing Readiness For Test 050-639

In addition to the general exam-readiness information in the previous section, there are several things you can do to prepare for the "NetWare 5 Administration" exam. As you're getting ready for Test 050-639, visit the Novell Education forums online. Sign up at **http://education.novell.com/general/forum-login.htm** (you'll need to agree to the terms and conditions before you can get in, but it's worth it). Once inside these forums, you'll find discussion areas for certification, training, and testing. These are great places to ask questions and get good answers, or simply to watch the questions that others ask (along with the answers, of course).

You should also cruise the Web looking for "braindumps" (recollections of test topics and experiences recorded by others) to help you anticipate topics you're likely to encounter on the test. The Novell certification forum at **http://www. saluki.com:8081/~2** is a good place to start, as are the Forums at **www.theforums.com**, and you can produce numerous additional entry points by visiting Yahoo! or Excite and entering "NetWare braindump" or "Novell braindump" as your search string.

When using any braindump, it's OK to pay attention to information about questions. But you can't always be sure that a braindump's author will also be able to provide correct answers. Thus, use the questions to guide your studies, but don't rely on the answers in a braindump to lead you to the truth. Double-check everything you find in any braindump.

Novell exam mavens also recommend checking the Novell Support Connection CDs for "meaningful technical support issues" that relate to your test's topics. Although we're not sure exactly what the quoted phrase means, we have also noticed some overlap between technical support questions on particular products and troubleshooting questions on the tests for those products. For more information on these CDs, visit **http://support.novell.com/** and click on the "Support Connection CD" link on that page.

Onward, Through The Fog!

Once you've assessed your readiness, undertaken the right background studies, obtained the hands-on experience that will help you understand the products and technologies at work, and reviewed the many sources of information to help you prepare for a test, you'll be ready to take a round of practice tests. When your scores come back positive enough to get you through the exam, you're ready to go after the real thing. If you follow our assessment regimen, you'll not only know what you need to study, but when you're ready to make a test date at Sylvan or VUE. Good luck!

Novell Certification Exams

Terms you'll need to understand:

√ Radio button

√ Checkbox

√ Exhibit

√ Multiple-choice question formats

√ Careful reading

√ Process of elimination

√ Adaptive tests

√ Form (program) tests

√ Simulations

Techniques you'll need to master:

√ Assessing your exam-readiness

√ Preparing to take a certification exam

√ Practicing (to make perfect)

√ Making the best use of the testing software

√ Budgeting your time

√ Guessing (as a last resort)

Exam taking is not something that most people anticipate eagerly, no matter how well prepared they may be. In most cases, familiarity helps offset test anxiety. In plain English, this means you probably won't be as nervous when you take your fourth or fifth Novell certification exam as you'll be when you take your first one.

Whether it's your first exam or your tenth, understanding the details of exam taking (how much time to spend on questions, the environment you'll be in, and so on) and the exam software will help you concentrate on the material rather than on the setting. Likewise, mastering a few basic exam-taking skills should help you recognize—and perhaps even outfox—some of the tricks and snares you're bound to find in some of the exam questions.

This chapter, besides explaining the exam environment and software, describes some proven exam-taking strategies that you should be able to use to your advantage.

Assessing Exam-Readiness

Before you take any more Novell exams, we strongly recommend that you read through and take the Self-Assessment included with this book (it appears just before this chapter, in fact). This will help you compare your knowledge base to the requirements for obtaining a CNE, and it will also help you identify parts of your background or experience that may be in need of improvement, enhancement, or further learning. If you get the right set of basics under your belt, obtaining Novell certification will be that much easier.

Once you've gone through the Self-Assessment, you can remedy those topical areas where your background or experience may not measure up to an ideal certification candidate. But you can also tackle subject matter for individual tests at the same time, so you can continue making progress while you're catching up in some areas.

Once you've worked through an *Exam Cram*, have read the supplementary materials, and have taken the practice test, you'll have a pretty clear idea of when you should be ready to take the real exam. We strongly recommend that you keep practicing until your scores top the 77 percent mark; you may want to give yourself some margin for error, though, because in a real exam situation, stress will play more of a role than when you practice. Once you hit that point, you should be ready to go. But if you get through the practice exam in this book without attaining that score, you should keep taking practice tests and studying the materials until you get there. You'll find more information about other practice-test vendors in the Self-Assessment, along with even more pointers on how to study and prepare. But now, on to the exam!

The Exam Situation

When you arrive at the testing center where you scheduled your exam, you'll need to sign in with an exam coordinator. He or she will ask you to show two forms of identification, one of which must be a photo ID. After you've signed in and your time slot arrives, you'll be asked to deposit any books, bags, cell phones, pagers, or other items you brought with you. Then, you'll be escorted into a closed room. Typically, the room will be furnished with anywhere from one to half a dozen computers, and each workstation will be separated from the others by dividers designed to keep you from seeing what's happening on someone else's computer.

You'll be furnished with a pen or pencil and a blank sheet of paper, or, in some cases, an erasable plastic sheet and an erasable pen. You're allowed to write down anything you want on both sides of this sheet. Before the exam, you should memorize as much of the material that appears on The Cram Sheet (in the front of this book) as you can, so you can write that information on the blank sheet as soon as you are seated in front of the computer. You can refer to your rendition of The Cram Sheet any time you like during the test, but you'll have to surrender the sheet when you leave the room.

Most test rooms feature a wall with a large picture window. This allows the exam coordinator to monitor the room, to prevent exam-takers from talking to one another, and to observe anything out of the ordinary that might go on. The exam coordinator will have preloaded the appropriate Novell certification test—for this book, that's Test 050-639—and you'll be permitted to start as soon as you're seated in front of the computer.

All Novell certification exams allow a certain maximum amount of time in which to complete your work (this time is indicated on the exam by an on-screen counter/clock, so you can check the time remaining whenever you like). Test 050-639, "NetWare 5 Administration," is what Novell calls a *form test* or a *program test*. This means it consists of a fixed set of questions (77). You may take up to 105 minutes to complete this exam. The Cut Score, or minimum passing score, for this test is 614 out of 800 (or 76.75 percent).

All Novell certification exams are computer generated and use a combination of questions that include several multiple-choice formats, interacting with illustrations (sometimes called exhibits), and operating simulations. In short, Novell provides plenty of ways to interact with the test materials, and not only check your mastery of basic facts and figures about NetWare 5, but they also require you to evaluate multiple sets of circumstances or requirements. Sometimes, you'll be asked to give more than one answer to a question (but in these cases, Novell almost always tells you how many answers you'll need to choose).

Sometimes, you'll be asked to select the best or most effective solution to a problem from a range of choices, all of which may be correct from a technical standpoint. Taking such a test is quite an adventure, and it involves real thinking. This book shows you what to expect and how to deal with the potential problems, puzzles, and predicaments.

Many Novell exams, but not the "NetWare 5 Administration" exam, employ more advanced testing capabilities than might immediately meet the eye. Although the questions that appear are still mostly multiple choice, the logic that drives them is more complex than form or program tests (like Test 050-639), which use a fixed sequence of questions. Most Novell tests that cover specific software products employ a sophisticated user interface, which Novell calls a *simulation*, to test your knowledge of the software and systems under consideration in a more or less "live" environment that behaves just like the original.

Eventually, most Novell tests will employ *adaptive testing*, a well-known technique used to establish a test-taker's level of knowledge and product competence. Adaptive exams look the same as form tests, but they interact dynamically with test-takers to discover the level of difficulty at which individual test-takers can answer questions correctly. Normally, when new tests are introduced in beta form (and for some time even after the beta is over), they are form tests. Eventually, most of these tests will be switched over to an adaptive format. That is, once Novell has run its question pool past enough test-takers to derive some statistical notion of how to grade the questions in terms of difficulty, it can then restructure the question pool to make a test adaptive.

On adaptive exams, test-takers with differing levels of knowledge or ability therefore see different sets of questions. Individuals with high levels of knowledge or ability are presented with a smaller set of more difficult questions, whereas individuals with lower levels of knowledge are presented with a larger set of easier questions. Even if two individuals answer the same percentage of questions correctly, the test-taker with a higher knowledge or ability level will score higher because his or her questions are worth more.

Also, the lower-level test-taker will probably answer more questions than his or her more knowledgeable colleague. This explains why adaptive tests use ranges of values to define the number of questions and the amount of time it takes to complete the test. Sooner or later, we expect this test, 050-639, to become adaptive as well.

Adaptive tests work by evaluating the test-taker's most recent answer. A correct answer leads to a more difficult question (and the test software's estimate of the test-taker's knowledge and ability level is raised). An incorrect answer leads to a less difficult question (and the test software's estimate of the test-taker's knowledge and ability level is lowered). This process continues until the test determines a test-taker's true ability level (presenting a minimum of 15 questions to all test-takers). A test concludes when the test-taker's level of accuracy meets a statistically acceptable value (in other words, when his or her performance demonstrates an acceptable level of knowledge and ability) or when the maximum number of items has been presented (in which case, the test-taker is almost certain to fail; no adaptive Novell test will present more than 25 questions to any test-taker).

Novell tests come in one form or the other—either they're form tests or they're adaptive. Thus, you must take the test in whichever form it appears; you can't choose one form over another. But if anything, it pays off even more to prepare thoroughly for an adaptive test than for a form test: The penalties for answering incorrectly are built into the test itself on an adaptive test, whereas the layout remains the same for a form test, no matter how many questions you answer incorrectly.

In the following sections, you'll learn more about what Novell test questions look like and how they must be answered.

Exam Layout And Design

Some exam questions require you to select a single answer, whereas others ask you to select multiple correct answers. The following multiple-choice question requires you to select a single correct answer. Following the question is a brief summary of each potential answer and why it's either right or wrong.

Question 1

Which of the following is not true concerning User objects?

○ a. You can create a User object in NetWare Administrator only.

○ b. You cannot create a User object without an entry in the Last Name field.

○ c. You can assign User objects absolute access to any object, and its properties, in the NDS tree.

○ d. In order to have access to a printer on the network, you must have a Printer object associated with your User object.

The correct answer is a. In addition to NetWare Administrator, you can create User objects in three other NetWare utilities: ConsoleOne, NETADMIN, and UIMPORT. Answers b, c, and d are true, and, therefore, incorrect.

This sample question format corresponds closely to the Novell certification test format—the only difference on the test is that questions are not followed by answers. In the real test, to select an answer, you would position the cursor over the radio button next to the correct answer, item a. Then, you would click the mouse button to select the answer.

Let's examine a question that requires choosing multiple answers. This type of question provides checkboxes rather than radio buttons for marking all appropriate selections.

Question 2

Which of the following are components of the NetWare file system? [Choose the four best answers]

❑ a. Volume

❑ b. Drive

❑ c. Subdirectory

❑ d. CD-ROM

❑ e. Directory

❑ f. File

The correct answers are a, c, e, and f. The five components that make up the NetWare file system are server, volume, directory, subdirectory, and file. A drive is a physical device and, although it contains file-system components, it is not really a component. Therefore, answer b is incorrect. A CD-ROM is not a component of the NetWare file system. Therefore, answer d is incorrect.

Although these two basic types of questions can appear in many forms, they constitute the foundation on which most of Novell's certification test questions rest. More complex questions include exhibits, which are usually screenshots of some kind of network diagram or topology, or simulations, which mock up some NetWare administrative utility, installation program, or other system component. For some of these questions, you'll be asked to make a selection by clicking on a checkbox, entering data into a text entry box, or by clicking on a radio button on a simulated screen. For others, you'll be expected to use the information displayed on a graphic to guide your answer to a question. Because software is involved, familiarity with important

NetWare 5 administrative tools and utilities are your keys to choosing the correct answer(s).

Other questions involving exhibits use charts or network diagrams to help document a workplace scenario that you'll be asked to troubleshoot or configure. Careful attention to such exhibits is the key to success. Be prepared to toggle frequently between the exhibit and the question as you work.

Test-Taking Strategy For Form And Adaptive Tests

When it comes to either kind of Novell test—be it a form test or an adaptive test—one principle applies: Get it right the first time. You cannot elect to skip a question and move on to the next one when taking either of these types of tests. In the form test, the testing software forces you to go on to the next question, with no opportunity to skip ahead or turn back. In the adaptive test, the adaptive testing software uses your answer to the current question to select whatever question it plans to present next. In addition, you can't return to a question once you've answered it on an adaptive test, because the test software gives you only one chance to answer each question.

On an adaptive test, testing continues until the program settles into a reasonably accurate estimate of what you know and can do, taking anywhere between 15 and 25 questions. On a form test, you have to complete an entire series of questions (77 for Test 050-639), which usually takes an hour or longer and involves many more questions than an adaptive test.

The good news about adaptive tests is that if you know your stuff, you'll probably finish in 30 minutes or less; in fact, Novell never schedules more than 60 minutes for any of its adaptive tests. The bad news is that you must really, really know your stuff to do your best on an adaptive test. That's because some questions are difficult enough that you're bound to miss one or two, at a minimum, even if you do know your stuff. So the more you know, the better you'll do on an adaptive test, even accounting for the occasionally brutal questions that appear on these exams.

Of course, it's also true on a form test that you must know your stuff to do your best. But for us, the most profound difference between a form test and an adaptive test is the opportunity to cover a broader range of topics and questions on the form test, versus the randomness of the adaptive test. If the adaptive test engine happens to hit a hole in your knowledge base early on in the testing process, that can make it harder for you to pass, as the test engine probes your knowledge of this topic. On a form test, if some questions hit a hole, you can assume that other questions will appear that you'll be able to answer.

Either way, if you encounter a question on an adaptive test or a form test that you can't answer, you must guess an answer immediately. Because of the way the adaptive software works, you may have to suffer for your guess on the next question if you guess right, because you'll get a more difficult question next! On a form test, at least, a lucky guess won't cost you in terms of the difficulty of the next question (but that may still not prevent that next question from being a real skull-buster, either).

Test-Taking Basics

The most important advice about taking any test is this: Read each question carefully! Some questions may be ambiguous, whereas others use technical terminology in incredibly precise ways. Your authors have taken numerous Novell exams—both practice tests and real tests—and in nearly every instance, we've missed at least one question because we didn't read it closely or carefully enough.

Here are some suggestions on how to deal with the tendency to jump to an answer too quickly:

➤ Make sure you read every word in the question. If you find yourself jumping ahead in the question impatiently, read the question again.

➤ As you read, try to restate the question in your own terms. If you can do this, you should be able to pick the correct answer(s) much more easily.

➤ Some questions may be long and complex, to the point where they fill up more than one screen's worth of information. You might find it worthwhile to take notes on such questions and to summarize the key points in the question so you can refer to them while reading the potential answers to save yourself the effort of ping-ponging up and down the question as you read.

➤ Some questions may remind you of key points about NetWare tools, terms, or technologies that you might want to record for reference later in the test. Even if you can't go back to earlier questions, you can indeed go back through your notes.

Above all, try to deal with each question by thinking through what you know about NetWare 5, the administrative utilities, and other aspects of the system—its characteristics and behaviors, plus all the facts and figures involved. By reviewing what you know (and what you've written down on your information sheet), you'll often recall or understand things sufficiently to determine the answer to the questions you'll encounter on the test.

Question-Handling Strategies

Based on exams we have taken, some interesting trends have become apparent. For those questions that take only a single answer, usually two or three of the answers will be obviously incorrect, and two of the answers will be plausible—of course, only one can be correct. Unless the answer leaps out at you (if it does, reread the question to look for a trick; sometimes those are the ones you're most likely to get wrong), begin the process of answering by eliminating those answers that are most obviously wrong.

Things to look for in obviously wrong answers include spurious menu choices or utility names, nonexistent software options, and terminology you've never seen. If you've done your homework for an exam, no valid information should be completely new to you. In that case, unfamiliar or bizarre terminology probably indicates a totally bogus answer. In fact, recognizing unlikely answers is probably the most significant way in which preparation pays off at test-taking time!

Numerous questions assume that the default behavior of some particular utility is in effect. If you know the defaults and understand what they mean, this knowledge will help you cut through many potentially tricky problems.

Mastering The Inner Game

In the final analysis, knowledge breeds confidence, and confidence breeds success. If you study the material in this book carefully and review all the practice questions at the end of each chapter, you should become aware of those areas where additional learning and study are required.

Next, follow up by reading some or all of the materials recommended in the "Need To Know More?" section at the end of each chapter. The idea is to become familiar enough with the concepts and situations you find in the sample questions that you can reason your way through similar situations on a real test. If you know the material, you have every right to be confident that you can pass the test.

You should also visit (and print or download) the Test Objectives page for Course 560, "NetWare 5 Administration." Here, you'll find a list of 62 specific test objectives that will help guide your study of all the topics and technologies that Novell thinks are relevant to Test 050-639. In fact, you can use this as a kind of road map to help guide your initial studying and to help you focus your efforts as you gear up to take your practice test(s)—and then, for the real thing when you're ready.

After you've worked your way through the book and the test objectives, take the practice test in Chapter 16. This will provide a reality check and help you identify areas to study further. Make sure you follow up and review materials related to the questions you miss on any practice test before scheduling a real test. Only when you've covered all the ground and feel comfortable with the whole scope of the practice test should you take a real one.

 If you take the practice test and don't score at least 77 percent correct, you'll want to practice further. Novell provides free practice tests on its The Guide CD. To obtain this CD, you must contact a local NetWare Authorized Education Center (NAEC) and request that one be sent to you. For more information on how to obtain this CD, you can use the Training Locator on the Novell certification pages at **http://education.novell.com** to locate the NAEC(s) nearest you.

Armed with the information in this book and with the determination to augment your knowledge, you should be able to pass the "NetWare 5 Administration" test. However, you need to work at it, or you'll spend the exam fee more than once before you finally pass. If you prepare seriously, you should do well. Good luck!

Additional Resources

A good source of information about Novell certification tests comes from Novell itself. Because its products and technologies—and the tests that go with them—change frequently, the best place to go for test-related information is online.

If you haven't already visited the Novell Education site, do so right now. The Novell Education home page resides at **http://education.novell.com** (see Figure 1.1).

Note: This page might not be there by the time you read this, or it may be replaced by something new and different, because things change on the Novell site. Should this happen, read the sidebar titled "Coping With Change On The Web."

The menu options on the left side of the home page point to the most important sources of information in these pages. Here are some suggestions of what to check out:

➤ **Training** Use this link to locate an NAEC in your vicinity, to learn more about available training, or to request The Guide CD (which includes practice tests, among other materials).

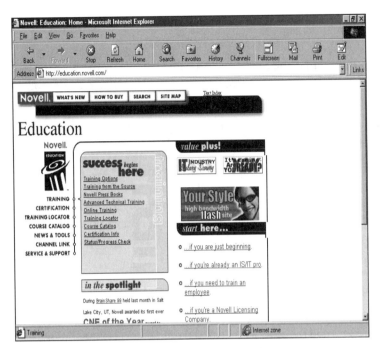

Figure 1.1   The Novell Education home page.

➤ **Certification** This option is the ultimate source of all information about the various Novell certifications. Use this menu entry to find a list of the courses and related tests, including test objectives, test data, a testing FAQ (a list of frequently asked questions about Novell's testing policies, strategies, and requirements), and more.

➤ **News & Tools** Check this item to get news about new tests, updates to existing tests, retirement of obsolete tests, and for information about software and practice tests.

These are just the high points of what's available on the Novell Education pages. As you browse through them—and we strongly recommend that you do—you'll probably find other informational tidbits mentioned that are every bit as interesting and compelling.

The following vendors offer practice tests for Novell certification topics:

➤ **www.bfq.com** is the Beach Front Quizzer Web site. This company makes practice tests for most of the Novell curriculum.

➤ **www.certify.com** is the Cyber Pass Web site. This company makes "CNEQuizr."

➤ **www.stsware.com** is the Self Test Software Web site. This company makes practice tests for most of the Novell curriculum.

➤ **www.syngress.com** is the Syngress Software Web site. This company has a set of NetWare 5 practice exams in the works. Visit the Web site for more information.

You can find still more sources of practice exams on the Internet if you're willing to spend some time using your favorite search engines.

Here's the bottom line about testing readiness: If you don't score 77 percent or better on the practice test in this book, you'll probably be well served by buying one or more additional practice tests to help get you ready for the real thing. It may even be cheaper than taking the Novell test more than once, and it will certainly increase the pool of potential questions to use as practice.

Coping With Change On The Web

Sooner or later, all the information we've shared with you about the Novell Education pages and the other Web-based resources mentioned throughout the rest of this book will go stale or be replaced by newer information. In some cases, the URLs you find here might lead you to their replacements; in other cases, the URLs will go nowhere, leaving you with the dreaded "404 File not found" error message. When that happens, don't give up.

There's always a way to find what you want on the Web if you're willing to invest some time and energy. Most large or complex Web sites—and Novell's qualifies on both counts—offer a search engine. On all of Novell's Web pages, a Search button appears along the top edge of the page. As long as you can get to Novell's Web site (it should stay at **www.novell.com** for a long time), use this tool to help you find what you need.

The more focused you can make a search request, the more likely the results will include information you can use. For example, you can search for the string

```
"training and certification"
```

to produce a lot of data about the subject in general, but if you're looking for the objectives for Test 050-639, "NetWare 5 Administration," you'll be more likely to get there quickly if you use a search string similar to the following:

```
"050-639" AND "objectives"
```

Also, feel free to use general search tools—such as **www.search.com**, **www.altavista.com**, and **www.excite.com**—to look for related information. Although Novell offers great information about its certification tests online, there are plenty of third-party sources of information and assistance that need not follow Novell's party line. Therefore, if you can't find something where the book says it lives, start looking around. If worse comes to worst, you can always email us. We just might have a clue.

Introduction To NetWare 5 Administration

2

Terms you'll need to understand:

✓ Network board

✓ Novell Directory Services (NDS)

✓ Novell Distributed Print Services (NDPS)

✓ Storage Management Services (SMS)

✓ Directory

✓ Object

✓ Property

✓ Value

✓ Object classes

Techniques you'll need to master:

✓ Identifying network components

✓ Understanding the NDS tree

✓ Describing the function of the NDS database

✓ Knowing the responsibilities of a network administrator

✓ Identifying and differentiating network resources and services

✓ Learning the advantages of shared resources

✓ Knowing NDS object classes and the rules that govern their functions

This chapter familiarizes you with the basic components of a network and the details Novell considers to be the necessary "base knowledge" to adequately administer a network. The latter part of the chapter introduces Novell's model for local and wide area network administration—Novell Directory Services (NDS).

You may also see NDS referred to as NetWare Directory Services (it even appears as such on Novell's own Web site). However, the official trademark name is Novell Directory Services.

With a surprisingly straightforward and logical construct, Novell's NDS model utilizes single-login/global access authentication and permits centralized as well as distributed management of network resources. NDS is Novell's answer to an enterprisewide network security system (restrictive or permissive) that allows a "single point of access" (one login ID and password) to all network resources and services—regardless of their locations on the network. Using the analogy of a hierarchical system is one of the best ways to understand NDS. Because NDS is a database of objects that is designed and organized graphically to reflect the structure of your organization, you never need to know on which server the resources are—or where the resources are located—to use or manage them. You can physically move, and even replace, resources, all without affecting the end user.

Network Components

Any functional network that requires administration consists of five major components:

➤ Server

➤ Workstation

➤ Network board

➤ Communication media

➤ Peripheral devices

Each component is itself a subsystem that has its own unique data-management protocols and characteristics. Figure 2.1 shows how these five components function in a network.

Server

A *server* or *file server* is a computer that shares resources and services with other computers that are connected to the same network. (NetWare servers are

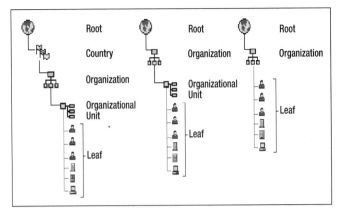

Figure 2.1   How the main components of a network work together.

computers that are running the NetWare operating system.) NetWare 5 must run on at least a 486MHz or Pentium CPU. Other servers or clients (workstations) may access services or resources connected to the NetWare 5 server. NetWare servers are always "dedicated" servers; that is, they cannot be used as workstations while NetWare is running. Servers also provide the following functions:

➤ They enable shared access to services and resources for clients requesting them.

➤ They employ a multitasking operating system that allows multi-user access.

➤ They store programs and data to be shared.

Workstation

Workstations are fully functional PCs that, as a minimum, have their own network board, CPU, and RAM. They usually have their own floppy and hard disk drive(s), but it's possible to have a workstation that has neither a floppy nor a hard drive. These workstations rely totally on the server for their hard-drive space and boot files. They use a "boot prom" on the network board that enables the network board to access the boot files on the server's hard drive. These stripped-down PCs, commonly called "diskless workstations," permit increased security and reduce hardware costs and administration expenses.

NetWare 5 supports the following workstation operating systems:

➤ DOS

➤ Windows 3.1

➤ Windows 95/98

➤ Windows NT 3.*x*, 4

➤ Macintosh

➤ Unix

➤ OS/2

Figure 2.2 shows a NetWare network using most of these operating systems.

Network Board

A network board is a circuit board that plugs into a workstation's or server's motherboard expansion slot; the network board is essential for a PC to connect to the rest of the network. This is accomplished through a media cable that plugs into the network board and conducts digitally formatted data to and from other network resources.

> *Note: A network board is also called a network interface card (NIC), network adapter, and network interface board. Novell uses the term network board most often.*

Communication Media

Typically, communication media consists of network cabling that connects the various devices used in a network, although communication media can also consist of "unbounded media" such as satellite or infrared devices. The type of

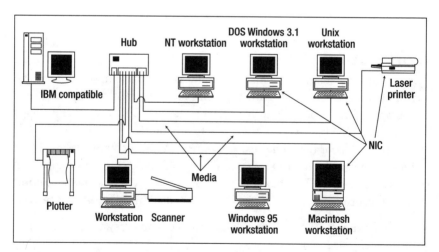

Figure 2.2   A NetWare network using multiple types of operating systems.

cable most commonly used (unshielded twisted pair, or UTP) is much like telephone cable, but it has slightly larger connectors that hold eight wires instead of a telephone line's four. Most cable installed in buildings today is category 5 specification (CAT5) UTP. Some other popular cable types are:

➤ Coaxial (TV) cable

➤ Coaxial (network) cable, in either AUI (thicknet) or BNC (thinnet) flavors

➤ Fiber optic cable

Peripheral Devices

Peripheral devices are any devices that are attached to a computer and are not an integral component of a workstation or server. Some peripheral devices include:

➤ CD-ROM drives

➤ Plotters

➤ Optical drives

➤ Printers

➤ Scanners

➤ Tape drives

➤ Jaz or Zip drives

➤ Jukebox storage devices

Network Administration

Once the network is installed, you'll perform several essential duties as a NetWare administrator to keep the network functioning properly. These duties involve setting up network services and configuring network resources. Understanding and executing these functions efficiently will largely determine whether the network serves the end users well—or whether it causes them grief. To properly administer a NetWare network, you need to understand the purposes of the NetWare server and operating system:

➤ **NetWare operating system** The purpose of an operating system is to provide a multiuser (and, hence, multitasking) engine that enables the connection of resources and includes interfaces that permit the management of those resources and their related services. The NetWare operating system's suite of components allows you to configure devices to communicate with each other, which facilitates the sharing of resources on the network.

➤ **NetWare server** The NetWare server console is unlike any workstation operating system you may have encountered. Typically, you use the server to load and unload server-based software modules, install and/or configure server components (such as storage devices, network boards, and tape drives), and set performance parameters that govern the efficiency of the server in handling client or device requests. Certain server utilities are also run on the server. An example is DSREPAIR, which is used to resolve NDS database corruption.

Administrative Responsibilities

As a NetWare administrator, you must maintain a variety of resources and services. Your two main areas of responsibility involve network resources and network services. A *network resource* is a physical or logical device, such as a shared plotter or a NetWare volume, whereas a *network service* is the means by which a network resource is delivered to the network.

You need to master several network resource management activities. You must be able to set up services on the network and organize, configure, and document your activities. You also need to know how to use the NetWare security systems to protect your applications and data. You should also be able to provide redundancy through some type of effective backup scheme.

As a network administrator, you must know how to set up, configure, organize, document, and otherwise manage the following NetWare 5 services:

➤ **Novell Directory Services (NDS)** NDS is a database of objects representing logical or physical resources on the network. It is responsible for authenticating objects, requesting access to resources, validating those requests against security assignments made to those objects, and permitting or denying access to those resources. While administering NDS, you'll have to create User objects, configure security assignments, and set up login procedures.

➤ **NetWare file system** The NetWare file system is NetWare's way of handling files and directories on a hard drive. Disk drives that are attached to file servers and configured for use by the NetWare server are shared by clients requesting access to the data stored on them. Information on NetWare networks is stored in files. As the administrator, it's your job to design the directory structure and secure the files and directories from accidental or intentional changes while, at the same time, making the appropriate applications and data files available to those clients and users authorized to access them.

➤ **Novell Distributed Print Services (NDPS)** NDPS is Novell's printing service. Printers can be shared on the network via a dedicated print-serving device, or they can be attached directly to a workstation or file server. It's your duty to configure printer access and to troubleshoot any situations that arise from a user's inability to access a printer.

➤ **Novell Application Launcher (NAL)** NAL is NetWare's answer to the vast amount of time network administrators spend installing applications. With this object-oriented approach to distributing applications to workstations on the network, end users can access applications simply by clicking on an object's icon. The main purpose of Application Launcher is to provide a pull technology that allows your end users to access applications with unprecedented ease.

➤ **Security** One of your most important duties as an administrator is to maintain control over who has—and doesn't have—access to network resources. Each network service has its unique application of security that you must learn and apply to secure every aspect of the network from accidental or intentional intrusion.

➤ **Storage Management Services (SMS)** SMS is a suite of services that communicates with backup devices and ensures that data is properly formatted for backup, thus allowing the data to be easily retrieved in case you need to restore lost or corrupted files.

Network Administration Duties

A NetWare administrator has many areas of responsibilities, such as network management, data protection, disaster recovery schemes, configuration of work-stations, clients, servers, print servers, printers, and applications. Some specific duties include the following:

➤ **Documentation** You need to maintain a current printed copy of the NDS directory structure, as well as a list of users and groups, and their rights and access privileges. You also need to keep a record of important security decisions and policies.

➤ **Backup** You should create, configure, and implement a system for maintaining duplicate copies of company data and applications so that any part of the network's data or configuration can be restored on short notice. You should also have a disaster recovery procedure that has been documented and tested before a disaster ever occurs.

➤ **Protection** You need to establish network-auditing procedures so that intrusive activities on the network are detected and dealt with appropriately. You're also responsible for monitoring and testing data integrity and security procedures.

➤ **Management** You need to consider the management of the network as a whole. Two key network management functions are security and printing. You'll generally collaborate with corporate managers and end users to design, implement, and maintain a functional security system. You'll also design, configure, test, and troubleshoot the network printing system.

Novell Directory Services (NDS)

The balance of this chapter concerns itself with the basic concepts that are the foundation of all NDS functionality created so far. We've discussed the resources and services you'll administer, and most of this administration is done using NetWare's graphical administration utility, commonly referred to as NetWare Administrator, or its text-based counterpart, NETADMIN.

NDS Design

Much has gone into the design of NDS to make it a streamlined, coherent model for organizing and managing network resources. Some fundamental aspects of NDS design that govern the function and operation of NDS are as follows:

➤ **Servers** All NetWare 5 servers include NDS.

➤ **Clients** All clients wanting access to a resource in the NDS tree must access that resource through NDS. This makes NDS a fundamental network service.

➤ **Resources** All NetWare 5 servers on the same network have access to every resource on that network because they all use the same directory.

➤ **Access** NDS is the means by which an administrator keeps track of and manages an entire network of resources from one access point instead of having to visit servers on an individual basis in different locations.

➤ **Location independent** NDS locates resources in its database, finds the resource, and provides it to a client that it has validated. It enables access to the resource without the user or client ever having to know the geographical location of the resource or on which server it resides.

In some Novell documentation, the Novell Directory Services (NDS) database is referred to simply as Directory. Therefore, when you see the word "Directory" capitalized in this book, it refers to the Novell Directory Services database—not a directory in the NetWare file system.

➤ **Naming** Resources in the NDS tree are differentiated by their name, with each object having a unique name. Novell has created a naming convention that identifies the object according to its location in the NDS tree.

➤ **Directory location** All NetWare 5 servers must use the NDS to function on the network. On any given server, you could have the entire NDS, segments of it, or none of it. Any server will, at the very least, contain references to the NDS's location that permit the server to access the entire Directory.

Directory Structure

The Directory structure consists of objects represented hierarchically by graphical symbols. There are really only three types of objects. The first two types are those that contain objects, called *container objects*, and those that represent resources or services on the network, called *leaf objects*. The third type of object is a superset of a container object that is referred to as the *[Root]* object, which basically contains the entire database and has its own characteristics. The directory is composed entirely of objects that have properties and values. Objects, properties, and values are defined as follows:

➤ **Objects** An *object* is a graphically represented collection of information about a resource. Every resource shared on the network is represented by its own object in the database. Objects can represent physical resources (such as servers or printers), organizational resources (which are container objects), or an NDS resource (such as a User, Group, or Profile object).

➤ **Properties** *Properties* are like database fields. For an object that is a User object, you could have properties like *first name*, *last name*, and *title*. All of the "types" of information that give the object its unique characteristics are its properties. (What distinguishes one type of object from another is the differences in its properties.)

➤ **Values** An object has properties that contain data called *values*. A value is data entered into a property. For example, the property *first name* in the User object could be the value Jim, Karen, Samantha, Alice, or Jack (or any other first name you could dream up). An object's values are the data entries that distinguish it from another object of the same type.

You can create some objects only if certain properties are filled in. For example, you can create a User object only if it has a login name and a last name. Multi-valued properties are properties that can contain more than one value. The User object property, for instance, can hold numerous telephone numbers.

Object Classes

As mentioned previously, NDS objects are of three classes or types: [Root], container, and leaf. Figure 2.3 illustrates the nature of these three object types, which we'll cover in more detail in the following sections.

[Root] Object

There will be only one [Root] object in any NDS tree, and its primary function is to contain other container objects. (The [Root] object is not generally classified as a container object but its properties are such that it's more like a container object than a leaf object because it contains other objects.)

 Because it's the base object that ultimately contains all other objects, the [Root] object really contains the entire NDS tree and is therefore called a container object.

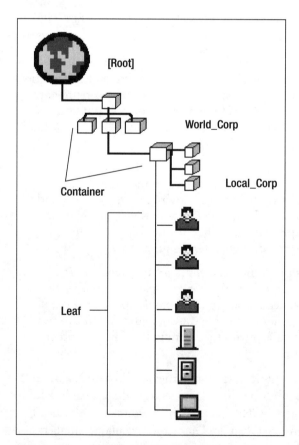

Figure 2.3   [Root], container, and leaf objects as they appear in NetWare Administrator.

The [Root] object has unique properties that make it different from other container objects:

➤ The [Root] object is generated automatically during the NDS installation. You cannot intentionally create a [Root] object without doing a complete installation of NDS.

➤ The [Root] object does not have any properties fields that can contain values.

➤ You cannot delete, rename, or move the [Root] object.

➤ The [Root] object has its name, [Root], assigned by NDS when the Directory tree is created; you cannot change it. It's the first and primary object in the tree and it's always called [Root], regardless of the tree name. Do not confuse it with the NDS tree itself, which has a name that you assign when you install NDS.

➤ You must use the square brackets, [ ], when referencing the [Root] object.

➤ Only Country, Organization, and Alias objects can be created directly under the [Root] object.

➤ You can grant trustee assignments to the whole NDS tree from the [Root] object.

Container Objects

Container objects are analogous to the DOS directories and Windows folders that organize your files. As their name implies, container objects are containers that hold other objects. This adds flexibility to NDS and makes organizing objects easier. Container objects typically represent countries, corporations, departments, or other logical divisions—such as cities, workgroups, or groups of network resources (like printers or volumes). Container objects can be grouped into three subsets or classes: Country, Organization, and Organizational Unit, as shown in Figure 2.4.

The Country object rules are:

➤ It uses only a valid two-letter international character code to name it, such as US, UK, CA.

➤ It can be created only in the [Root] object.

➤ It's not a required object.

➤ It's used to divide the NDS tree by countries.

The Organization object rules are:

➤ The object name must be 64 characters or fewer.

➤ It can exist only in the [Root] or Country object.

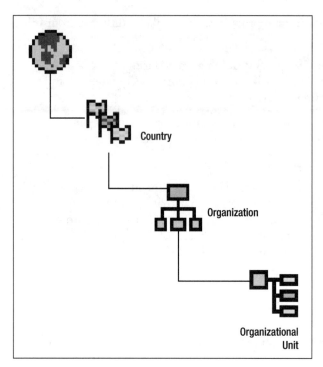

Figure 2.4 The three classes of container objects: Country, Organization, and Organizational Unit.

➤ It's a required object. NetWare will not let you create the NDS tree without creating an Organization object.

➤ It's used to divide the NDS tree by organizational groups, such as city, company, college, or department.

The Organizational Unit object rules are:

➤ Its object name must be 64 characters or fewer.

➤ It can only exist in Organization objects or Organizational Unit objects.

➤ It's not a required object.

➤ It's used to divide the NDS tree into convenient groups. Some typical groups would include departments, workgroups, project teams, object types, or network resource groups, such as printers, plotters, backup devices, and servers.

Leaf Objects

From an NDS point of view, leaf objects do not contain anything. Leaf objects represent network resources such as printers, User objects, workstations, file

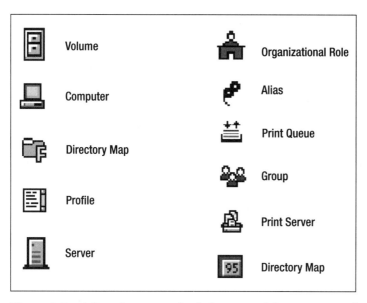

Figure 2.5   A list of common leaf objects and their associated icons.

servers, Group objects, and so on. A more complete list is referenced in the examples of common leaf objects shown in Figure 2.5.

 A common mistake is to think of an NDS Volume object (which is a leaf object) as a container object. Although a Volume object seems to contain the files and directories on a server, it does not actually contain any NDS objects. Therefore, it's not a container object.

The Directory Tree Structure

The purpose of NDS is to provide a sophisticated layer of security that protects the entire network but yet allows access to various network resources without burdening the user with multiple passwords and IDs. To access NDS, you log in with a single username and password. NDS verifies that the object name (login ID) you entered exists in the database. Once NDS verifies your login ID, it grants you access to all of the network resources assigned to your ID.

The process by which NDS grants user permission is described in the following steps:

1. A client makes a request for a resource.

2. The NetWare server responds to the request.

3. NDS locates the object in its directory.

4. The physical location of the object is identified.

5. The existence and security assignments of the client are verified.

6. The client is connected to the requested resource.

The NDS tree is best viewed through the NetWare Administrator utility, which is a graphical interface that runs on Windows (version 3.1 and later). It's used as an administrative tool to view, organize, and otherwise manage NDS objects. The tree is hierarchical in nature because the properties of the various object classes tend to enforce it. Figure 2.6 shows a simple NDS tree with the [Root] object, a single Organization object (CSC), and several leaf objects.

A popular method of analogy for the NDS tree is to compare it with the DOS directory structure. Although there are similarities, only three are of any consequence:

➤ DOS has a root directory on every drive that contains all the other directories, and the NDS tree has a [Root] object that effectively contains all the other objects.

➤ DOS has directories that hold other objects (files and directories), and NDS has container objects that also hold other objects (container and leaf).

➤ DOS objects (files and directories) require names to exist, and NDS objects require names to exist.

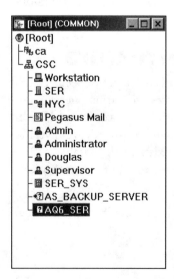

Figure 2.6   The NDS tree from the NetWare Administrator.

Sometimes the analogy tends to confuse more than it helps. The reason is that the differences outnumber the similarities, and it's precisely these differences that make NDS the tool that it is. The analogy tends to break down quickly for the following reasons:

➤ The NDS tree container objects do not contain data files.

➤ The DOS directory structure does not support object classes. All directories are the same in nature: There are no directory "types."

➤ Trustee security assignments don't exist in DOS.

➤ Excluding the name, DOS directories do not have property fields that contain user-definable parameters.

➤ DOS is a disk operating system, whereas NDS is a security system.

➤ NDS is a relational database, whereas DOS could be compared as "the most basic of flat file databases."

➤ NDS uses a graphical depiction of its objects, and DOS uses only text.

➤ DOS uses typed commands to execute management functions, whereas NDS uses mouse-enabled drag-and-drop technology, point-and-click selection, and execution of sophisticated tasks (as well as many more features too numerous too list).

➤ NDS is not a tool for organizing data, whereas DOS is. NDS is a network-resource management tool used to assign or revoke rights to objects attempting to access network resources. If security were not an issue, there would be no need for NDS.

➤ Files in DOS, which are often analogized to leaf objects, are quite different from leaf objects. A file generally contains either data or executable code, whereas a leaf object is representative of a network resource in that it contains information and access rights for that specific resource.

NDS's Hierarchical Structure

Because of the design of the objects in the NDS tree structure, users are forced to employ a hierarchical layout when they organize NDS objects. Each of the three classes of container objects has been designed around different rules that determine where these objects can exist in the NDS tree. Each class has different properties that enhance the usefulness of these organizational tools.

Three major hierarchical structures result from using the NDS container objects, as shown in Figure 2.7. Note the use of both Country and Organizational Unit objects in the left tree and the absence of them in the right tree.

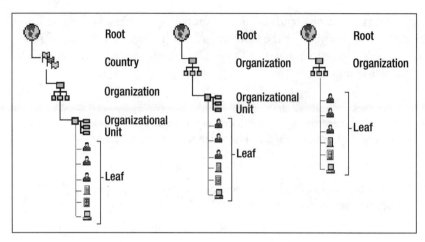

Figure 2.7 Three configurations of the NDS tree structure, made possible by the use of hierarchically differentiated container objects.

NDS Container Object Rules

Rules that govern the NDS container objects form the basis of the entire organizational structure of the NDS tree. The restrictions placed on each container object result in the following conditions:

➤ The [Root] object can only be at the top. You can create only Alias, Country, and Organization objects in the [Root] object.

➤ In a Country object, you can create only Alias and Organization objects.

➤ In an Organization object, you can create only leaf and Organizational Unit objects.

➤ In an Organizational Unit object, you can create only leaf and Organizational Unit objects.

Practice Questions

Question 1

> Which of the following components are peripheral devices? [Choose the three best answers]
>
> ❑ a. External CD-ROM drive
>
> ❑ b. Network board
>
> ❑ c. Laser printer
>
> ❑ d. Scanner

The correct answers are a, c, and d. Network boards are internal to a PC or server. Therefore, answer b is incorrect.

Question 2

> Which of the following are characteristics of a NetWare server? [Choose the three best answers]
>
> ❑ a. A NetWare server has a multitasking operating system.
>
> ❑ b. A NetWare server can act as a server and workstation at the same time.
>
> ❑ c. A NetWare server is used primarily to store and share programs and/or data.
>
> ❑ d. Access to file server resources is done through a client.

The correct answers are a, c, and d. NetWare servers don't have workstation capabilities. Therefore, answer b is incorrect.

Question 3

Which of the following duties are typically the responsibility of a NetWare administrator? [Choose the three best answers]

❏ a. Setting up network printing

❏ b. Installing clients on workstations

❏ c. Installing NetWare 5 on file servers

❏ d. Repairing workstation PCs

The correct answers are a, b, and c. Administrators are generally expected to install operating systems and clients, and also to set up printing. Repairing PCs is strictly a hardware problem and is not typically assigned to a network administrator. Therefore, answer d is incorrect.

Question 4

Which statement is true of the responsibilities normally assigned to a network administrator?

○ a. An administrator must document security decisions and policies.

○ b. An administrator must keep track of the IS budget.

○ c. An administrator should set up training sessions for end users.

○ d. An administrator is responsible for exchanging defective PCs.

The correct answer is a. Part of an administrator's responsibility is to document security issues. Budget, training, and PC replacement could be assigned to a network administrator, but they usually are not. Therefore, answers b, c, and d are incorrect.

Question 5

Which of the following are NetWare services or network resources? [Choose the three best answers]

❏ a. NetWare File System

❏ b. Application Launcher

❏ c. Storage Management Services

❏ d. Novell Distributed Directory Services

The correct answers are a, b, and c. There's no such thing as Novell Distributed Directory Services. Therefore, answer d is incorrect.

Question 6

Which of the following are characteristics of the NDS design? [Choose the three best answers]

❏ a. All NetWare 5 servers on any given multiserver network contain NDS.

❏ b. All NetWare 5 servers on any given multiserver network have access to any part of the NDS tree.

❏ c. No resource on a NetWare 5 network may be accessed except through NDS.

❏ d. NetWare 5 can run without NDS, if it's run as a standalone server.

The correct answers to this question are a, b, and c. NDS is required on all servers or you cannot be authenticated to access resources. Therefore, answer d is incorrect.

Question 7

NDS has only three types of leaf objects.

○ a. True

○ b. False

The correct answer is b, false. There are more than three types of leaf objects.

Question 8

The Country object is not a required object.

○ a. True

○ b. False

The correct answer is b, false. The Country object is required.

Question 9

Which of the following statements are true concerning the [Root] object? [Choose the three best answers]

❑ a. It's a container object that contains the entire NDS tree.

❑ b. It can only be replicated using other third-party utilities.

❑ c. It's impossible to delete.

❑ d. It's impossible to create.

❑ e. It can only be renamed when the tree is reinstalled.

The correct answers are a, c, and d. The [Root] object cannot be replicated at all, and it cannot be renamed. Therefore, answers b and e are incorrect.

Question 10

What type of objects can an Organization object contain? [Choose the two best answers]

❑ a. [Root]

❑ b. Country

❑ c. Organization

❑ d. Organizational Unit

❑ e. Leaf

The correct answers are d and e. Organization objects may contain only Organizational Unit objects or leaf objects. An Organization object cannot contain itself, [Root], or Country objects. Therefore, answers a, b, and c are incorrect.

Question 11

What objects can an Organizational Unit object not contain? [Choose the two best answers]

❑ a. [Root]

❑ b. Country

❑ c. Organization

❑ d. Organizational Unit

❑ e. Leaf

The correct answers are a, b, and c. Organizational Unit objects can only contain other Organizational Unit objects or leaf objects. Therefore, answers d and e are incorrect.

Question 12

What types of objects can a leaf object contain?

○ a. None

○ b. Organizational Unit

○ c. Organization

○ d. Leaf

○ e. Container

The correct answer is a. Leaf objects cannot contain other objects. Therefore, answers b, c, d, and e are all incorrect.

Question 13

Which statement is true regarding NDS objects?

○ a. They all have definable properties and values.

○ b. They may all be named using 64 or fewer characters.

○ c. All three types of container objects are not required to create an NDS tree.

○ d. All container objects may contain leaf objects.

The correct answer is b. The rule is that NDS objects can be named using 64 or fewer characters. The [Root] object does not have definable properties and values. Therefore, answer a is incorrect. Country and Organizational Unit objects are not required objects. Therefore, answer c is incorrect. Country objects cannot contain leaf objects. Therefore, answer d is incorrect.

Question 14

What was the NDS tree designed to accomplish? [Choose the two best answers]

- ❑ a. Provide a single user ID and password to gain access to any peripheral
- ❑ b. Provide superior network security
- ❑ c. Provide global management from a centralized location
- ❑ d. Provide enhanced file access

The correct answers are b and c. NDS was designed to provide more global access to "shared" resources—not just any peripheral. Therefore, answer a is incorrect Answer d is incorrect because NDS is not concerned with file access.

Question 15

Which of the following are main similarities between DOS and NDS? [Choose the three best answers]

- ❑ a. DOS has a root directory and NDS also has a [Root] object.
- ❑ b. Both DOS and NDS have directories that contain other objects.
- ❑ c. DOS has data files in directories and NDS has data files in volume objects.
- ❑ d. DOS and NDS objects both require names to be created.

The correct answers are a, b, and d. DOS and NDS both have root objects. Therefore, answer a is correct. DOS has directories, which are containers, and NDS has container objects. Therefore, answer b is correct. DOS files and directories require names and NDS objects require names. Therefore, answer d is correct. Answer c is incorrect because data files are not NDS objects.

Need To Know More?

 Novell course 560 manual. *Netware 5 Administration*. Novell, Inc., 1998. This manual is available from Novell (1-800-NetWare) or from any authorized Novell training center.

 Search the Help menu in the NetWare Administrator utility. Choose Find and then type in "object." Then choose the object type, such as "Organizational Unit" or "leaf."

 www.novell.com/documentation/en/nw5/nw5/docui/index.html contains a copy of the NetWare 5 documentation.

 www.novell.com/netware5/demo.html is Novell's Web site where you can order your own live copy of NetWare 5. You may also call 1-800-NetWare to order live demo copies of NetWare 5.

Using NetWare Administrator

Terms you'll need to understand:

√ NDS objects

√ Container objects

√ Leaf objects

√ Context

√ Common name

√ Current context

√ Relative distinguished name

√ Distinguished name

√ Trailing periods

√ Typeful and typeless naming

Techniques you'll need to master:

√ Using NetWare Administrator to modify the NDS tree structure

√ Finding objects with the NetWare Administrator utility

√ Understanding object-naming terminology

The NetWare Administrator utility is one of the most important and most commonly used utilities in NetWare 5. All objects within your network, including users, groups, security, printing, and the file system, are managed by this utility. In this chapter, you'll learn the basics of NetWare Administrator and how to use it.

Running NetWare Administrator

The NetWare Administrator utility is stored on the server, rather than on each of the individual client machines. When you first install NetWare, a shortcut is not created for NetWare Administrator. You should create a shortcut manually on machines that will be used to administer the network. To do this, go to the SYS:Public\win32 directory, right-click on the NWADMN32.EXE application, drag it to the desktop, and select Create Shortcut from the drop-down menu.

To start NetWare Administrator, follow these steps:

1. Log into the network and connect to the NetWare server. This ensures that the Public directory is mapped to your client.

2. Click on the Start menu and select the Run option.

3. Click on the browse button and find the application named NWADMN32.EXE. This application is located in the win32 directory under Public.

When NetWare Administrator starts, you're shown a graphical representation of the Novell Directory Services (NDS) tree, as shown in Figure 3.1.

 | The NDS Directory tree is also known as either the *Directory tree* or the *NDS tree*.

Novell Directory Services Objects

Everything in the NDS tree is treated as an object. You can create new objects in several ways:

➤ By clicking on the Object menu

➤ By right-clicking on an existing object, and selecting Create from the drop-down menu

➤ By clicking on the Create A New Object button on the button bar

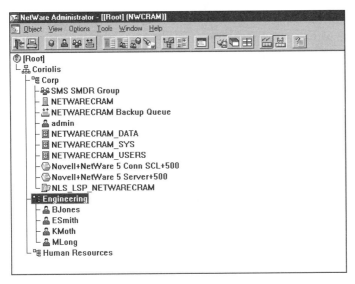

Figure 3.1   The NDS tree.

Creating An Object

When you create a new object, make sure that you select the container object in which you would like the object created. (Once you create the object, it will be placed in the selected container.) Once the Create option is selected, a New Object dialog box appears, as shown in Figure 3.2.

The New Object dialog box allows you to create any type of object that is supported by the NDS tree. To create a specific object, simply highlight the desired object and click on OK. If you are unsure as to where in the tree the object will be created, you can click on the Context button and NetWare Administrator will notify you of the target container. If the container context is not where you would like the object created, you can simply click on Cancel, select the correct container object, and choose the Create Object option.

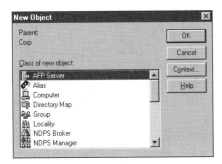

Figure 3.2   The New Object dialog box.

You can create several different objects with the NetWare Administrator application. (Many of the objects are covered in detail in later chapters.) The following lists some of the objects:

➤ AFP Server

➤ Alias

➤ Computer

➤ Directory Map

➤ Group

➤ Locality

➤ NDPS Broker

➤ NDPS Manager

➤ NDPS Printer

➤ NetWare Server

➤ Organizational Role

➤ Organizational Unit

➤ Print Queue

➤ Print Server (non-NDPS)

➤ Printer (non-NDPS)

➤ Profile

➤ SLP Directory Agent

➤ SLP Scope Unit

➤ Template

➤ User

➤ Volume

Once you select one of these objects and click on OK, you are presented with a dialog box in which you can enter properties for an object. The properties presented will vary from object to object. Because the User object is one of the most common objects used, we're going to use it as an example. The Create User dialog box asks you to specify the login name and last name (see Figure 3.3). It's important to note that both the Login Name and the Last Name are required properties. The Create button won't function unless you enter a value for both.

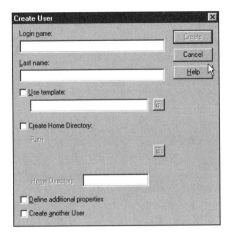

Figure 3.3   The Create User dialog box.

 The User object requires, at a minimum, both the Login Name and Last Name fields in the Create User dialog box be filled in. If you want to create a User object but not assign it a last name, simply type a space in the Last Name field. The Create button becomes active and you may continue.

You can also set four additional options in the Create User dialog box:

➤ **Use Template**   Copies user properties from a previously created template.

➤ **Create Home Directory**   Sets up a directory on a NetWare server that will be the user's Home directory.

➤ **Define Additional Properties**   Allows you to define more properties for the user.

➤ **Create Another User**   Allows you to create an additional user.

The process of creating different objects is relatively the same as that for creating User objects. The main difference is that each object has its own set of properties and values that you can specify. (Subsequent chapters will provide greater detail on the User object and several other objects as well.)

NetWare Administrator allows you to delete, move, and rename objects. You can also use NetWare Administrator to print the entire NDS tree structure or to search the tree for a particular object.

Finding An NDS Object

Searching the NDS tree for an object is one of NetWare Administrator's most powerful features. To use its search capabilities, simply select the Search option

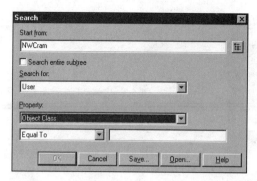

Figure 3.4   The NetWare Administrator Search dialog box.

from the Object menu. The Search dialog box (shown in Figure 3.4) allows you to start the search from anywhere in the NDS tree.

Once you select the starting location, you can specify the objects for which you want to search (such as User, Groups, or Volume objects). The next field is the Property field, which is a drop-down menu. The Property drop-down menu varies depending on which object you select. It includes information, such as phone number or ZIP code, that you can use when searching for a User object. Next, you can choose to compare the object and the property. The options include Equal To, Not Equal To, Present, or Not Present.

Naming An NDS Object

You need to understand how objects are tracked and accessed within the NDS, because it is this organization that allows you to access objects efficiently.

In an NDS structure that contains multiple containers, you must be able to efficiently locate and use objects. NDS must have precise information to find the correct object. The context is important when using DOS-based commands, such as **MAP** or **LOGIN**. If the context is incorrect, it can be very difficult to locate resources.

As shown in Figure 3.5, the NDS can include two User objects with the same name (in this case BSmith). These two User objects exist in different containers within the directory. In this case, if you were to attempt to log into the NDS tree as BSmith, the NDS wouldn't know which User object to use.

When you access NDS objects, you must provide enough information to NDS so it knows which object you're referring to. For example, if we were to tell you about a city named "London," you wouldn't know whether we were talking about London, England, or London, Ontario (Canada). Without the specifics of the location (or country) in which the city is located, you could access incorrect information.

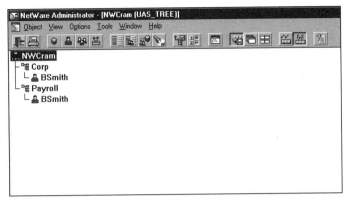

Figure 3.5   Duplicated object names in the NDS tree.

You can specify object names via two methods: distinguished name and relative distinguished name. Both of these methods are discussed in the following sections.

Object-Naming Under NetWare

Before you can truly understand the difference between a distinguished name and a relative distinguished name (discussed in the following sections), you must be familiar with the following object-naming terms (which are also covered in the following sections):

➤ Common name

➤ Context

➤ Current context

➤ Distinguished name

➤ Relative distinguished name

➤ Typeful naming

➤ Typeless naming

➤ Trailing periods

Common Name

An object's common name (also known as its CN) is a relative distinguished name that appears in the NDS tree to the right of the icon. For example, BSmith is the common name for the BSmith User object. It's most commonly written as CN=BSmith.

Context

Context refers to an object's position or location in the NDS tree. It's a map that starts at the [Root] object and finishes at the object. Context is similar to locating a file in the directory path. For example, in the directory structure shown in Figure 3.6, the context of the NETSCAPE.EXE file is C:\Program Files\Netscape\Communicator\Program.

Within the NDS tree, two leaf objects with the same name cannot coexist in the same container. However, two leaf objects with the same name can exist in the same NDS tree, as long as they reside in different containers.

If you refer back to Figure 3.5, the difference between the two objects named BSmith is that one exists within the OU=Corp.O=NWCram (the Corp Organizational Unit within the NWCram Organization) context, whereas the other exists within the OU=Payroll.O=NWCram (the Payroll Organizational Unit within the NWCram Organization) context.

> *Note: For an example of the naming convention shown here, refer to the "Typeful Naming" section later in this chapter.*

Current Context

The current context is your current location in the NDS tree structure. Obviously, you have to know where you are to get to a remote destination. In the same way, you need to know your current position in the NDS tree to access an object in a different part of the tree. You need to know that the current context does not correspond with where your User object exists in the NDS tree structure.

If you know your current context, you can refer to any object that exists in your current location by the common name only, without having to enter the distinguished name. This is true because the object's context and your current context would be exactly the same.

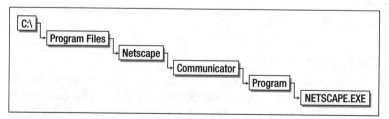

Figure 3.6   The directory structure of the NETSCAPE.EXE file.

The current context also dictates how much of an object's distinguished name you would have to provide to access the object.

Note: The current context is also known as the current name.

Distinguished Name

When we combine an object's common name with its context, we end up with the object's distinguished name.

If we refer to the example in the "Context" section, the User object that resides in Organizational Unit Payroll in the Organization NWCram would read

```
.CN=BSmith.OU=Payroll.O=NWCram
```

whereas the User object that resides in the organizational unit Corp in the organization NWCram would read:

```
.CN=BSmith.OU=Corp.O=NWCram
```

 A distinguished name always starts with a leading period.

In the same way that a TCP/IP address is separated by periods and a DOS directory path is separated by backslashes (\), the distinguished name is separated by periods. Also, the distinguished name always starts with a trailing period (covered in the section "Trailing Periods" later in this chapter).

Once you understand distinguished names, you'll see that two objects cannot have the same distinguished name in the same NDS tree (because if two objects have the same distinguished name, then they exist in the NDS tree in exactly the same location). This would be akin to assigning a single parking spot at work to two people who both drive midsized cars.

Relative Distinguished Name

A relative distinguished name is the location of the object from the current position in the NDS tree (or the current context). A relative distinguished name has several attributes:

➤ It doesn't have a leading period.

➤ It lists the path from the current context to the final object.

➤ It is able to use trailing periods.

➤ Objects in the name are separated by periods. For example, assume that you have a User object (JohnS) within the Organizational Unit Payroll. The current context would be the NWCram Organization. The relative distinguished name would be JohnS.Payroll.

So, as a rule: The relative distinguished name plus the current context equals the distinguished name. Referring to the previous example, this would be:

```
JohnS.Payroll + NWCram. = JohnS.Payroll.NWCram.
```

Typeful Naming

A typeful name uses attribute type abbreviations to distinguish between the different container types and leaf objects in the distinguished or relative name. The following lists these abbreviations:

➤ **CN** Common Name (all leaf objects)

➤ **OU** Organization Unit

➤ **O** Organization

➤ **C** Country

Attribute types are not mandatory, but they do help you avoid confusion as to container types. Attribute types have three different properties:

➤ They always appear before the object they represent.

➤ They're always separated from the object they represent by an equal sign (=).

➤ They distinguish between container types and leaf objects.

Typeless Naming

A typeless name does not use the attribute types as described in the previous section. For example, take the following distinguished name:

```
.CN=BSmith.OU=Boston.OU=Corp.O=NWCram
```

The typeless name would simply remove the attribute types and the equal sign, as seen here:

```
.BSmith.Boston.Corp.NWCram
```

It's really up to you to decide which method to use in your naming of objects in NetWare. Find a method that you like and run with it. You'll most likely start with a typeful name and move to a typeless name when you are more comfortable with the NDS tree.

Trailing Periods

Trailing periods in NetWare work in a similar way as they do in DOS. Just as a period informs DOS to move up one level in the directory tree, trailing periods tell NDS to remove object names from the left side of the current context. NDS removes one object name for each trailing period.

If, for example, your current context is

```
OU=Sales.OU=Boston.O=Widgets
```

and you enter the relative distinguished name, "CN=Admin.", NDS removes the Sales object from the current context and appends the relative distinguished name to the left of the remaining name. This returns the following result:

```
.CN=Admin.OU=Boston.O=Widgets
```

Every trailing period that you enter causes NDS to remove an object name from the left side of the current context.

Practice Questions

Question 1

> Which of the following are container objects? [Choose the two best answers]
>
> ❑ a. [Root]
>
> ❑ b. Volume
>
> ❑ c. User
>
> ❑ d. Organization

The correct answers are a and d. Both the [Root] object and the Organization object are containers. Any object that can contain other objects is a container object. Even though a Volume object contains directories and files, it's not considered a container because it cannot contain leaf objects, such as User or Group objects. Therefore, answer b is incorrect. A User object cannot hold any other objects. Therefore, answer c is incorrect.

Question 2

> What is the typeless name for the following typeful name?
> ```
> .CN=BSmith.OU=Engineering.OU=NewYork.O=Widgets
> ```
>
> ○ a. BSmith
>
> ○ b. Engineering.NewYork.Widgets
>
> ○ c. OU=Engineering.NewYork.Widgets
>
> ○ d. BSmith.Engineering.NewYork.Widgets

The correct answer is d. A typeless name does not contain the object type abbreviations. BSmith is not a complete name because it does not specify the context for the object. Therefore, answer a is incorrect. Engineering.NewYork.Widgets is not complete because it lacks the leaf object name (BSmith). Therefore, answer b is incorrect. OU=Engineering.NewYork.Widgets uses object type abbreviations on some of the objects but not on others, and the leaf object name is missing. Therefore, answer c is incorrect.

Question 3

Your current context is OU=Sales.OU=Chicago.O=Sprockets. You would like to use trailing periods to move up to the Chicago Organizational Unit. Your common name is Admin. Which relative distinguished name would you enter?

○ a. CN=Admin.OU=Sales.

○ b. CN=Admin.

○ c. CN=Admin.OU=Sales.OU=Chicago.

○ d. O=Sprockets.

The correct answer is b. By entering "CN=Admin.", NDS removes the Sales object and appends the relative distinguished name to the left of the remaining name. Therefore, answers a, c, and d are incorrect.

Question 4

Which tasks can be completed using NetWare Administrator? [Choose the two best answers]

❑ a. Modifying software installed on the server

❑ b. Creating User objects

❑ c. Setting object rights

❑ d. Modifying client configurations

The correct answers are b and c. To modify server software, you must run the configuration utility on the server. Therefore, answer a is incorrect. The NetWare Administrator does not allow for client configurations. Therefore, answer d is incorrect.

Question 5

> Which of the following defines an NDS context?
>
> ○ a. The name assigned to the object in the NDS tree
>
> ○ b. The location of the [Root] object in relation to the current location
>
> ○ c. The current location in relation to the [Root] object
>
> ○ d. The location of the NetWare Administrator program

The correct answer is c. The context defines your current location in the NDS tree with regard to the [Root] object. The name assigned to the object is its common name. Therefore, answer a is incorrect. Because the context is in relation to the [Root] object and not the reverse, answer b is incorrect, thus making this a trick question. The NetWare Administrator program is located in the Public directory of the SYS: volume. Therefore, answer d is incorrect.

Question 6

> What is the typeful distinguished name for the user JJonas who is located in the HR organizational unit of the Sprockets organization?
>
> ○ a. JJonas.HR.Sprockets
>
> ○ b. U=JJonas.OU=HR.O=Sprockets
>
> ○ c. N=JJonas.OU=HR.O=Sprockets
>
> ○ d. CN=JJonas.OU=HR.O=Sprockets

CN=JJonas.OU=HR.O=Sprockets is a typeful distinguished name. Therefore, the correct answer is d. JJonas.HR.Sprockets is a typeless name. Therefore, answer a is incorrect. Both U and N are not valid object type abbreviations. Therefore, answers b and c are incorrect.

Need To Know More?

 For more information on the NetWare Administrator and the NDS object naming criteria, check the NetWare 5 online documentation with keyword searches on "NetWare Administrator," "context," "distinguished name," "objects," and "NDS."

 www.novell.com/documentation/en/nw5/nw5/docui/ index.html contains a copy of the NetWare 5 documentation.

 Search for "NetWare Administrator" or "NWAdmin" in your favorite search engine for more information.

Using A Workstation

Terms you'll need to understand:

- √ Workstation
- √ Network board
- √ Network cable
- √ Novell Client software
- √ Password
- √ Login process
- √ Login ID
- √ Login name

Techniques you'll need to master:

- √ Understanding the Novell Client software installation procedures
- √ Learning the differences between workstation hardware and software
- √ Logging into the network

We have examined how NetWare 5 creates and uses objects, but we're still missing one part of the equation. Once these objects are created, how do we access them? The answer to that is simple: by using a computer, which, in the Novell world, is referred to as a *workstation*. A workstation is a computer that can access the NetWare network resources, such as printing and file sharing. In this chapter, you'll discover the differences between the software and hardware components of the workstation, and how these resources are used to access the network.

Workstation Communication

An everyday PC that has the necessary hardware and software components to participate on a computer network is called a *workstation*. The workstation's hardware and software components work together to allow it to interact with other systems and resources that are on the network.

All network communication by workstations involve several different tasks, such as:

➤ The physical connection of the workstation to the network, which is accomplished using network boards and cables.

➤ The software component that allows for communication between the user and the physical hardware—for example, the workstation's operating system (DOS, Windows, and so on) and the client software (the Novell Client).

➤ The transfer of information between the servers and the workstations on the network.

Hardware's Role In Networking

The workstation's hardware is what allows the communication with the rest of the network. This hardware also makes sure that the data sent and received is free of errors and has not been corrupted.

A workstation requires several components to function on a network. Two of the most important components are the network cable and the network board.

> *Note: A network board is often called a network interface card (NIC), a network adapter, or a network interface board. Novell uses the term network board most often, but network board vendors usually use the term NIC.*

The *network cable*, or network architecture, is the physical cable that connects all the devices on the network so that they may communicate. It's the cable itself that carries the communication or data on the network, and this communication can use light (visible and invisible) or electrical impulses. The network cable could be an Ethernet cable, a token ring cable, a Fiber Distributed Data Interface (FDDI), an Asynchronous Transfer Mode (ATM), or any other type of networking architecture. Each of the network architecture components must be compatible with each other (or gateway systems must connect the dissimilar architectures).

The *network board* is the device that connects the workstation to the network architecture or cable. The network board translates the digital impulses from the workstation so they can be transmitted on the network.

Although the network hardware is crucial in the communication among different devices on a network, it's important to note that the workstation hardware is not responsible for several tasks, such as:

➤ The actual data or the information within the data

➤ How the workstation translates the information and how it transfers it to the applications

➤ Security on the network

All of these tasks are the responsibility of the workstation *software*, which is covered in the following section.

Software's Role In Networking

The software components complete the process of transferring information among network devices. Like a network's hardware component, the network software is incomplete as a singular device. As an analogy, take a look at today's new cars: What happens if the computer that controls the car fails? Most likely, tasks that we take for granted (such as using the power windows and door locks, and starting the car) would not be possible without both the hardware (the starter, the key, the power window motor) and the software (the programming that allows the hardware to function).

The workstation software includes the following components:

➤ The Novell Client software (covered in the following section)

➤ The actual operating system, such as DOS, Windows, or OS/2

➤ The applications, such as a word processor, a spreadsheet program, and an email program

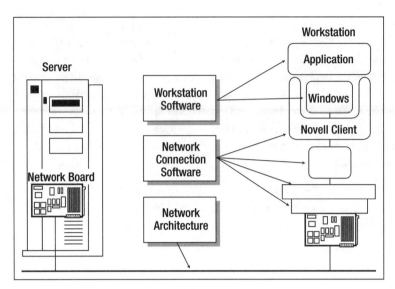

Figure 4.1 The workstation software.

Figure 4.1 illustrates how the workstation software is used in the workstation.

The Workstation Operating System And Its Functions

The operating system provides the users with a common interface for all their files and applications. Once a user has learned to control an application (using a mouse and a keyboard, for example), it's very straightforward for the user to control a new application.

The operating system also controls how data travels between the applications, the operating system components, and the network. It also allows users to store information and files on the local hard drives, as well as on the server's remote locations. The operating system also redirects print jobs to either a local printer (a printer physically connected to the workstation) or to a remote printer (either a network printer or a printer connected to a remote workstation or server). Both the operating system and the Novell Client software share the actual network services.

Note: *NetWare 5 supports all versions of Windows, including Windows 98.*

The Workstation Applications And Their Functions

The applications on the workstation are what actually create the data that is sent to and from the workstation. The applications can request data stored on remote network resources or send data to those locations.

For example, a database program may access a shared database that's stored on a NetWare server somewhere on the network. It can both read data from the database and write data to it. Another example is an email application, which creates messages that are transmitted to various locations on a network.

It's very important, however, to understand that the applications do not actually communicate between the workstation and the network. In order to accomplish this communication, the applications rely on three components: the workstation's hardware, the Novell Client program, and the workstation's operating system.

As an example, let's look at an email application. When a message is completed and the user clicks on the Send button, the application then communicates with the operating system for delivery. The operating system, through the Novell Client, resolves any addressing issues and sends the message to the remote location. At the receiving end, the Novell Client and the operating system receive the information, decide that it belongs to the email application, and route it accordingly.

The Novell Client Software And Its Functions

Without the Novell Client, workstations wouldn't be able to communicate with the NetWare server. The Novell Client is the heart of the network communication process. It ties into other workstation software components, especially the operating system, to enable the following features:

➤ **NetWare services access** Some of the NetWare services include storage and access of files on the server, printing to network printers, and running applications from the server.

➤ **Network security** This feature makes sure that files and resources are secure and limits access to them to authorized users only.

Note: Novell does not have a client operating system. It relies on other operating systems, such as DOS, Windows, and OS/2. The Novell Client adds functionality to the operating system to allow access to Novell NetWare servers and services.

To provide users with the full functions of the network, you must install the Novell Client program on each workstation. Once the Novell Client is installed, the user is prompted to provide a username and a password.

The Novell Client program is included with the NetWare 5 installation CDs, or it can be downloaded from Novell's Web site (**www.novell.com/download/**) by clicking on the appropriate link for your operating system. Once the client is installed, it's virtually transparent to the user.

Flow Of Information Between The Workstation Software And Hardware

In this section, we illustrate how data flows between the different components (as previously illustrated in Figure 4.1). Figure 4.2 shows the different components of the workstation model and the data flow.

In the lower section of Figure 4.2, you'll see the hardware components. These include the network board and the network cable (and, ultimately, the motherboard, CPU, RAM, and so on). The higher levels of the figure include the software components, including the network board drivers, the network architecture (Ethernet, token ring, and so on), the Novell Client, the operating system, and finally, the application at the top of the figure.

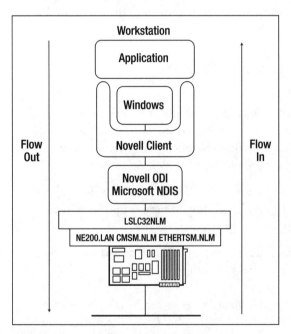

Figure 4.2 Workstation data flow.

The best way to understand how data flows within this diagram is with a database example. Assume that you have a database client that is accessing information from the network and then committing information back to the database. Also assume that you have initiated a request for data to be sent to us from the database server. The steps would be similar to the following:

1. The database server sends the information as requested.

2. The network cable carries the data to your workstation based on the Media Access Control (MAC) address.

3. The network board in your workstation receives the data and passes it to the network board driver.

4. The network board driver gathers this information and passes it to your workstation's operating system. The network board drivers convert the data as received by the network board into a format that your operating system recognizes.

5. The operating system, via the Novell Client, processes the data and decides which application requested it. It then sends the data to the proper application.

6. The application (the database client, in this case) receives the information.

7. The database client then converts the data into an understood format and displays it on the screen.

8. You read the information, make changes, and commit these changes back to the database. This causes the database client to convert your information into data that is recognized by the operating system and the Novell Client, and to then send it to the client.

9. The operating system and the Novell Client process the data, decide on its destination, and send it to the network board drivers for transmission.

10. The network board drivers send the data to the network board.

11. The network board sends the data to the network cable.

12. The network cable carries the data back to the server, and the process repeats at the server.

Note: This process is similar to any type of data, not just database queries. For example, sending email, transferring files, and printing to a network printer all follow a similar process.

Installing The Novell Client Software

As you may have guessed by now, the Novell Client is the key to communicating in a Novell NetWare network. In this section, you'll learn how to install the Novell Client, often called the Novell Client 32 program.

To install the Novell Client, you must run a program called WINSETUP.EXE. The program must be installed on every workstation. WINSETUP.EXE is located on the NetWare 5 Novell Client Software CD-ROM. You can access the software by simply inserting the CD into the CD-ROM drive and waiting for the Installation screen (see Figure 4.3) to appear. If this screen does not appear, simply browse the CD, find the WINSETUP.EXE program (in the root directory), and double-click on it.

The only two options on this initial screen are to select the language of the installation or to exit the installation program. If you select a language to install, you will be prompted with the options screen illustrated in Figure 4.4. At this point, you get to select which application to install. The options are as follows:

➤ Windows 95/98 Client

➤ Windows NT Client

Figure 4.3 The initial WINSETUP.EXE screen.

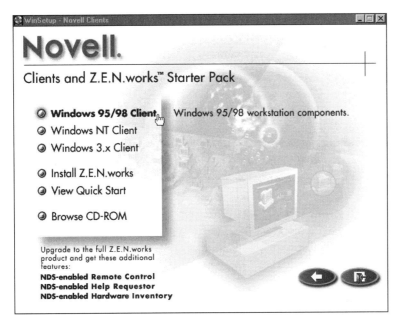

Figure 4.4   The Install Options screen.

➤ Windows 3.x Client

➤ Install Z.E.N.works

➤ View Quick Start

The first three options are fairly straightforward. Select the option based on your operating system. (For example, if you have Windows 95, then you should select that option.) The fourth option installs Z.E.N.works, whereas the fifth, View Quick Start, will help you with the Z.E.N.works installation. (Z.E.N.works is covered in detail in Chapters 11, 12, and 13.)

> *Note: From this screen, you can also select to browse the contents of the CD, return to the previous screen, or exit the installation program.*

Once you choose which client to install (Windows 95/98, Windows NT, or Windows 3.x), you're given a choice of applications that are available for your operating system. For example, you can install the following components for Windows NT:

➤ **Install Novell Client** Installs the Novell Client for the selected operating system.

➤ **Documentation** Installs the documentation set for the Novell Client.

➤ **Install Netscape** Installs Netscape Navigator 4.04.

➤ **Install Win2NCS** Installs the Novell Win2NCS application. This application allows you to dial out of the network through the server's pool of modems.

➤ **Install Java** Installs Sun's Java runtime environment.

Note: *This installation program is "smart." If you select a client that's not compatible with your operating system, the installer will display the components screen, but the links will not work.*

When you click on the Install Novell Client option, the installer (WINSETUP.EXE) will launch the actual installation program and terminate. If you would like to install the clients without using the WINSETUP.EXE program, you can run the installers directly. Their paths on the CD are listed in Table 4.1.

The actual installation of the Novell Client is very easy. You have to select whether you would like to perform a typical or a custom installation, agree to the licensing agreement, and finally reboot the system.

Once the system is rebooted, you'll notice that your workstation will have a new login screen. (This is most noticeable if you are running Windows NT.) The Novell Client program will place a login icon in the Start menu under Programs|NetWare. If you're installing the Novell Client program under Windows NT, you are given the option to log into the NetWare network and the Windows NT network, or just into the Windows NT network. (This is explained in more detail in the section titled "Understanding How The Login Process Works" later in this chapter.)

A regular installation of the Novell Client program takes between 10 and 15 minutes, depending on your hardware configuration.

Table 4.1 Novell Client installation program locations.		
Operating System	**Path (from the CD)**	**Program**
Windows 95/98	\PRODUCTS\WIN95\IBM_ENU	SETUP.EXE
Windows NT	\PRODUCTS\WINNT\I386	SETUPNW.EXE
Windows 3.x	\PRODUCTS\DOSWIN32	INSTALL.EXE

As an example, we'll go through the Novell Client for Windows NT installation. Because the typical installation is extremely easy to complete, we'll look at the custom installation:

1. Run the Novell Client Installer.

2. Select the Custom Installation radio button, and click on the Next button.

3. Next, you're given the choice to select which options you would like to install. These options and their definitions are included in the following list, and the component's installation screen is shown in Figure 4.5.

   ➤ **Novell Client For Windows NT (Required)** This is the actual Novell Client application. This is the only component that is required to complete the installation.

   ➤ **Novell Distributed Print Services** Allows for bidirectional communication between the workstation and network print services.

   ➤ **Novell IP Gateway** Allows for Internet access on IPX or private IP networks.

   ➤ **Novell Target Service Agent** Automatically backs up selected hard drives from the server.

   ➤ **Novell Workstation Manager** Allows administrators to configure and manage workstations using Novell Directory Services (NDS).

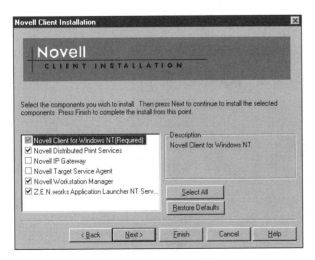

Figure 4.5   Installing the Novell Client components.

➤ **Z.E.N.works Application Launcher** Allows the Application Launcher to install applications on secure Windows NT workstations.

Select the options that you would like to install and click on the Next button.

4. This next screen, as seen in Figure 4.6, allows you to select which protocol(s) to use with the Novell Client program when communicating on the network. The options include:

➤ **IP Only** Installs the IP protocol only.

➤ **IP With IPX Compatibility** Allows IPX applications to run in an IP network by converting the IPX packets to IP packets.

➤ **IP And IPX** Installs both the TCP/IP and IPX protocols.

➤ **IPX Only** Installs the IPX protocol only.

If you choose protocols that are not currently installed on your workstation, the installation program may prompt you to insert the original Windows NT media so the needed components can be installed. Select the protocol(s) you would like to install, and click on the Next button.

5. The next screen gives you the ability to select which type of Novell server to connect to. You can choose to use NDS (NetWare 4.x or higher) or bindery (NetWare 3.x). Choose the selected connection method, and click on the Next button.

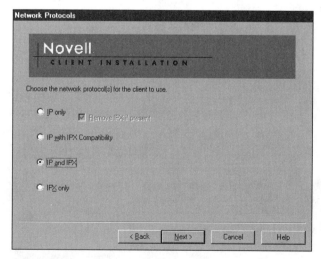

Figure 4.6 Installing the Novell Client protocols.

6. Enter the name of the NDS tree, and click on the Next button.

7. Click on the Finish button to start the installation.

8. Click on the Reboot button to complete the installation, and reboot the server.

Understanding How The Login Process Works

Once you have installed the Novell Client software, you can use the login procedure to access the network. If you understand the login process and how NetWare 5 deals with it, you'll be able to troubleshoot login problems in the future.

As with many network operating systems, NetWare 5 will allow only authorized users to access the network. The login procedure ensures that a user attempting to access the network and its resources is authorized to do so.

When users log into the network, their identity is verified, and the rights and permissions they might have to different resources are checked before they are granted access to the network. You need to remember a few things about the network login process. First, as mentioned earlier, the login is mandatory. Second, NetWare 5 uses the single login feature. This means that once a user enters his or her credentials, he or she will usually not be required to enter them again.

Before you can log into the network, you need to verify the following:

➤ The Novell Client software is installed.

➤ The password you have been assigned and your username are valid.

➤ The workstation is online and able to connect to the network.

➤ The workstation is able to communicate with the network. This means that it must have a network board that is compatible with the network cable and the architecture, and that it has the correct drivers installed.

You can log into the network in many ways, and the method you use depends on the configuration of your workstation. Here are three ways to log into the network:

➤ When you first turn on your computer, the login screen (shown in Figure 4.7) appears.

➤ Right-click on the red "N" icon in the Windows system tray, and select the NetWare Login option from the menu.

➤ You can also select the Login option from the Start menu.

Figure 4.7 The Novell Login screen.

You can also run the LOGINW95.EXE program from the NOVELL\
CLIENT32 directory if you are running Windows 95, or press Ctrl+Alt+Del
if you are running Windows NT.

 Your login name or ID and your User object name are the same. Until the administrator has created a User object for you in the NDS tree, you cannot log in. By default, a User object does not require a password; therefore, your User object name should be changed to something unique and not easy to guess.

Most users will use the login dialog box as it appears in Figure 4.7. Advanced
users can modify the login process by clicking on the Advanced button.

In this screen, you can control which tree, context, and server to use; configure
login scripts; configure dial-up networking; and, if a Windows NT domain is
present, configure the domain information as well (see Figure 4.8).

Figure 4.8 The Advanced Login screen.

Accessing Network Resources

Once the Novell Client software is installed, you can browse and connect to network services, such as file and print services. There is only one client available for Windows 95/98 and Windows NT that allows you to *fully* browse and control the NDS tree—the Novell Client. (To browse the NDS tree, you can use either Network Neighborhood or Windows Explorer.)

It's important to note some of the added functionality that the Novell Client software adds to browsing:

➤ It's fully integrated with Network Neighborhood, Windows Explorer, and other Windows programs. If you right-click on Network Neighborhood, you'll notice that several options have been added. All the Novell Client options have a red "N" to the left of their names.

➤ A red "N" appears in the Windows system tray. By right-clicking on it, you can access many Novell options.

➤ It supports long filenames (LFNs).

Practice Questions

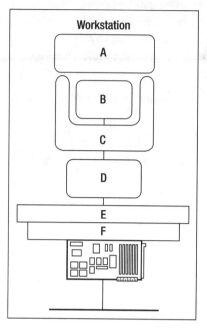

Figure 4.9 Use this figure for questions 1 through 4.

Question 1

The TCP/IP and IPX protocols are located in which portion of the workstation shown in Figure 4.9?

○ a. A

○ b. B

○ c. C

○ d. D

○ e. E

The correct answer is d. The TCP/IP and IPX protocols are located in the fourth section: section D. The components of the workstation, from the network board up, are the LAN driver, the TCP/IP and IPX protocols, the Novell Client software, the operating system, and the application. Therefore, answers a, b, c, and e are incorrect.

Question 2

> The LAN driver is located in which portion of the workstation shown in Figure 4.9?
>
> ○ a. A
>
> ○ b. B
>
> ○ c. C
>
> ○ d. D
>
> ○ e. E

The correct answer is e. The LAN driver is located in the fifth section: section E. The components of the workstation, from the network board up, are the LAN driver, the TCP/IP and IPX protocols, the Novell Client software, the operating system, and the application. Therefore, answers a, b, c, and d are incorrect.

Question 3

> The operating system is located in which portion of the workstation shown in Figure 4.9?
>
> ○ a. A
>
> ○ b. B
>
> ○ c. C
>
> ○ d. D
>
> ○ e. E

The correct answer is b. The operating system is located in the second section: section B. The components of the workstation, from the network board up, are the LAN driver, the TCP/IP and IPX protocols, the Novell Client software, the operating system, and the application. Therefore, answers a, c, d, and e are incorrect.

Question 4

> The application is located in which portion of the workstation shown in Figure 4.9?
>
> ○ a. A
>
> ○ b. B
>
> ○ c. C
>
> ○ d. D
>
> ○ e. E

The correct answer is a. The application is located in the first section: section A. The components of the workstation, from the network board up, are the LAN driver, the TCP/IP and IPX protocols, the Novell Client software, the operating system, and the application. Therefore, answers b, c, d, and e are incorrect.

Question 5

> Which of the following are required for a user to be able to log into the network? [Choose the two best answers]
>
> ❑ a. The user must have a valid ID and password (if the User object has been assigned a password).
>
> ❑ b. The workstation must be running TCP/IP only.
>
> ❑ c. The Novell Client must be installed.
>
> ❑ d. The workstation must be directly connected to the server via a crossover cable.

The correct answers are a and c. Both a valid ID (or username) and password, as well as the Novell Client software must exist before a user will be authorized to access the network and its resources. The login process is not limited to the TCP/IP protocol; IPX can be used as a protocol as well. Therefore, answer b is incorrect. To be able to connect to the server and the network, the workstation needs only to be connected to the network and have the network board driver installed and configured. Therefore, answer d is incorrect.

Question 6

What is a network board? [Choose the best answer]

○ a. The network interface card and the network card drivers

○ b. The network interface card

○ c. An Ethernet card

○ d. A token ring card

The correct answer is b. The network board is simply the card that connects the computer to the network. By definition, the network board does not include the network board drivers. Therefore, answer a is incorrect (and the reason why this is a trick question). The network board can be an Ethernet card, a token ring card, or any other type of network card that has NetWare network board drivers available. Therefore, answers c and d are incorrect.

Need To Know More?

 For more information on the NetWare Administrator and the NDS object-naming criteria, check the NetWare 5 online documentation with keyword searches on "Novell Client," "workstation," "login," "network board," and "LAN drivers."

 www.novell.com/documentation/en/nw5/nw5/docui/index.html is where you can find a copy of the NetWare 5 documentation.

 Search for "Novell Client" in your favorite search engine for more information.

 www.novell.com/search is Novell's search page. Search for "Novell Client," "login," and "workstation."

User Management, Licensing, And Logins

5

Terms you'll need to understand:

√ NetWare Administrator

√ ConsoleOne

√ UIMPORT

√ Template object

√ Admin object

√ License container object

√ License Certificate object

√ User License container

√ Server License container

√ Authentication

Techniques you'll need to master:

√ Creating and modifying user accounts

√ Creating and managing multiple User objects

√ Creating and configuring objects using ConsoleOne

√ Creating User objects using UIMPORT

√ Managing NetWare user licenses

√ Understanding login security

The User object is considered the key to all of the resources attached to the network. In other words, without a User object you cannot access any network resources. In a properly designed network, all network resources are arranged and configured so they support users in as transparent a manner as possible. To be an effective administrator, you must understand the User object and the utilities to manage it. In this chapter, you'll examine User objects and the various utilities NetWare has available to administer them.

Administrating Network Access For Users

As a NetWare administrator, you're responsible for maintaining a database of objects that govern access to the network. The Novell Directory Services (NDS) database is a sophisticated security system that permits or denies access to the resources that are represented by objects in the database. If there were no need for security, there would be no need for NDS. NDS is not a file management system, nor is it a tangible resource. Think of NDS as an "access management" system.

You'll be expected to understand this security system and develop it so the resources on your network are protected from accidental or intentional intrusion. The four main types of network security that you need to understand (login, NDS, file system, and printing) are covered in the following section.

Understanding The User Object

In this chapter, you'll become familiar with the most fundamental object in the NDS tree—the User object. It's the single point of entry that you must use to access any network resource. Without a User object, you cannot log into the network and are therefore prevented from accessing any network resources.

 Novell will occasionally refer to the NDS tree as the *NDS Directory* or the *Directory tree*.

Your User object must be associated with a resource for you to access it. The following four types of security access are assigned through the User object:

➤ **Login security** Login security requires a valid username and password to gain access to any network resources.

➤ **NDS security** This security system of database objects is used to assign or revoke access to network resources on a granular basis.

➤ **File system security** File system security protects the data on file servers from unauthorized manipulation or destruction.

➤ **Printing security** Printing security allows you to prevent the unauthorized use of print resources by restricting a User object's access to print devices.

NetWare has three utilities that can be used to create, modify, and manipulate User objects: NetWare Administrator, ConsoleOne, and UIMPORT. You must be familiar with each utility's characteristics and capabilities to effectively manage a NetWare network.

➤ **NetWare Administrator** You use this graphical user interface (GUI) to create and manipulate NDS objects. NetWare Administrator has a text-based counterpart, NETADMIN.

 Novell will sometimes refer to NetWare Administrator as *NWAdmin*.

➤ **ConsoleOne** You use this utility (which is not found in previous versions of NetWare) to create User and container objects from the file server (or a browser running on a Java-enabled workstation).

➤ **UIMPORT** Many companies already have a database of usernames and associated information, such as telephone numbers, addresses, and related information. You use this utility to create large numbers of users from an existing database without reentering the data.

Using NetWare Administrator

NetWare Administrator is the primary utility used to manage NDS objects. The following steps show how to create an NDS user account using NetWare Administrator:

1. Log in to NDS and supply a username and password (if a password is required). Then, click on OK to log in to the network. Figure 5.1 shows the Novell Login screen.

2. Launch NetWare Administrator and select the container in which you want to create the User object. Figure 5.2 shows the NDS tree with the NYC container selected.

3. Select Object|Create, or right-click on the selected container and choose Create.

Figure 5.1 The Novell Login screen.

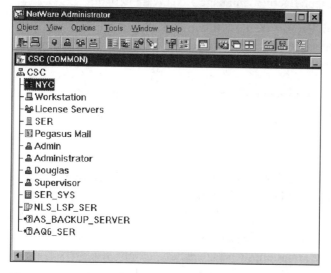

Figure 5.2 The NDS tree with the NYC container selected.

4. In the New Object dialog box, scroll down and select the User object as shown in Figure 5.3. Click on OK.

Instead of scrolling, you may type the letter "u" in the dialog box and go immediately to the User object.

5. In the Create User dialog box (shown in Figure 5.4), enter a login name and a last name. These are required fields, and the User object cannot be created without them. If you do not want to enter a last name, you must enter at least a blank space.

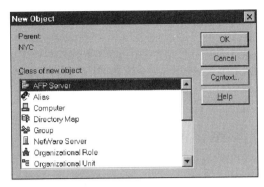

Figure 5.3   The New Object dialog box.

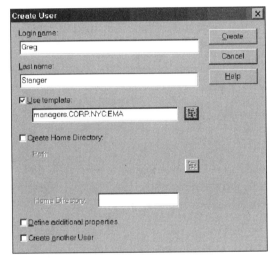

Figure 5.4   The Create User dialog box.

 The Create Another User checkbox allows you to continue entering and creating User objects.

Creating Multiple Users With The Same Properties

Administrators often need to create large numbers of users at the same time (for example, when a network is first implemented). If these user accounts have similar properties, the Template object is ideal for minimizing data entry.

The Template object provides a way to distribute data or properties to User objects without opening each object individually to enter the same data over and over. Users with the same file and directory rights, printing rights, security equivalencies, fax numbers, ZIP or postal codes, and other such properties are more efficiently created and managed through the use of a Template object.

Use the following steps to create and use the Template object:

1. Log in to the network, launch NetWare Administrator, and navigate to the container in which you want to create the Template object.

2. Select Object|Create (or right-click on the container and choose Create). The New Object dialog box appears.

3. Choose the Template object. The Create Template dialog box, shown in Figure 5.5, appears. In the Name field, enter a name for the template, such as "Managers." (The only required field is the Name field.)

   Note: *If the Use Template Or User checkbox is checked, you cannot create the template until you've chosen a template or user. Therefore, the Create button will remain grayed until you've selected a template or user.*

4. If the Use Template Or User checkbox is checked, select the template or user whose properties you want to use for this Template object. To do this, click on the browse button to the right of the Use Template Or User field. The Select Object dialog box appears.

5. Select the Template object or user whose properties and values you want to acquire, as shown in Figure 5.6. Click on OK, which will take you back to the Create Template dialog box.

6. In the Create Template dialog box, click on Create to create the Template object with the User object or Template object that you assigned to your new template. If the Define Additional Properties checkbox is selected, you need to define additional properties.

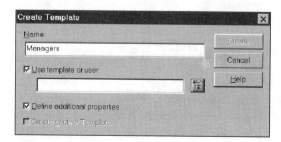

Figure 5.5   The Create Template dialog box.

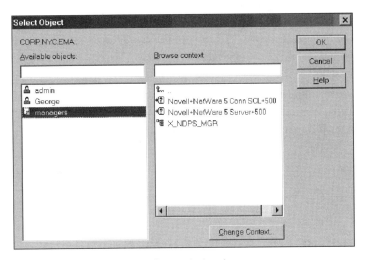

Figure 5.6   The Select Object dialog box.

7. In the resulting dialog box, select the Members Of Template tab (see Figure 5.7) of your Template object. This page is where you'll add members to the Template object so it will know to which users or templates to assign properties. Click Add.

8. From the Select Object dialog box, select the users or templates you want as members of your Template object. Click on OK.

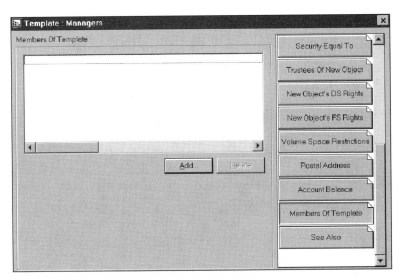

Figure 5.7   The Members Of Template tab of your Template object.

Note: *To select a range of User objects, highlight the first object, press Shift, and highlight the last object. To select individual User objects, select the User object followed by the Control key.*

Figure 5.8 shows the members of the Template object added to the new Managers template you created. These members are the User objects or other Template objects you'll manage with the newly created Template object.

You can make global changes to User objects using the Details On Multiple Users option (which is discussed later in this chapter). When creating a user account, you may select a Template object from which you'd like to acquire properties.

Understanding The Admin Object

The Admin object is the only User object created by default when the NDS tree is installed. You must have at least one user account for any NDS tree, or you won't be able to log in. By default, the Admin account has supervisory authority throughout the NDS tree. You use the Admin account to begin the initial network setup.

The Admin object is like any other User object: You can delete and rename it, and reduce its rights to the status of any other user. However, if you do and you don't have another user with the same privileges as Admin, you'll permanently lose access to some parts of the tree. Depending on the security settings of

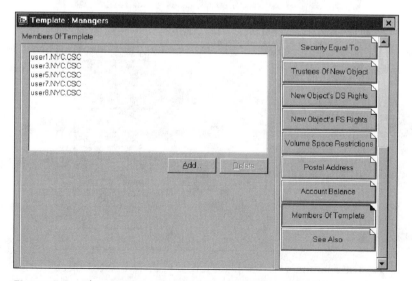

Figure 5.8 The new members of the Managers template.

other accounts, you may even be prevented from managing other objects at all. This may even require reinstalling the NDS tree to gain access to file server data. If you reinstall the NDS tree, you'll lose all previously assigned security access and begin again with one Admin User object.

 For additional security, some administrators choose to immediately create another account with the same rights as Admin and disable or delete the Admin account. This prevents an intruder from trying to determine the password of a known account.

Modifying The Properties Of User Objects

As the administrator of a network that utilizes NDS, you'll constantly be making changes to user accounts, either individually or in groups. To modify groups of users, you use the Details On Multiple Users option, which is covered later in this section.

Note: Fields requiring unique information cannot be modified in groups.

You modify the properties of all users in a container by selecting the container. If you use this feature, however, you also change the properties of all groups and Template objects in that container.

The following steps show you how to automatically create home directories when you create a user, and how properties are filled in by the Template object when you create users with it:

1. In the Create User dialog box (refer back to Figure 5.4), enter a login name and a last name and select the Create Home Directory checkbox.

2. Click on the Home Directory Path button (the button to the right of the Create Home Directory checkbox), which tells NetWare Administrator where to put the user's home directory. (Notice that the Home Directory field is filled in with the login name, which NetWare Administrator does automatically when you check the Create Home Directory checkbox.)

3. Select the Users directory to tell NetWare Administrator where to put the home directory. Click on OK, which returns you to the Create User dialog box.

4. The path should now be displayed on the Create User dialog box, the Define Additional Properties checkbox is selected, and the Managers Template object is associated with the new user. Click on Create.

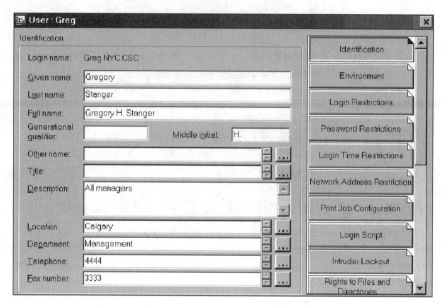

Figure 5.9 The description information is filled in from the Managers Template object.

5. In the Identification page that appears (see the example in Figure 5.9), fill in the information that is unique to this user (such as first name, last name, full name, and middle initial). Notice that the Description, Location, Department, Telephone, and Fax Number sections are filled in by data from the Managers Template object. Click on OK to create the user.

6. To update the properties of multiple users, select the Managers Template object and then choose Object|Details On Multiple Users. (Note that the Department field that was changed in the Template object will also be changed in all the users who are members of the Template object at the time the Template object is created.)

Using ConsoleOne To Create Objects

ConsoleOne is a Java-based GUI interface that runs on the server or in a browser from a Java-enabled workstation. It's a new feature of NetWare 5 that allows you to browse the NDS tree and to create objects. With ConsoleOne, you can create the following objects:

➤ Organization

➤ Organizational Unit

➤ Users

➤ Groups

You use ConsoleOne to modify the properties of any of these objects, as well as the properties of other classes of objects already created in the NDS tree.

You must install a Java runtime environment to use ConsoleOne properly. To install Java, do the following:

1. Run the NetWare client installation by choosing WINSETUP.EXE from the CD or the directory the client is in.

2. Select the client that matches your workstation (for example, Windows NT client).

3. Choose Install Java and follow the prompts.

4. Reboot your workstation for the Java configuration to take effect.

5. Navigate to the *servername*\sys\public\mgmt subdirectory.

6. Run the CONSOLE1.EXE file to execute ConsoleOne.

Figure 5.10 shows ConsoleOne running from a workstation.

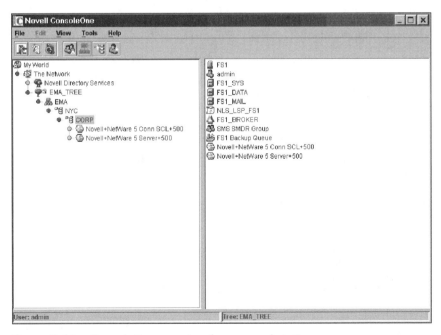

Figure 5.10   ConsoleOne running from a workstation.

You create a user account with ConsoleOne in much the same way as in NetWare Administrator. First, you click on the container in which you want to create the object. Then, you select the type of object you want to create, fill in the username and last name, choose whether you want to define additional properties, and select Create.

Using UIMPORT To Create User Objects

UIMPORT is a text-based utility that has been designed expressly for creating large numbers of users from a database of users and related properties, such as telephone numbers, addresses, fax numbers, titles, login names, and other User object properties.

UIMPORT is also used to globally update groups of existing users as changes occur in data common to those users. UIMPORT requires a delimited ASCII file from which to read its data. (Delimiters are defined in the control file you set up to tell UIMPORT how to handle incoming data. The default delimiter is a comma.)

A home directory location may be specified and home directories may be created when creating users with UIMPORT.

The two components that are needed to run UIMPORT are:

➤ **A control file** A control file is composed of headers and format information. The headers tell UIMPORT what type of format information to expect from the indented information to follow, and the format information tells UIMPORT how to handle the incoming data.

➤ **A delimited ASCII file** The delimited data file contains user information that is processed by UIMPORT using the conditions that are specified in the control file.

A typical control file looks like this:

```
Import Control
      Name Context=.SALES.MKTG.ORG
      User Template=y
      Create home directory=y
      Home directory path="\users"
      Home directory volume=".sys.org"
      Separator=,
      Name Context = .OU=NYC.O=EMA
Fields
```

```
Last Name
Name
Title
Department
```

A typical delimited ASCII data file looks like this:

```
Smith,John,Engineer,R & D
Jackson,Frederic,Manager,Marketing
Johnstone,Mary,President,Sales
```

The following rules must be followed to create users with UIMPORT:

➤ If you do not specify a context in which to create the users, UIMPORT will create them in the current context by default.

> *Note:* *Context is covered in detail in Chapter 3.*

➤ A comma delimiter in the ASCII data file tells UIMPORT to create a new property in the matching control-file field.

➤ If changes occur in your data file, you can run UIMPORT and update existing users with the changes.

➤ The control file ends in a .CTL extension and the ASCII file ends in a .DAT extension.

➤ The syntax necessary to use UIMPORT is:

```
UIMPORT CONTROL_FILE.CTL USER_DATA.DAT
```

NetWare License Management

Administrating user accounts also involves assigning licenses to users. These licenses allow the users to connect to the network. NetWare is a licensed application, which means that the number of users that log in cannot exceed the number of licenses currently installed.

NetWare has developed a new client/server model for licensing server connections. Previously, a NetWare server had connection licensing only at the server. If a server had a 500-user license, it would allow any of 500 users to access the server. If you tried to log in as the 501st user, you would be refused a connection. With NetWare's new client/server licensing model, you can guarantee access to a specific user or container by assigning a specific license to that user or container. A license that is assigned to a user or container is not available to anyone until that assignment is revoked.

Managing NetWare License Connections

When you manage NetWare license connections, you must decide whether you need to guarantee a license to certain users, groups, or containers, or whether you just permit anyone to access the licenses on a first-come/first-serve basis. If your have more licenses than users, you do not need to make any assignments. (Your server connection licenses will allow more users than presently exist, so no guaranteed license assignments have to be made to ensure that certain users always have a license.)

If you have more users than server licenses (which is common in large multi-server networks), you have to make specific license assignments to those users who must have a connection whenever they request it.

When you install NetWare, two types of License objects are created:

➤ **License container objects** These objects contain the license certificates that grant access to the NetWare server.

 Note: License container objects are actually leaf objects.

➤ **License Certificate objects** These objects *are* the licenses.

 When you install a NetWare license, two types of License objects are created:

 ➤ **User License container** This object contains the user licenses.

 ➤ **Server License container** This object contains the server licenses.

License container objects can contain numerous License Certificate objects. As illustrated in Figure 5.11, the names of the objects consist of the publisher, product, number of licenses, and version.

Figure 5.11   The names of the objects consist of the publisher, product, number of licenses, and version.

Assigning License Certificates To Objects

You don't need to assign licenses to specific users or containers for them to be granted access to the network. If you do not make license assignments, the total number of licenses will be available to any user who can access the NetWare 5 server (if the number of users is less than the number of server licenses). If you choose to specifically assign licenses to NetWare objects, the licenses will not be available to any other objects.

You can make licenses available to users by assigning them to any of the following objects:

➤ Organization

➤ Organizational Unit

➤ User

➤ Group

The following rules apply when assigning a container object to a license certificate:

➤ All users in that container will be granted a license from the license certificate.

➤ Any users in child container objects of the container object that is assigned to the License object may also access the license container that contains the license certificate and be granted a connection. (A license container is not an NDS container object like an Organization or Organizational Unit.)

➤ The right for users to use the licenses flows down the NDS tree.

Installing Licenses

You install licenses from either the server or a workstation. Follow these steps to assign licenses from a server:

1. From the server console, exit the GUI by clicking on Exit GUI from the start button.

2. Type "NWCONFIG" at the server prompt.

3. Select License Options.

4. Select Install Licenses.

5. Change the path if you are installing from a floppy disk.

6. Press Enter.

To install licenses from a workstation, you log in as the Admin user (or equivalent) and do the following:

1. Put the floppy disk that contains the new license certificate in the server's floppy drive.

2. Using the NetWare Administrator utility, choose Tools|Install License| Install License Certificate.

3. In the dialog box that appears, browse for the NLF certificate file on the disk.

4. Type in the NDS context for the License Certificate object by browsing the tree and selecting the parent container of the User License container object.

Network Security

Network security is not controlled by any single security system. As mentioned previously in this chapter, the four security systems are:

➤ Login security

➤ NDS security

➤ Printing security

➤ File-system security

Two features you must understand about network security are login security and its subset, authentication. These two features work together to protect user accounts from unauthorized access while providing speedy access to authorized security clearances. You must understand user account restrictions to provide the granular levels of privilege needed to make a network as secure as necessary.

Login Security

Three main sections—authentication, intruder detection, and user account restrictions—of login security work together to provide continuous verification of network access:

➤ **Authentication** This is the process by which NetWare examines the entities that are attempting to access its resources and determines if they are forgeries. Authentication is so vast in its technical construct that we will look at only its main process.

➤ **Intruder detection** This process is designed to prevent would-be
intruders from guessing passwords in attempts to break into the system.
It locks out requests for network authorization when the number of
failed attempts exceeds the number of authorized attempts.

➤ **User account restrictions** These restrictions prevent users from logging
in from specified workstations, or at various times of the day or week.
The restrictions are a layer of security that you need to understand so
you can create the maximum protection from login attempts that should
not be occurring during certain times or from certain locations.

Figure 5.12 shows the login process that NetWare executes when a user tries to
log in.

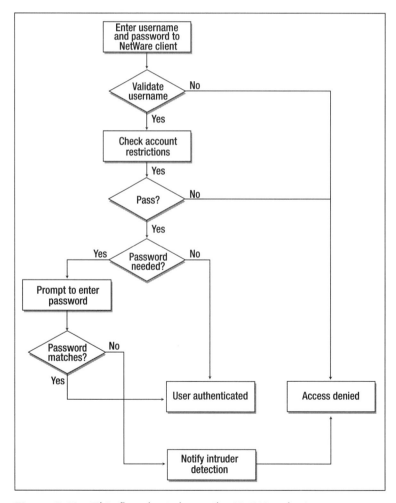

Figure 5.12   This flowchart shows the NetWare login process.

Understanding Authentication

Authentication is a continuous process that is performed as a series of background checks that are not noticeable to the user. These background checks verify the authenticity of any client request that arrives at a NetWare server. The process involved in authentication is as follows:

1. A user makes a login request.

2. The operating system returns a unique code.

3. The code is combined with the login information (time, MAC address, and password) to make a unique key that is used to authenticate the client when it makes a network request.

4. The key is used to check for authenticity at any time during the communication process.

The purpose of authentication is to verify the following:

➤ The message is coming only from the workstation where the authentication key was created.

➤ Only the sender built the message being sent.

➤ The message has not been corrupted or tampered with.

➤ The message was initiated from the current session.

➤ The message contains no counterfeited data from another session.

Understanding Intruder Detection

Intruder detection offers another level of security to prevent unauthorized users from guessing the password to a user account. The following are also features of the intruder detection security system:

➤ Prevents users from breaking into the system by guessing passwords.

➤ Records the network address of the workstation from which the intruder attempted to log in.

➤ Determines the number of failed attempts a user is permitted before locking the account.

➤ Locks the account until the lock expires or until the administrator unlocks it.

Understanding User Account Restrictions

User account restrictions are properties that limit the account's initial access to the network. You set up restrictions in the properties pages of a User object for the following:

➤ **Account Balance** Users are given an account that has units of time that are "spent." The account balance represents the unused time before the credit limit expires. When you have used all the time in the account balance, the account is automatically disabled. This property may also be assigned to an entire group instead of just to individual users in the group.

➤ **Connections** By default, users are not limited to the number of workstations that they can be logged into simultaneously. However, you can set the number of simultaneous logins a user may have.

➤ **Disable/Enable** An account may be disabled or reenabled using this option, as when, for example, the intruder detection system disables an account after detecting fraudulent login attempts. That account must then be reenabled before the user can log in.

➤ **Expiration Date** If an expiration date is set in this field, the account is disabled on the date entered.

➤ **Network Address** This option specifies from which workstations users may log in. It does so by specifying the network address of stations from which they are authorized to log in.

➤ **Password** When the option is set to require a password, any combination of the following restrictions can be applied to that user:

➤ **Force Periodic Password Changes** This option determines how often you require the user to change his or her password.

Although frequent changes of passwords are a simple and effective security procedure, the downside is that users tend to write down their passwords in obvious places because they cannot remember them.

➤ **Minimum Password Length** This option sets the required number of characters a password must be. The default is five characters, although it can be set higher or lower.

➤ **Unique Password** This option forces the user to use new passwords instead of allowing him or her to reuse the same ones. NetWare memorizes the last eight passwords, forcing the user to have at least eight original passwords.

➤ **Grace Login** This option sets the number of logins a user may execute after being reminded to change his or her password. After the number of grace logins are exhausted, the account is disabled and the user must contact an administrator to unlock the account.

➤ **Time** Also referred to as "time of day," this feature limits the hours of the day that a user can be logged into the network. Time can also be set for groups. If a user has an account that is individually restricted—and also has a group account that restricts time of day—the time-slot assignments are added together to produce a "least restrictive" assignment encompassing the total of the multiple time allotments.

If a user breaches any of these conditions, NetWare disables the user account and the account cannot be used to log into the network with that username.

Practice Questions

Question 1

> There is no object in the NDS tree more fundamental than the User object.
>
> ○ a. True
>
> ○ b. False

The correct answer is a, true. The User object is the most fundamental object in the NDS database.

Question 2

> Which of the following is not true concerning User objects?
>
> ○ a. You cannot create a User object in NetWare Administrator.
>
> ○ b. You cannot create a User object without an entry in the Last Name field.
>
> ○ c. You can assign User objects absolute access to any object, and its properties, in the NDS tree.
>
> ○ d. In order to have access to a printer on the network, you must have a Printer object associated with your User object.

The correct answer is a. You can create User objects in the following NetWare utilities: NetWare Administrator, ConsoleOne, NETADMIN, and UIMPORT. Answers b, c, and d are true and, therefore, incorrect.

Question 3

Which of the following are the NetWare utilities used to create User objects?
[Choose the three best answers]

❑ a. NetWare Administrator and its text-based counterpart, NETADMIN

❑ b. UIMPORT

❑ c. UserConsole

❑ d. ConsoleOne

The correct answers are a, b, and d. There's no such utility as UserConsole.
Therefore, answer c is incorrect.

Question 4

You can run the ConsoleOne utility from the file server or from a workstation.

○ a. True

○ b. False

The correct answer is a, true. You can run the ConsoleOne utility from both
the file server and from a workstation.

Question 5

The Admin user account is always the default account used to begin setting
up the NDS tree.

○ a. True

○ b. False

The correct answer is a, true. Although the Admin account may be renamed
and have its security modified, it's still the default account created during the
installation of NDS.

Question 6

> Which of the following statements are true about a Template object? [Choose the three best answers]
>
> ❏ a. You use the Template object to manage the property fields of large groups of users.
>
> ❏ b. You use the Template object to create multiple users from a database of usernames.
>
> ❏ c. You may alter the properties of many User objects at the same time by making the changes to the Template object.
>
> ❏ d. You can modify objects created and assigned to a Template object by making changes to the Template object.

The correct answers are a, c, and d. You use the UIMPORT utility to create users from a database. Therefore, answer b is incorrect.

Question 7

> If you delete the Admin user without assigning appropriate rights to another user, you are still able to manage the NDS tree properly.
>
> ○ a. True
>
> ○ b. False

The correct answer is b, false. If you delete the Admin object without having the same Admin rights assigned to another object, you'll lose access to part or all of the NDS tree.

Question 8

> Which of the following statements are true concerning the ConsoleOne utility? [Choose the two best answers]
>
> ❏ a. ConsoleOne is a Java application.
>
> ❏ b. ConsoleOne permits the renaming of a new NDS tree.
>
> ❏ c. ConsoleOne permits the renaming of the [Root] object.
>
> ❏ d. ConsoleOne permits the renaming of container and User objects.

The correct answers are a and d. ConsoleOne doesn't permit the renaming of a new NDS tree. Therefore, answer b is incorrect. The [Root] object cannot be renamed under any condition. Therefore, answer c is incorrect.

Question 9

Which objects can be created in ConsoleOne? [Choose the four best answers]

- ❏ a. Organization
- ❏ b. Organizational Unit
- ❏ c. User
- ❏ d. Group
- ❏ e. Country

The correct answers are a, b, c, and d. The Country object cannot be created in ConsoleOne. Therefore, answer e is incorrect.

Question 10

Which of the following items are necessary to create User accounts with UIMPORT? [Choose the three best answers]

- ❏ a. A delimited ASCII file of usernames and related data
- ❏ b. An ASCII control file
- ❏ c. Statements defining the fields to be imported
- ❏ d. A control statement telling UIMPORT what context to put the users in

The correct answers are a, b, and c. UIMPORT will create users in the current context if no context has been defined. Therefore, d is incorrect.

Question 11

If the number of users logged into a NetWare server exceeds the number of connection licenses, the server will permit the connection but it will be a violation of the license agreement.

- ○ a. True
- ○ b. False

The correct answer to this question is b, false. The NetWare operating system prevents you from connecting if you do not have a valid license connection.

Question 12

> Which of the following are valid components of the NetWare licensing system?
> [Choose the four best answers]
>
> ❑ a. License Certificate object
>
> ❑ b. User license
>
> ❑ c. Container license
>
> ❑ d. Server license
>
> ❑ e. Server License container

The correct answers to this question are a, b, d, and e. There is no such thing as a container license. Therefore, answer c is incorrect.

Question 13

> License container objects are actually leaf objects.
>
> ○ a. True
>
> ○ b. False

The correct answer to this question is a, true. Although License container objects contain licenses, they are actually leaf objects because they do not contain other NDS objects. They only contain License Certificate objects.

Question 14

> How many of the following items are contained in a License Certificate?
> [Choose the three best answers]
>
> ❑ a. Product name
>
> ❑ b. Product version
>
> ❑ c. License connection parameters
>
> ❑ d. Number of license units available

The correct answers to this question are a, b, and d. There's no such thing as a license connection parameter. Therefore, answer c is incorrect.

Question 15

When creating a Template object in ConsoleOne, you must fill in which of the following mandatory fields? [Choose the best answer(s)]

❏ a. Template Name

❏ b. Members

❏ c. Define Additional Properties

❏ d. None of the above

The correct answer is d. You cannot create a Template object in ConsoleOne. Therefore a, b, and c are incorrect.

Need To Know More?

 Novell course 560 manual. Netware 5 Administration. Novell, Inc., 1998. This manual is available from Novell (1-800-NetWare) or from any authorized Novell training center.

 www.novell.com/documentation/en/nw5/nw5/docui/ index.html contains a copy of the NetWare 5 documentation.

 www.novell.com/netware5/ is Novell's NetWare Web page. You can order the NetWare 5—3 user demo from this page. You may also call 1-800-NetWare to order live demo copies of NetWare 5.

 www.flashcards.com is an inexpensive but excellent study resource to help prepare for Novell exams. Select Novell QSets and scroll down to 560 NetWare 5 Administration.

Novell Distributed Print Services Configuration

Terms you'll need to understand:

√ Novell Distributed Print Services (NDPS)

√ NDPS Broker

√ Printer Agent

√ Public access printer

√ Controlled access printer

√ Novell Printer Manager

Techniques you'll need to master:

√ Creating NDPS Manager objects

√ Creating Printer Agents

√ Creating controlled access printers

√ Creating NDPS Printer objects

√ Configuring Printer Agents

√ Configuring printer access

√ Configuring print jobs

As an administrator, one of the most time-consuming responsibilities is printing, a feature of networked computers that users often take for granted. Printers are among the few devices used in networking that have actual moving parts, such as rollers, fusers, and drums. In addition, the devices are fairly sophisticated. A laser printer, for example, takes digital information, changes it to electrical charges, applies the toner to the paper, and then fuses the toner to the paper to produce the printed text or image.

To make matters more difficult, users from across the network—with different computers, operating systems, and applications—are allowed to print to a shared printing device. In addition, multiple users will often be printing to one device at the same time. With all of these factors working against us, it's not a surprise that most administrators spend much of their time on printing issues.

NetWare offers considerable improvement in network printing with Novell Distributed Print Services (NDPS). In this chapter, you'll learn to create and configure NDPS in NetWare Administrator. You'll learn how to set up the NDPS manager, Printer Agents, gateways, and brokers. You'll also discover how to create public and controlled access printers, how to configure and manage printing from workstations, and how to manage printer access and print jobs.

Printing On A Network Using NDPS

Before you can fully comprehend how a network printer operates, you need to understand how standalone—non-network—printing works. In standalone printing, the printer and the computer are connected directly to each other, usually by a printer cable. (In some cases, the computer may be communicating with the printer via an infrared connection.) The actual communication is accomplished with driver software that is stored on the computer. Normally, each type of printer requires a different printer driver; even printers from the same manufacturers will need different drivers. (For example, although an HP LaserJet 6P will most likely function properly with the driver for the HP LaserJet 6L, you may find that you lose some functionality.) So, to make full use of all of your printers' features, you should use their specific drivers.

The print driver converts messages from a format that the computer understands to a format that the printer understands. This driver also makes the application attempting to print independent of the printer. When PCs were in their infancy (when DOS was the prevalent operating system), each application had to know how to "talk" to the printer. Every time you got a new printer, you needed a patch for each application that required the capability to print.

Now, this communication is accomplished by the operating system and the printer driver.

Another drawback of early print technology was that each user who needed to print required his or her own printer. This, of course, was an expensive solution. The alternative was network printing. Although a network printer is usually more expensive that the standalone printer, it's also usually faster and has greater paper-handling capabilities.

In a networked environment, a printer is usually shared between several users and workstations. When a user prints, the print job travels through a print driver on the local workstation (in a very similar manner to a standalone installation) to a print queue on the network. The print jobs are stored in the print queue until a print server sends them to the actual printer.

Printers can be connected to a network in three different ways, as shown in Figure 6.1. They can be attached either through a workstation or a server that does not contain printing software, directly to the network, or to the network through a server running the printing software.

When a printer is connected through a workstation, the workstation's network board is responsible for the communication between the print server and the printer. This communication is transparent to the user. If, however, the attached printer is heavily used, the communication between the print server and the printer will noticeably slow the workstation. If a printer's high volume begins to affect the performance of the workstation, the printer should be upgraded to either a direct connection or a dedicated print server.

> *Note:* *A network board is also called a network interface card (NIC), network adapter, and network interface board. Novell uses the term network board most often. However, network board vendors usually call it a NIC.*

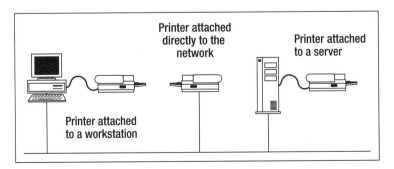

Figure 6.1 Methods for connecting network printers.

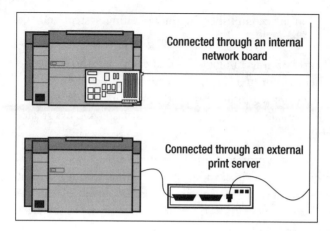

Figure 6.2 Methods to connect printers directly to the network.

There are two ways to connect a printer directly to the network, as shown in Figure 6.2:

➤ The first method is to purchase a specialized network board that installs directly in the printer. This network board will not install in just any printer: The printer must be a network-capable printer. This board allows you to configure different protocols for the printer and also allows the printer to communicate on the network (as if it's a workstation or a server).

➤ The second method involves an external box, called a *printer server box*. The printer server box has one or more parallel-port connectors and one or more network connections. Using this method, you can use any printer, because you can simply connect the printer in the same way that you connect it to a computer. The printer server box acts as the workstation or server and allows the printer to communicate on the network.

When configuring printers in a NetWare 4 environment, you had to configure the print queue, the print server, and the printer individually because they were represented by separate objects in Novell Directory Services (NDS). Only after each of these components was configured properly would they work together properly. This task (called *queue-based printing*) was at times, and can still be, difficult.

Note: Queue-based printing is discussed in Exam Cram for Advanced NetWare 5 Administration CNE, *also published by Certification Insider Press.*

Queue-based printing has been replaced by Novell Distributed Print Services (NDPS). You're no longer required to create, configure, and connect print queues, print servers, and printers. You simply use NDPS to manage all these tasks, which are centered on the printer itself. The printer is configured and managed through the NDS using NetWare Administrator.

NDPS brings several benefits to NetWare 5. It reduces problems that are normally associated with network printing and the amount of your time that is required to manage and administer the network, and it improves network performance. Another advantage is that the three components used in the previous versions of NetWare—the printer, print server, and print queue—are all combined into a single object called the *Printer Agent*. As the user sends print jobs, the jobs are routed directly to the printer instead of the print queue.

NDPS has also replaced the need to install the printer driver at each workstation. Instead, NDPS downloads the printer drivers to each workstation as they are needed. From a management standpoint, this is a huge timesaver if the drivers need to be replaced. For example, let's say that you are administering a network with 50 workstations that share a single printer. A new version of the driver is released that fixes some bugs in the old driver. With NetWare 4, you would have had to visit each of the workstations and physically install the new printer driver. With NetWare 5 and NDPS, all you have to do is replace the printer driver on the Printer Agent. The next time users attempt to print, a new version of the driver is automatically downloaded to the workstations.

For backward compatibility with previous version of NetWare, the older queue-based printers will still work. Remember, however, that queue-based printing is no longer required.

Setting Up NDPS On The Network

The NDPS Manager is a software module that you'll use to create and manage Printer Agents. You must load it on a NetWare 5 server either by batch file or by manually typing a command (such as **LOAD NDPSM** *manager_name_and_context*) at the server console. Nevertheless, it must be running on the server to perform its tasks, which include the following:

➤ Acts as a repository for Printer Agents

➤ Controls access to Printer Agents

➤ Controls Printer Agents

➤ Functions as the NDS object in which you create Printer Agents

Creating The NDPS Manager

NDPS was loaded on your server's hard drive when you installed NetWare 5, but it must be configured before it can become a useful network resource. The NDPS Manager is the first object you create when you set up NDPS, and it's the tool that you use to set up and manage all other parts of NDPS. The NDPS Manager is to NDPS as NetWare Administrator is to NDS.

To configure NDPS on the network, you create an NDPS Manager using the following steps:

1. In NetWare Administrator, select the container object in which you want to create the NDPS Manager.

2. Right-click on the container object and select Create|NDPS Manager from the pop-up menu. Click on OK. The Create NDPS Manager Object dialog box appears, as shown in Figure 6.3.

3. Type a name for the NDPS Manager in the NDPS Manager Name field.

4. Select the browse button beside the Resident Server field and choose the server on which you want the NDPS Manager to reside.

5. Use the browse button beside the Database Volume field to choose the volume on which you want to create the NDPS Manager database.

6. Click on Create to create the NDPS Manager.

Printer Agents

Printer Agents are the resource that the NDPS Manager was designed to manage. The two classes of Printer Agents are a public access printer and a controlled

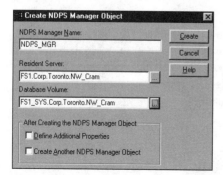

Figure 6.3 The Create NDPS Manager Object dialog box.

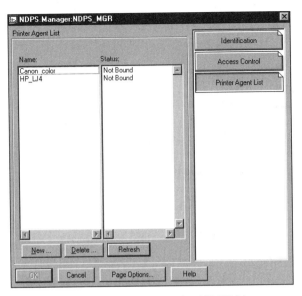

Figure 6.4   Printer Agents in the NDPS Manager.

access printer. A public access printer is represented as a Printer Agent in the NDPS Manager (as shown in Figure 6.4). A controlled access printer shows up in the NDPS Manager list of Printer Agents, and it's additionally represented by an NDS object called an *NDPS Printer object*.

Creating Public Access Printers

Novell created public access printers to simplify the administration of security assignments. In previous versions of NetWare (4.x and newer), printers were always NDS objects, which meant that only controlled access to these printers was available. You had to make or manage NDS trustee assignments to anyone needing to use a printer.

Public access printers are not represented by NDS objects, and therefore have no security assigned to them. These printers, as the name implies, are available to anyone who has access to the network. The following steps detail how to create a public access printer:

1. Use NetWare Administrator to navigate to the NDPS Manager from which you want to manage the printer.

2. Right-click on the NDPS Manager you selected and select Details.

3. In the NDPS Manager property page, select Printer Agent List.

4. Select New. The Create Printer Agent dialog box appears (as shown in Figure 6.5).

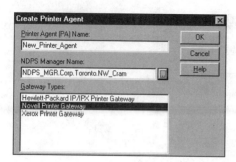

Figure 6.5 The Create Printer Agent dialog box.

5. Enter a name in the Printer Agent (PA) Name field.

6. Choose the appropriate gateway type: Hewlett-Packard, Novell, or Xerox.

7. Configure the gateway appropriately for the type of gateway you chose. (See the following sections to learn how to configure the different printer gateways.)

Configuring NDPS Printer Gateways

Printers that are "NDPS-aware" have an imbedded Printer Agent that recognizes and connects directly to the NDPS Manager. If you do not have an NDPS-aware printer, you need a gateway that allows your workstation client to connect to other printers. The three types of printer gateways that ship with NetWare 5 are Hewlett-Packard IP/IPX, Novell, and Xerox, each of which is explained in the following sections.

Hewlett-Packard IP/IPX Printer Gateway

The Hewlett-Packard IP/IPX printer gateway allows you to use all Hewlett-Packard JetDirect print servers or printers with internal JetDirect cards that are connected directly to the network. When you select this gateway, the Configure HP Printer Gateway dialog box appears, as shown in Figure 6.6.

Use the following steps to configure the Hewlett-Packard IP/IPX printer gateway:

1. Select the type of printer you're using.

2. Choose the protocol you want to use: either IP or IPX.

3. Select the JetDirect card from the list of print servers, or specify the IP or MAC address of that device.

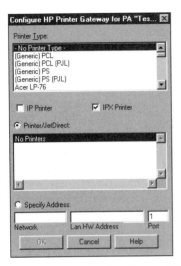

Figure 6.6   The Configure HP Printer Gateway dialog box.

4. Click on OK.

5. In the dialog box that appears, select the printer drivers (for each operating system) that you want automatically downloaded to a user's workstation when the printer is installed on that station. Click on Continue.

The Printer Agent is created.

Novell Printer Gateway

The Novell printer gateway is designed to be used for all printers that are not NDPS-aware. You'll also use this gateway with any printers whose manufacturers did not provide a gateway. Most legacy printers have to be set up using this gateway. Choose the Novell gateway selection from the Create Printer Agent dialog box, and the configuration screen appears, as shown in Figure 6.7.

Follow these steps to configure the Novell Print Device Subsystem (PDS) for the Printer Agent:

1. Choose the type of printer from the Printer Type list.

2. Choose the Novell Port Handler in the Port Handler Type section of the dialog box and click on OK.

3. Select the type of connection and port type.

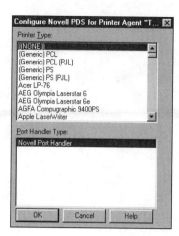

Figure 6.7 The Configure Novell PDS For Printer Agent configuration screen.

4. Click on Next.

5. You are required to supply details, such as queue name, depending on the type of port you selected. Fill in the appropriate details.

6. Click on Finish. The Printer Agent loads, and the Select Printer Drivers dialog screen appears.

7. Select the printer drivers (for each operating system) you want automatically downloaded to a user's workstation when the printer is installed on that station. Click on Continue.

The Printer Agent appears in the Printer Agent list in the NDPS Manager screen.

Xerox Printer Gateway

The Xerox printer gateway is for Xerox printers that are not NDPS-aware. Select the Xerox printer gateway from the Create Printer Agent dialog box and the Xerox Setup Wizard screen appears, as shown in Figure 6.8.

To install this gateway, click on Next in the wizard dialog box. The Xerox Printer Installation Wizard searches the network for network-aware Xerox printers. It then produces a list of printers from which you select the appropriate one. If you have Xerox printers that are not network-aware, they will not be detected by the wizard. You'll need to configure non-network-aware printers with the Novell printer gateway.

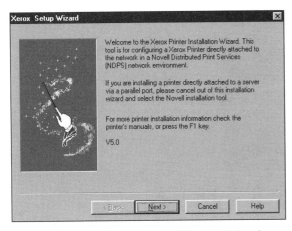

Figure 6.8   The Xerox Setup Wizard dialog box.

Note: After creating each gateway, you're given the option to select the printer drivers you want downloaded whenever you install a printer at a workstation. This allows you to update your NDPS Manager with the latest drivers and mitigates the extra work of installing printer drivers on individual workstations. The drivers are pulled off the server whenever you install a printer.

Creating A Controlled Access Printer

Frequently, you'll restrict access to specific printers. You may have plotters, color laser printers, sign-cutting devices, or other specialized imaging equipment that has significant costs associated with its operation. You control access to these devices so that only certain users or workstations can use them. The following steps guide you through the process of creating a controlled access printer:

1. In NetWare Administrator, select the container object in which you will create the printer.

2. Right-click on the container object and select Create|NDPS Printer from the pop-up menu. Click on OK to call up the Create NDPS Printer dialog box (see Figure 6.9).

3. Enter a name for the printer and then click on the radio button for Create A New Printer Agent (or you can choose an existing NDPS Printer object by selecting the checkbox for Existing NDPS Printer Object In NDS). Click on Create.

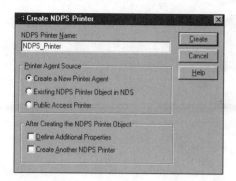

Figure 6.9 Creating a controlled access printer.

4. Link the printer to an NDPS Manager by selecting One in the NDPS Manager Name field.

5. Choose a gateway and configure it as illustrated previously in the "Configuring NDPS Printer Gateways" section of this chapter.

6. Select the appropriate printer driver for each operating system you want supported.

7. Make security trustee assignments, such as users or groups, to the printer's access control list (ACL).

The NDPS Broker Object

When you first install NetWare 5 on a computer, you are given the option to install NDPS as part of the server installation. If you did not choose to install NDPS when you created the server, you can do it later using the NWCONFIG utility that resides on the server. When NDPS is installed, an object called an *NDPS Broker object* is created automatically and appears in the same container object where your File Server object is created. The NDPS Broker object handles the following functions:

➤ **Event Notification Services** This service enables printers to deliver event and status notifications through a variety of delivery methods.

➤ **Service Registry Services** This service allows public access printers to advertise themselves and maintains a database of device identifications.

➤ **Resource Management Services** This service allows you to maintain a centralized repository of network-related software resources for device configuration—such as drivers or clients—that you would otherwise have to install manually.

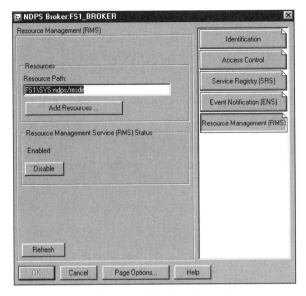

Figure 6.10 The NDPS Broker dialog box.

To view the layout and function of the NDPS Broker object, perform the following steps:

1. Double-click on the NDPS Broker object, and the NDPS Broker dialog box appears. (See Figure 6.10.)

2. Click on the Resource Management (RMS) tab.

3. Click on the Add Resources button, and the Manage Resources dialog screen appears.

4. In the Resource Types area, click on one of the resource types.

5. In the Current Resources area, click on the Add button. From here, you can browse to the disk and directory that contain the updated or new printer drivers. You install the printer drivers from this location so they are available for updates across the network.

Printing From Workstations To NDPS Printers

The whole point of all this network paraphernalia is to provide end users sitting at their workstations with a simple, yet flexible, method of getting their print jobs to the printer. As the administrator, you must efficiently install and configure printer drivers on workstations so that all the users have to do is to send their print jobs to the printer of their choice. End users should not be concerned with loading or installing printer drivers.

You use NDPS to configure your network printing system so when users log in, they automatically receive the correct drivers installed and configured on their workstation. The users never need to install or configure anything to do with printing—they don't even have to set the default printer. You configure all this in advance when you set up NDPS Printer Agents. The next time the user logs into the network, NDPS takes over, downloads the correct drivers, and configures them on the user's workstation.

Where user requirements are more varied and specific, you also have the option to manually configure each station from Novell Printer Manager, which is discussed in the section titled "Manual Printer Configuration" later in this chapter.

Automatic Printer Configuration

For large networks with many users, automatic printer configuration is obviously the ideal option. To set a printer driver to download and configure on users' workstations automatically, you must do the following:

1. In NetWare Administrator, select the container that contains the users who will use the printer you want configured.

2. Right-click on the container object, and select Details.

3. Select the NDPS Remote Printer Management page. The NDPS Remote Printer Management screen appears, as shown in Figure 6.11.

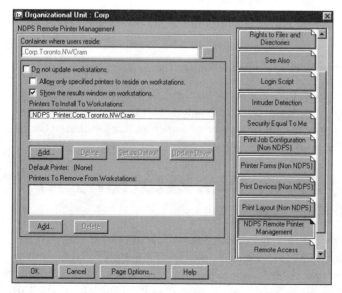

Figure 6.11 The NDPS Remote Printer Management screen.

4. Click on Add under Printers To Install To Workstations, choose an available public access or controlled access printer from the list provided, and click on OK to return to the NDPS Remote Printer Management dialog box.

5. Select the Update Driver button.

6. Optionally, set the default printer.

Now, when users who reside in this container log into the network again, their printer drivers are installed automatically and configured, or are updated with the latest drivers.

Manual Printer Configuration

To understand manual printer configuration, you need to use a workstation utility called *Novell Printer Manager*. This utility enables users to completely manage their printing tasks from their workstations. The following steps explain how to install this utility:

1. Execute the file NWPMW32.EXE from the SYS:PUBLIC\WIN32 directory on your NetWare 5 server. The Novell Printer Manager interface screen appears, as shown in Figure 6.12.

   You manage the following tasks from the Novell Printer Manager interface:

   ➤ Adding or deleting printers

   ➤ Changing the order of jobs

Figure 6.12   The Novell Printer Manager interface.

Figure 6.13 The Novell Printers dialog box for adding printers.

➤ Checking status information of jobs

➤ Pausing, resuming, and deleting jobs

➤ Receiving event notification

➤ Updating printer lists

2. In the Novell Printer Manager interface, choose Printer|New. The Novell Printers dialog box appears, as shown in Figure 6.13.

3. Click the Add button.

4. Select the printer you want to install, select Install, and click on OK.

5. Close the dialog box. Your printer driver is installed.

NDPS Printing Management

You manage printer access to determine who does what with which printers. To determine who has access to printers, you use the Access Control tab on an NDPS Printer object. You determine what a user can do by selecting a role and adding users, groups, or containers to that role.

Access management and print-job management encompass the two main aspects of NDPS printing management. They are covered in the following sections.

Printer Access

You'll choose one of three roles when you assign access control to a user or group:

➤ **User** A user can send, reconfigure, or remove his or her own print jobs.

➤ **Operator** An operator can pause, restart, abort, set configuration defaults, reinitialize, and change the order of jobs.

➤ **Manager** A manager can add and delete users from the printer. A manager can also create, modify, and delete printer configurations, and configure notification profiles. The manager role is a troubleshooting role.

Print Job

You manage print jobs by changing the jobs' status. To perform any of the following printing tasks you must be assigned the role of either operator or manager for the printer in question. Typical tasks include modifying, deleting, moving, and copying print jobs, changing the order or priority of print jobs, viewing information details about print jobs, and modifying a printer's configuration.

Modifying, Deleting, Moving, And Copying A Print Job

A print job sent to the queue inherits the configuration settings of the installed printer. The job's owner and the printer operator can make modifications to the job itself, and these modifications will override any properties that the job may have inherited from the printer configuration.

To modify a print job, perform the following steps:

1. In Novell Printer Manager, right-click on the printer to which the job was sent, and select Jobs|Job List.

2. Right-click on the job you want to modify, and select Configuration.

3. Select the tab that corresponds with where, how, or when you want to affect the job's execution.

4. Alter the properties that you wish to change, and click on OK.

You delete a print job by performing the following steps:

1. In Novell Printer Manager, right-click on the printer to which the job was sent.

2. Select Jobs, and right-click on the job you want to delete.

3. Choose Cancel Printing or press the Delete key on the keyboard.

You may move or copy a print job if it meets the following three conditions:

➤ You're the print job's owner or an operator.

➤ Both the current and target printers are on the same NetWare 5 server.

➤ The target printer is compatible with the current printer.

To copy or move a print job from one printer to another:

1. In Novell Printer Manager, right-click on the printer to which the job was sent, and select Jobs.

2. Right-click on the job you want to copy or move and select Copy Or Move.

3. In the Copy Job Or Move Job dialog box that appears, select the printer to which you want the job moved or copied.

4. Select Copy or Move.

Note: *When changing the order of the print jobs, and copying or moving print jobs, you can press F5 to automatically update the information.*

Changing The Order Of Print Jobs

When there are several jobs in the queue and you need one of them printed before the others, you can change its priority. As an administrator, you're allowed to move print jobs up and down the order list. For example, you may want to move a particularly large print job to the lowest priority in the queue. The following steps detail how to change the order of a print job:

Note: *Users can't move jobs up the list. They can only move them down.*

1. In Novell Printer Manager, right-click on the printer to which the job was sent.

2. Select Jobs, and right-click on the job you want to reorder and choose Reorder.

3. Select the number that corresponds with the position in the queue that you want the job to have, and click on OK.

Viewing Print Job Information

To view information about a print job:

1. In Novell Printer Manager, right-click on the printer to which the job was sent.

2. Select Jobs, and right-click on the job you want to view.

3. Select Information to view the status, job owner, job name, submission date, and the size of the print job.

Modifying A Printer's Configuration

You can modify the printer configuration on your workstation before sending any print jobs. If you do so, every job you send to that printer will use the properties of the modified configuration as the job is processed.

To modify a printer's configuration:

1. From the Novell Printer Manager (see Figure 6.12 earlier), select Printer|New|Configuration.

2. Select any of the tabs and make whatever configuration changes you wish.

Practice Questions

Question 1

> To create an NDPS printer queue, which of the following conditions must be met?
>
> ○ a. You must be logged into the network and have NetWare Administrator running.
>
> ○ b. You must be in the container object in which you want the queue created.
>
> ○ c. You must have a valid container license.
>
> ○ d. You must supply a valid name for the NDPS printer queue.
>
> ○ e. None of the above are correct.

The correct answer to this question is e. There is no such object as an NDPS printer queue, which is why this is a trick question. Therefore a, b, c, and d are incorrect.

Question 2

> Which of the following are valid components of the NDPS printing system? [Choose the three best answers]
>
> ❑ a. Printer Agent
>
> ❑ b. Printer object license
>
> ❑ c. NDPS Manager
>
> ❑ d. NDPS Broker

The correct answers to this question are a, c, and d. There's no such thing as a "printer object license." Therefore, answer b is incorrect.

Question 3

The NDPS Broker object is created automatically when the NetWare 5 server is installed.

○ a. True

○ b. False

The correct answer to this question is b, false. The Broker object is created only if you select the option to install NDPS on the server.

Question 4

Which of the following statements describe the NDPS Manager? [Choose the three best answers]

❑ a. It's a repository for Printer Agents.

❑ b. It controls access to Printer Agents.

❑ c. It controls printer icons.

❑ d. It's used to create Printer Agents.

The correct answers to this question are a, b, and d. The NDPS Manager does not control printer icons. Therefore, answer c is incorrect.

Question 5

Which of the following does not describe a public access printer?

○ a. It's an NDS object.

○ b. It has no security.

○ c. It's a Printer Agent.

○ d. It was not available in NetWare 4.11.

The correct answer to this question is a. Public access printers are not NDS objects. Therefore, answers b, c, and d are incorrect.

Question 6

Which of the following are valid gateways that ship with NetWare 5 NDPS?
[Choose the three best answers]

❏ a. Xerox gateway

❏ b. Hewlett-Packard gateway

❏ c. IBM gateway

❏ d. Microsoft gateway

❏ e. Novell gateway

The correct answers to this question are a, b, and e. IBM and Microsoft do not ship gateways with NetWare 5. Therefore, answers c and d are incorrect.

Question 7

The Novell gateway is used for all printers that are NDPS-aware.

○ a. True

○ b. False

The correct answer to this question is b, false. The Novell gateway is used for all printers that are not NDPS-aware.

Need To Know More?

 Go to the Help screen in NetWare Administrator and select the Table of Contents. Scroll down to Novell Distributed Print Services—Managing Printers.

 support.novell.com is the Novell Support Connection page. Click on Knowledgebase and search for documents 2930094 (which is an NDPS white paper) and 2929349 (which is the NDPS release notes).

File-System Management

Terms you'll need to understand:

√ NetWare Administrator

√ Volume

√ Directory

√ Subdirectory

√ File

√ Salvage

√ Purge

√ FILER

√ **NCOPY**

√ **NDIR**

√ NETADMIN

√ Drive pointer

√ Drive mapping

Techniques you'll need to master:

√ Using NetWare Administrator to manage volumes and files

√ Using FILER and other utilities to manage volumes and files

√ Using NetWare Administrator and FILER to salvage and purge deleted files

One of the main tasks you ask a server to do is to share files. Although the way that each network operating system actually accomplishes this task is different, the way that you see it is usually the same. NetWare—as well as DOS, Windows, and Unix—uses a system that is analogous to a filing cabinet. In this chapter, you'll learn how NetWare's file system is used. You'll also learn about some of the utilities available to you, as an administrator, to manage these resources. And, finally, you'll learn how to manage volume space on your NetWare servers.

Understanding The NetWare File System

As mentioned previously, most operating systems (and not just network operating systems) use a system whose structure and methods are familiar to anyone who has used a filing cabinet. The reason for this is simple: People tend to understand—and be comfortable with—things they've seen in the past. If a system is foreign to you, you find it harder to learn and master. For this reason, the file system used in the industry today is similar between the various operating systems. But, because this is a book about Novell NetWare Administrator 5, you'll obviously look at how NetWare deals with files and folders.

Designing a network filing system is easy. Designing a file system that is efficient and makes sense to the end user is more difficult. It's up to you, as an administrator, to decide how users will manage this information. In this chapter, we cover just the file system itself—the permissions you assign to the file system are covered in Chapter 8.

The File-System Components

The five major components of the NetWare file system are:

➤ NetWare server

➤ Volume

➤ Directory

➤ Subdirectory

➤ Files

Figure 7.1 shows a NetWare network file system.

The *NetWare server* can be compared to the actual filing cabinet. In the same way that a filing cabinet contains folders, documents, and documents within folders, the NetWare server can contain directories, files, and files within the directories.

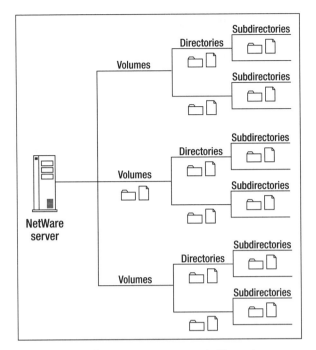

Figure 7.1   The NetWare network file system.

The *volume* is analogous to the drawers of the file cabinet. Most filing cabinets have multiple drawers: For example, you can store personal information in one drawer and business information in the other drawer. The same is true with volumes—a NetWare server can contain one or more volumes, and the volume can contain both directories and files.

A Novell NetWare server must have, at the very least, a single volume. This volume is known as the *SYS volume*, and it contains the binary and configuration files used by NetWare to initialize and run. NetWare will not install if this volume does not exist.

The third component, the *directory*, is very much like a folder within the filing cabinet drawer. In the same way that a physical folder contains documents (such as reports, letters, memos, forms, and so on), so can a directory. The directory can store any type of file, and it can also store other directories, known as subdirectories.

The *subdirectory* is the hardest component to compare to the filing cabinet. In real life, you wouldn't normally have a folder within a folder; instead you would likely have a second folder at the same "level" as the first. With computers, this is different. A folder can have a folder, which can have another folder, and so on. The best way to compare a subdirectory in our filing cabinet analogy is to call it a *divider*. For example, you may have a folder named "Novell-1998". This folder contains all Novell documents created in 1998. You could now place a divider behind the last document named "Novell-1999". Any document placed behind this divider will be known to deal with Novell and have been created in 1999. A subdirectory can have other subdirectories (this is where the analogy falls apart) and files.

The *files* are the smallest unit in a file system. As a rule, a file cannot contain other files: It can contain only information. The file is analogous to the individual pages or documents that are stored within the file folder.

> *Note: It was previously stated that documents could not contain other documents. You may ask, What about compressed archive files, such as ZIP files? The answer is simply that files contained within a ZIP file cannot be accessed "on the fly," that is to say, you must uncompress the files before they can be used. For this reason, a ZIP file does not truly contain files; it contains information that can be used to re-create the files.*

Managing The NetWare File System With The Administration Utilities

To completely manage the file system, you must know how to manage the files, directories, subdirectories, and volumes. Several of the necessary utilities to do this are built into NetWare 5.

Anyone that has used DOS or Windows will realize that Novell NetWare emulates the Windows (or DOS) file system. For this reason, you can use any built-in or third-party tool you prefer for managing this system. You can use either command-line DOS programs or the user-friendly Windows Explorer to complete these tasks. However, you should know that to take advantage of some of the Novell services, you must have the client software installed. As you learned before, the client software integrates with Windows Explorer, giving you extra features that are not normally available.

NetWare utilities that add functionality when managing the file system include:

➤ NetWare Administrator

➤ FILER

➤ NCOPY

➤ NDIR

➤ RENDIR

➤ FLAG

Only two of these utilities, NetWare Administrator and FILER, give you full functionality when managing the file system. We'll cover these two utilities in great detail and look briefly at the other four utilities.

NCOPY and **NDIR** are simply "NetWare-aware" versions of the DOS commands **COPY** and **DIR**. **NCOPY** allows you to copy files and directories between NetWare volumes while maintaining all NetWare security information and ownership attributes. **NDIR** returns all the information that the regular DOS **DIR** command does, including NetWare-specific information (such as the owner of the file). Some of the advanced features of this command allow you to search whole volumes or to search according to specific criteria, such as the file owner.

The **RENDIR** command renames directories, whereas the **FLAG** command allows you to modify the attributes for directories and files. This command is similar to the DOS **ATTRIB** command, only it's NetWare-aware in that it allows you to modify NetWare attributes, such as read-only, shared, read-write, and so on.

Of all the utilities available to you, only NetWare Administrator and FILER provide you the tools that will completely manage the file system for you.

NetWare Administrator

As you have seen in previous chapters, NetWare Administrator was developed as an all-in-one management tool. It is, by far, the most complete tool for the management of NetWare file systems. NetWare Administrator allows you to complete the following tasks:

➤ Copy, move, and delete files and directories.

➤ View and manage all NetWare file and directory properties and attributes.

➤ Control data migration.

➤ Copy, move, and delete multiple files.

➤ Delete and move directory structures.

➤ Manage file-system attributes.

➤ Salvage and purge deleted files.

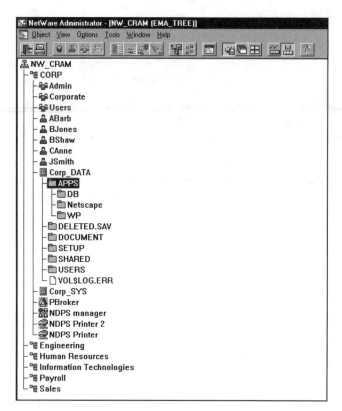

Figure 7.2 File-system management using NetWare Administrator.

Figure 7.2 illustrates the way NetWare Administrator displays the file system.

A common mistake that administrators who are new to the Novell Directory Services (NDS) tree make is to assume that the file system is part of the tree. The NetWare Administrator program helps clear up this misconception. This is because you can view the Volume objects in the NDS tree right along with the file-system information (the directories and files). This leads many to believe that they are the same, when they are most definitely not.

Refer to Figure 7.3 and notice the horizontal line. This line represents the barrier between the NDS tree and the file system. Everything above the line belongs to the NDS, whereas every-thing below it is the file system. Remember this point, memorize it, and etch it into your brain. It's extremely important that you understand the difference.

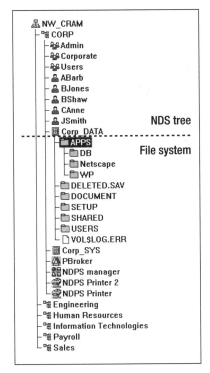

Figure 7.3 NDS and file-system differences in NetWare Administrator.

The Volume object is an object that exists in the NDS tree, and the directories and files are items that exist within the volume. For an analogy, remember when we defined files: A ZIP file contains (in a sense) other files, although they are compressed and cannot be easily accessed by applications. This does not break the rule that states that files cannot contain other files.

Although a volume resembles a container object, it's actually a leaf object. Remembering the definition of a leaf object (a leaf object cannot contain other objects within it), this rule would hold true.

FILER

FILER is a text-based application that allows you to manage the file system. It has much of the same functionality as the file-system management component of the NetWare Administrator program. Figure 7.4 illustrates the FILER application.

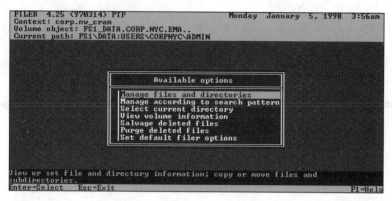

Figure 7.4 The FILER application.

 Although you'll probably use NetWare Administrator most of the time, you should become familiar with FILER. You'll find that if you can't run the NetWare Administrator program, the FILER utility will work just fine.

As with many of NetWare's "blue" utilities (those with the blue background), the keys used in the program are standard. Once you learn how to navigate in one of these utilities, you can navigate in most of them. In this section, we'll cover some of the most common command keys.

If you can use the arrow keys, the F5 and F6 keys, the Insert and Delete keys, the Enter key, and the Escape key, you can very quickly become proficient in these utilities. The keys and the tasks they accomplish are listed in Table 7.1.

Table 7.1	The keys used in FILER and their purposes.
Key	**Purpose**
Arrow	Navigates through the menus. Usually, only the up and down arrow keys are used.
F5	Selects/deselects entries.
F6	Selects/deselects entries based on search criteria, such as a wildcard character.
Insert	Presents a list of available entries to select.
Delete	Removes an entry from the current selection.
Enter	Moves down one menu level or accepts the selection.
Esc	Moves up one menu level.

As an example, lets change the current directory:

1. Start FILER from the \PUBLIC directory on the SYS volume.

2. Press the down arrow key twice so Select Current Directory is highlighted. Press the Enter key. The main menu will be grayed out and a field will appear with your current directory.

3. At this point, you can either enter the location manually or navigate to it. To navigate, press the Insert key, and Figure 7.5 appears.

4. Press the Enter key to select the highlighted entry. If you select the ".." entry, you move up one level in the directory structure.

5. Once you're at the desired location, press the Esc key to jump back to the current Directory Path dialog box, and press the Enter key to return to the main menu. Notice that your current directory has changed.

Various Ways To View File-System Information

One of the most powerful features of the NetWare file system is its abundance of available information. This is also true with most other objects, especially User and Group objects. Novell has given the administrator some powerful tools to take full advantage of these features. It also added functionality to the operating system (DOS, Windows 95/98, and Windows NT) that gives the administrator the ability to leverage these features.

With this information at hand, your task of assigning access rights to file-system objects becomes much easier. You have the ability to view the file system in a graphical way and in a "from above" view.

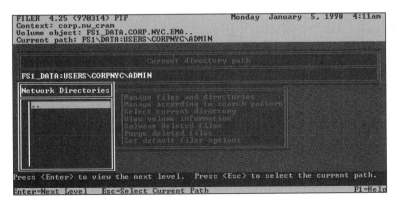

Figure 7.5 Navigating using FILER.

Using NetWare Administrator To View File-System Information

As you may have already guessed, the tool that is most often used to control and configure the file-system information is NetWare Administrator. As you'll see in the following sections, it can be used to configure all of the file-system information that is available to you as an administrator. As with other objects in the NDS tree, you want to become familiar with how the NetWare Administrator program interacts with the file system, as well as the options that are available to you.

When you install a NetWare server, regardless of whether it's installed with a new NDS tree or into an existing one, a Server object is created in the NDS tree at the selected context. The same is true when you create the SYS volume (or any other volume for that matter). If you refer to Figure 7.6, you'll see not only the Server and Volume objects, but also the Directory, Subdirectory, and File objects in the file system.

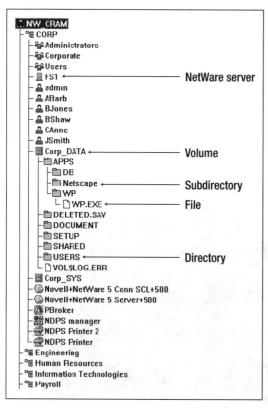

Figure 7.6 File-system objects in NetWare Administrator.

Viewing Volume Information

Although some DOS-based utilities allow you to view the volume information, NetWare Administrator presents the information in a manner that is easier to understand. Figure 7.7 illustrates one of the informational screens, the Statistics window, available to you with the NetWare Administrator program.

 To access the volume informational windows, highlight and right-click on the desired volume, and select Details from the menu.

The following is a sample of the information that's available about a volume from the NetWare Administrator program:

➤ Identification information, such as volume name, the server to which the volume is assigned, the volume's location, and the department to which it belongs

➤ Statistical information, such as disk space used and available, the number of directory entries, the name spaces installed, and the number of deleted and compressed files in the volume

➤ User space limitations

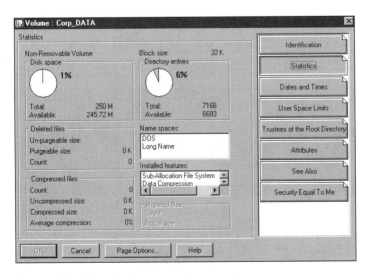

Figure 7.7   The Statistics window.

➤ Trustee assignments

➤ Volume attributes, such as hidden, immediate compress, purge, and system

Viewing Directory Information

You can view directory information in NetWare Administrator in the same way that you view volume information. Figure 7.8 shows the directory informational screens.

> To access the directory informational windows, highlight and right-click on the desired directory, and select Details from the menu.

Among some of the directory details these screens give you are:

➤ The directory name in the different name spaces that are installed on the volume

➤ The owner of the directory, the maximum and restricted sizes, and when it was last modified

➤ The trustee assignment information

➤ Directory attributes, such as system, purge, and delete inhibit

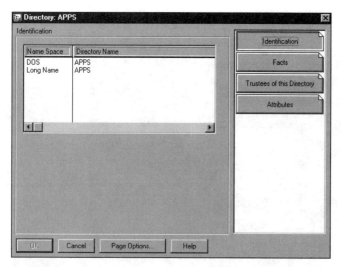

Figure 7.8 The Directory Identification window.

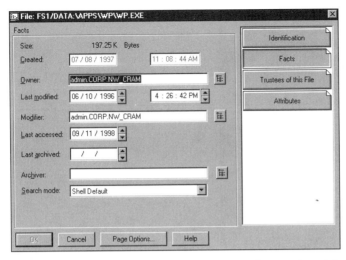

Figure 7.9   The file information as seen with NetWare Administrator.

Viewing File Information

Viewing file information is similar to viewing both volume and directory information. Some of the information available to you when using the NetWare Administrator program (as shown in Figure 7.9) includes:

➤ Access date

➤ Access rights

➤ Archive information

➤ File attributes

➤ File name and extension

➤ Modification date and time

➤ Owner name

➤ Search mode

Using Windows To View File-System Information

When you install the NetWare client software, it adds functionality to Windows. Part of this functionality is evident when you look at the properties of a NetWare volume through Network Neighborhood, as seen in Figure 7.10.

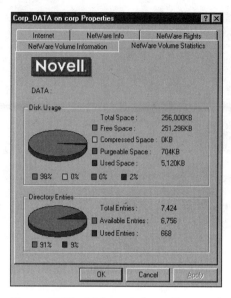

Figure 7.10 Volume information as viewed through Network Neighborhood.

The information you can view in these windows includes:

➤ Disk usage

➤ Directory entries

➤ Server the volume exists on

➤ Block size

➤ User restrictions

➤ Name space

➤ Volume's owner

➤ Volume attributes

➤ Access rights

For you to be able to access the NetWare file system, you must be able to access the desired volume. Any application that is NetWare-aware can simply use the server and volume names to access this information, in the form *server\volume*.

You run into a problem, however, when dealing with legacy or obsolete applications. These applications may not be network-aware, let alone NetWare-aware. For these applications, you use a process known as *drive mapping*. To understand drive mapping, you must first know what a *drive pointer* is.

When you access a file in Windows, you may look on the C: drive. This is the drive pointer. Drive mapping creates a virtual link between a letter—the C: drive, for example—and points it to a directory/volume combination on a NetWare server. (See Chapter 9 for more information on drive mapping.)

Selecting The Correct File-System Utility

After you've become more familiar with the utilities mentioned in this chapter, you'll know automatically which one can complete the tasks that you need to complete. Novell constructed a couple of tables to help you determine which utility to use (until you get familiar with their capabilities). The first table deals with some of the management tasks that you would perform on the directory structure, whereas the second deals with file management. We discuss these, as well as copying, salvaging, and purging files in the following sections.

Utilities For Managing The Directory

Although we cannot cover all of the directory-management tasks that you may be required to perform, Table 7.2 lists the most-common ones.

Table 7.2	Directory-management tools and their utilities.				
Task	NetWare Admininistrator	FILER	NDIR	RENDIR	NCOPY
Copy directory structure and its attributes	X	X			X
Create a directory	X	X			
Delete directories and their structure	X	X			
Delete files and subdirectories	X	X			
Modify information such as owner	X	X			
Move a directory structure	X	X			
Rename a directory	X	X		X	
View directory information	X	X	X		

Table 7.3 File-management tools and their utilities.

Task	NetWare Administrator	FILER	NDIR	NCOPY
Copy files (preserving NetWare attributes)	X	X		X
Modify file information	X	X		
Purge deleted files	X	X		
Salvage deleted files	X	X		
View file information	X	X	X	

Utilities For Managing Files

As with directory management, Table 7.3 outlines some common file-management tasks.

Copying Files

If all you need to do is copy files, you can use just about any file-management software that you have available, including ones built into the Windows operating system or the DOS **COPY** command. You may wonder why you would want to bother with the NetWare utilities. They do offer some advantages over their counterparts, including:

➤ You can copy not only directories, but also entire file structures.

➤ When you copy files with the NetWare utilities, you maintain all NetWare-specific information.

➤ You are notified if a problem occurs during the copy process, such as name space limitations or extended attributes not being copied.

➤ These utilities verify that the copy was not only completed, but was also completed successfully and correctly.

➤ You can copy a directory to a volume rather than only to drive letters, as with the built-in utilities. For example, you would copy the files from the current directory to the volume DATA by entering the following command:

```
NCOPY FILE5.TXT FS1_DATA:\DIR2\FILE4.txt
```

Salvaging Files

Similar to the recycle bin in Windows, when you delete a file, it's not actually deleted from the system. Instead, one of two things happens. First, if files and/or subdirectories are deleted from a directory, they will still exist (in a deleted format) in the directory. Second, if the directory is deleted along with the files and subdirectories, then they would be moved to a hidden directory—called DELETED.SAV—on the volume.

As long as the deleted files have not been purged, they can be recovered using the NetWare Administrator and FILER utilities.

 Two NetWare file rights and one NetWare directory right are required before a user can salvage a file. These rights are the Read and File Scan rights (to the file) and the Create right (to the directory). These rights are discussed in Chapter 8.

Figure 7.11 shows the Salvage Files dialog box. To salvage deleted files using NetWare Administrator, complete the following tasks:

1. Highlight the directory from which the file (or subdirectory) has been deleted (or the DELETED.SAV directory, if the directory has been deleted).

2. Choose Tools|Salvage.

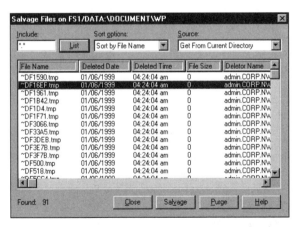

Figure 7.11   Salvaging files using NetWare Administrator.

3. In the dialog box that appears, enter your search criteria and click on the List button. This builds a list of the deleted files in the directory.

4. Select the desired file or files and click on Salvage.

To salvage deleted files using FILER (see Figure 7.12), follow these steps:

1. Navigate to the directory from which the files have been deleted.

2. Choose the Salvage Deleted Files option.

3. If the directory from which the files have been deleted still exists, choose the View/Recover Deleted Files option; otherwise, choose the Salvage From Deleted Directories option. (This second option lets you choose the volume from which to salvage the files.)

4. Choose the desired files and recover them by selecting the files and pressing the Enter.

Purging Files

Deleted files can be purged in only one of three ways: A user deliberately purges them, the server runs out of disk allocation blocks on the volume, or the Purge attribute is set on the directory.

If the server runs out of disk allocation blocks, it purges files on a first-in first-out basis. (The files are purged in the order in which they were deleted.)

Volume Space Management

As a system administrator, you'll need to perform several volume space-management tasks. If you leave users unchecked, you can be almost certain that they will gobble up valuable disk space on your system. Although hard

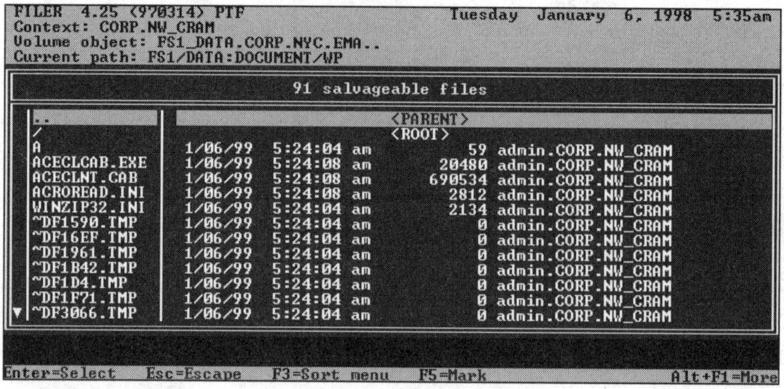

```
FILER  4.25 <970314> PTF                    Tuesday  January  6, 1998  5:35am
Context: CORP.NW_CRAM
Volume object: FS1_DATA.CORP.NYC.EMA..
Current path: FS1/DATA:DOCUMENT/WP

                         91 salvageable files

                                    <PARENT>
                                    <ROOT>
/
A                1/06/99  5:24:04 am           59 admin.CORP.NW_CRAM
ACECLCAB.EXE     1/06/99  5:24:08 am        20480 admin.CORP.NW_CRAM
ACECLNT.CAB      1/06/99  5:24:08 am       690534 admin.CORP.NW_CRAM
ACROREAD.INI     1/06/99  5:24:08 am         2812 admin.CORP.NW_CRAM
WINZIP32.INI     1/06/99  5:24:04 am         2134 admin.CORP.NW_CRAM
~DF1590.TMP      1/06/99  5:24:04 am            0 admin.CORP.NW_CRAM
~DF16EF.TMP      1/06/99  5:24:04 am            0 admin.CORP.NW_CRAM
~DF1961.TMP      1/06/99  5:24:04 am            0 admin.CORP.NW_CRAM
~DF1B42.TMP      1/06/99  5:24:04 am            0 admin.CORP.NW_CRAM
~DF1D4.TMP       1/06/99  5:24:04 am            0 admin.CORP.NW_CRAM
~DF1F71.TMP      1/06/99  5:24:04 am            0 admin.CORP.NW_CRAM
~DF3066.TMP      1/06/99  5:24:04 am            0 admin.CORP.NW_CRAM

Enter=Select   Esc=Escape   F3=Sort menu   F5=Mark            Alt+F1=More
```

Figure 7.12 Salvaging files using FILER.

drives have dropped in price, remember that to add disk space you must take the server offline to add these drives. This downtime can be extremely costly in some organizations.

In this section, we'll cover the following tasks:

➤ Monitoring a volume's space-usage statistics

➤ Locating a file by its attributes

➤ Restricting available volume space

Using Volume Space Effectively

A good administrator can make his or her job seem obsolete. Such an administrator uses the "act" method instead of the "react" one. This is our goal as administrators. If we can fix the problems before they occur, we reduce our workload and our stress (if that is at all possible). Monitoring volume space usage is a task administrators should perform regularly to prevent problems. If they monitor volume space, and act accordingly (by adding hard drives, purging files, and so on), they can minimize problems due to insufficient disk space. Remember that users would rather deal with scheduled downtime than with unscheduled outages. So, as you can see, the efforts of a good administrator can be almost invisible, because he or she acts on problems before the problems have a chance to occur.

Several of the aforementioned utilities can be used to monitor volume space information, including:

➤ NetWare Administrator

➤ NETADMIN

➤ FILER

➤ NDIR

If you refer back to Figure 7.7, you'll see how NetWare Administrator presents information to you, including:

➤ Available disk space

➤ Number of directory entries

➤ Deleted files information

➤ Name space information

➤ Compressed files information

If you are required to find volume statistics from a DOS prompt, use the **NDIR /VOLUME** command. Just be sure that the drive from which you run the command is on a NetWare volume, because that is the volume that it will check. Figure 7.13 illustrates a sample output of this command.

Location Of Files

One of the easiest and quickest ways to free up disk space on your servers is to delete and purge old files. Deciding which files to get rid of can become a difficult and tedious process. Fortunately, NetWare provides tools to help with this task, namely the **NDIR** command. Using this command, you can search for files based upon several criteria including, file size, creation date, access date, and so on. Table 7.4 gives examples of **NDIR** searches based on specific tasks.

Restricting Volume Space

An easy way to control volume disk space is to create what are normally known as *quotas*. Quotas simply limit the amount of space that is allocated. The two

```
Z:\>ndir /volume

Statistics for fixed volume FS1/SYS:
Space statistics are in KB (1024 bytes).

Total volume space:                       976,512   100.00%
Space used by 61,205 entries:             303,424    31.07%
Deleted space not yet purgeable:               64     0.01%
                                          _____
Space remaining on volume:                673,088    68.93%
Space available to .admin.CORP...:        673,088    68.93%

Maximum directory entries:                 75,264
Available directory entries:               14,059    18.68%

Space used if files were not compressed:  432,640
Space used by compressed files:           176,128
                                          _____
Space saved by compressing files:         256,512    59.29%

Uncompressed space used:                  177,728

Name spaces loaded: OS/2

Z:\>_
```

Figure 7.13   A sample **NDIR /VOLUME** command.

Table 7.4 The NDIR command options.	
Command	**Task**
NDIR . /SIZE LT 300000	Lists all files less than 300,000 bytes in size.
NDIR . /ACCESS BEF 01-01-98	Lists all files accessed before January 1, 1998.
NDIR . /OWNER EQ ADMIN	Lists all files owned by the ADMIN user object.
NDIR . /REV SORT SIZE	Sorts files according to size.

distinct ways you can limit volume space are by user and by directory. We cover these methods in the following sections.

Volume Restrictions By User

When you limit the amount of space assigned to a user, be aware that this must be done on each volume that the user has access to. For example, if you assign Bob a limit of 1,024K on the SYS volume and leave the DATA volume alone, Bob will have unlimited disk space on DATA.

> *Note:*   *Unlimited is a relative term. It does not mean that the user can use disk space forever. What it does mean is that the user can use up to and including all of the disk space available on the volume.*

Two utilities allow you to modify a user's volume space limitation: NetWare Administrator and NETADMIN. Figure 7.14 shows the User Space Limits property page in NetWare Administrator.

Volume Restrictions By Directory

The process of restricting volume space by directory is similar to that of restricting according to a user. The main difference is that you use NetWare Administrator and FILER.

Limiting space according to a directory controls the amount of disk space the directory in question can use. Figure 7.15 illustrates where the Restrict size

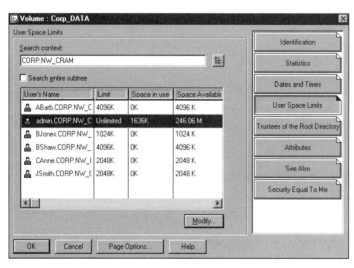

Figure 7.14   The User Space Limits property page in NetWare Administrator.

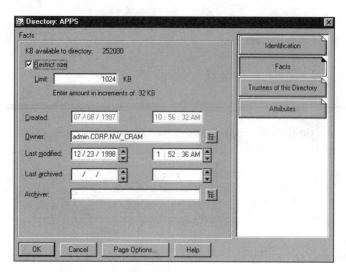

Figure 7.15 Directory volume restrictions.

option is found in NetWare Administrator. Simply highlight the desired directory, right-click on it, select Details, and choose the Facts button.

File Compression, Data Migration, And Disk Block Suballocation

NetWare has three extra features in its file system: file compression, data migration, and disk block suballocation. With *file compression* enabled, you can control which files and directories are compressed and when they are compressed. The NetWare compression scheme uses the "on-the-fly" method. This means that users may access a compressed file and not realize they are doing so because NetWare will compress the file to disk and then uncompress it transparently when the file is requested.

The ability to compress files is configured during (or after) the NetWare 5 installation process. However, you want to be certain that you want compression on your system because once compression is enabled, it cannot be disabled without re-creating the volume.

Any file that has the Immediate Compress (IC) attribute set will be compressed immediately, as long as compression has been enabled on the volume. If compression is not enabled, set the file with IC; then if it's not accessed after a certain amount of time, IC will compress it. The Days Untouched Before Compression parameter is used by the operating

> system to decide which files need to be compressed. Once this parameter is met, NetWare automatically compresses the data. The Days Untouched Before Compression parameter can be modified using the **SET** command.

It's common for organizations to build a large repository of data over time. With large amounts of data, it becomes impossible to keep all of it available online. To solve this problem NetWare uses a method known as *data migration*. Data migration simply transfers some of the older files from the online volumes to an offline storage device, such as a tape drive or an optical jukebox drive. One of the best features of this process is that it's done in the background without the user realizing that it occurred. When the user requests a directory listing, he or she will see the migrated files as though they are still physically in the volume. If the user requests a migrated file, NetWare will go to the jukebox and copy it back to the volume.

Block suballocation allocates a smaller block size (512K) than in previous versions of NetWare, which results in greater storage efficiency because it doesn't waste as much disk space.

Practice Questions

Question 1

> Which of the following are components of the NetWare file system? [Choose the four best answers]
>
> ❑ a. Volume
>
> ❑ b. Drive
>
> ❑ c. Subdirectory
>
> ❑ d. CD-ROM
>
> ❑ e. Directory
>
> ❑ f. File

The correct answers are a, c, e, and f. The five components that make up the NetWare file system are server, volume, directory, subdirectory, and file. A drive is a physical device and, although it contains file-system components, it is not really a component. Therefore, answer b is incorrect. A CD-ROM is not a component of the NetWare file system. Therefore, answer d is incorrect.

Question 2

> Which tools allow you to view volume space? [Choose the four best answers]
>
> ❑ a. FILER
>
> ❑ b. **NCOPY**
>
> ❑ c. **NDIR**
>
> ❑ d. NETADMIN
>
> ❑ e. Windows Explorer
>
> ❑ f. NetWare Administrator

The correct answers are a, c, d, and f. **NCOPY** allows you only to copy files between directories and volumes. Therefore, answer b is incorrect. Windows Explorer does not give you the functionality to view volume space information. Therefore, answer e is incorrect.

Question 3

> Only the system administrator can salvage and purge deleted files.
>
> ○ a. True
>
> ○ b. False

The correct answer is b, false. As long as a user has Read, File Scan, and Create rights, he or she can salvage and purge deleted files. Therefore, answer a is incorrect.

Question 4

> If older applications are not aware of the NetWare file system, they cannot access the volumes.
>
> ○ a. True
>
> ○ b. False

The correct answer is b, false. The process of drive mapping allows legacy applications to access NetWare file system information. Therefore, answer a is incorrect.

Question 5

> You delete a directory and the files contained within it. You now have to salvage one of the files that existed within this deleted directory. Where will you have to look for the file?
>
> ○ a. In the SALVAGE directory
>
> ○ b. In the DELETED.SAV directory on the SYS volume
>
> ○ c. In the directory directly above the old location of the deleted one
>
> ○ d. In the DELETED.SAV directory on the volume where the directory existed

The correct answer is d. If you delete the directory itself, all the deleted files are moved to the DELETED.SAV directory on that volume. If the deleted

directory was on the SYS volume, answer b would be correct, which is why
this is a trick question. There is no SALVAGE directory; it's known as the
DELETED.SAV directory. Therefore, answer a is incorrect. You cannot assume that the DELETED.SAV directory will always be on the SYS volume.
Therefore, answer b is incorrect. When the entire directory is deleted, the only
location where you'll find the deleted files is in the DELETED.SAV directory.
Therefore, answer c is incorrect.

Question 6

Which tools can be used to restrict volume space usage for a directory? [Choose
the two best answers]

❑ a. FILER

❑ b. NETADMIN

❑ c. Windows Explorer

❑ d. NetWare Administrator

The correct answers are a and d. Only FILER and NetWare Administrator
give you that functionality. NETADMIN does not allow you to restrict volume space usage for a directory. Therefore, answer b is incorrect. Windows
Explorer does not have the functionality to control NetWare volume limits
built into it. Therefore, answer c is incorrect.

Question 7

Which tools can be used to limit volume space usage for a user? [Choose the
two best answers]

❑ a. FILER

❑ b. NETADMIN

❑ c. Windows Explorer

❑ d. NetWare Administrator

The correct answers are b and d. Both NETADMIN and the NetWare Administrator program can be used to limit volume space by users. FILER can
only limit space usage by directories, not by user. Therefore, answer a is incorrect. Windows Explorer does not have the functionality built into it to control
NetWare volume limits. Therefore, answer c is incorrect.

Need To Know More?

 For more information on the NetWare Administrator and the NDS object-naming criteria, check the NetWare 5 online documentation with keyword searches on "file system," "FILER," "NDIR," and "NCOPY."

 www.novell.com/documentation/en/nw5/nw5/docui/ index.html is where you can find the NetWare 5 documentation online. Again, search for "file system," "FILER," "NDIR," and "NCOPY."

 Search for "NetWare file system" in your favorite search engine for more information.

File-System Security

8

Terms you'll need to understand:

√ File and directory rights

√ File and directory attributes

√ Inheritance

√ Trustee

√ Effective rights

√ [Public] trustee

√ Inherited Rights Filter (IRF)

Techniques you'll need to master:

√ Calculating effective rights

√ Blocking inherited rights

√ Granting explicit rights

√ Planning and implementing file-system rights

Whereas Novell Directory Services (NDS) security is the basis of all the access security for network resources, file and directory security is the basis of all access security for data. In this chapter, you'll acquire a thorough understanding of file and directory security so you'll be able to adequately protect your data, which includes applications as well as information.

You must lock your applications to prevent accidental or intentional corruption, to prevent unwanted reconfiguration, and to minimize the likelihood of virus infection in the event your existing virus protection fails. You also need to lock your data to prevent unauthorized tampering or the theft of sensitive information. In this chapter, you'll examine the concepts, procedures, and functions related to managing NetWare file and directory rights.

Understanding File And Directory Concepts

Regardless of its sophistication, file-system security ultimately involves permitting, controlling, and denying access to users. File and directory security is really about who has access to what data, and what they can do with the data they have access to. To effectively tailor and implement a security model for your organization, you must master four concepts:

➤ **File and directory rights** These are the permissions that are associated with each file or directory. A file or directory right is like a specific permit that allows users to perform a singular activity (or a set of activities)—such as deleting or renaming—on a file or directory.

➤ **Trustee** This is an object that appears in the access control list (ACL) of a file or directory. The ACL is a list of objects (trustees) that have been granted or denied permissions to perform operations on a particular object.

➤ **Inheritance** This concept enables rights to flow through the directory structure according to certain rules that ease the process of granting file and directory permissions. You master the concept of inheritance instead of controlling a user's access by explicitly assigning rights to every file or directory.

➤ **Effective rights** These are the rights that result from the combined rights that an object has obtained from any source minus those rights that have been blocked by the Inherited Rights Filter (IRF).

Describing File And Directory Rights

Files and directories use the same rights. You need to know the description of each file and directory right to adequately combine them in a useful security scheme. Each task that you perform on a file or directory has corresponding rights that make that task possible. (Tasks and their associated rights are covered later in this section.)

The rights you assign to a trustee at any specific directory level are known as *explicitly assigned rights*. The definitions and abbreviations of the specific file and directory rights are:

➤ **Supervisor (S)** Allows you to grant or revoke rights to all files and directories at or below the directory to which the right is granted. You cannot block this right with the IRF. When you grant the Supervisor right to a file, it applies to that file alone; the right does not flow to any other files or directories.

➤ **Read (R)** Allows you to open files and view their contents. It also lets you execute a program file.

➤ **Write (W)** Allows you to open and modify the contents of a file.

➤ **Create (C)** Allows you to create new files and directories.

➤ **Erase (E)** Allows you to delete directories and files.

➤ **Modify (M)** Allows you to change file attributes or to rename a file or directory.

➤ **File Scan (F)** Allows you to view a file name in a directory through a GUI (such as Windows Explorer), or to view it during a directory scan using the DOS **DIR** command.

➤ **Access Control (A)** Allows you to add or remove trustee assignments to the ACL of a file or directory. You can also grant rights or use the IRF to block inherited rights (except the Supervisor right in either case).

Certain default rights for system-generated User and Group objects are built into NetWare 5. You can change these rights at any time, but they are applied by default when certain objects are created. The default rights are:

➤ The user's home directory receives RWCEMFA (Read, Write, Create, Erase, Modify, File Scan, and Access Control) rights automatically when you have NetWare Administrator create a user's home directory at the time of the User object's creation.

Note: When referring to multiple rights, Novell typically uses the first letter of the rights rather than spelling them out repeatedly.

If a trustee is granted Supervisor rights to a Server object, the rights automatically apply to the entire file and directory structure of all volumes on that server. This occurs under the following conditions:

➤ If you are the user who creates a Server object, you are granted Supervisor rights to that object.

➤ If you are assigned Supervisor rights to a Server object, you have Supervisor access to all volumes, files, and directories on that server.

➤ If you are assigned the Write right to the Object Trustees property of a Server object, you're granted the Supervisor right to the root directory of all volumes on that server. A user in the same container as SYS: gets Read (R) and File Scan (F) rights to SYS:PUBLIC by default. Other users must be explicitly granted these rights to log in.

If an object obtains file and directory rights through any of these methods, that object cannot be found in the ACL of any file or directory. You must understand this to prevent a potentially significant security problem with your server's data. Imagine the consequences if a user (with Supervisor rights to all of a server's data) accidentally drags a system directory and all its contents to some other place as he or she is moving the mouse across the Windows Explorer screen. All it takes is a careless click of a mouse button and your server is suddenly inoperable.

As mentioned previously in this section, a user needs a specific right or combination of rights to accomplish a specific task. A list of common tasks and the abbreviation for their rights is shown in Table 8.1.

Table 8.1   A list of common tasks and their required rights.

Task	Required Right(s)	Abbreviation
Display a file name or search for it	File Scan	F
Open a file and view its contents	Read	R
Run a program (COM or EXE file)	Read, File Scan	RF
Create a file and write to it	Create	C
Open an existing file and write to it	Write, Create, Erase, Modify	WCEM

(continued)

Table 8.1	A list of common tasks and their required rights (continued).		
Task	**Required Right(s)**	**Abbreviation**	
Delete a file or directory	Erase	E	
Create a directory	Create	C	
Rename a file or directory	Read	R	
Copy files from a source directory	Read, File Scan	RF	
Copy files to a destination directory	Write, Create, File Scan	WCF	
Salvage deleted files	Read, File Scan, Create (on the directory)	RF(C)	
Modify directory or file attributes and rename a file or directory	Modify	M	
Alter trustee assignments	Access Control	A	
Change a user's disk space on a directory	Access Control	A	
Update the IRF	Access Control	A	

Understanding Inheritance

Inheritance is the means by which rights can be assigned to a directory so they flow unhindered to subdirectories below it. To make efficient use of inherited rights, you must understand some simple rules:

➤ True to the definition of *inheritance*, explicitly assigned rights flow downward. When explicitly assigned rights flow to the next directory, the rights are inherited by that directory. For example, if you assign the Create right to an object at the "data" directory in a directory structure like the following

```
\data\acctg\spreadsheets\excel
```

the Create right is automatically granted at the acctg, spreadsheets, and excel directories. This feature of inheritance lends itself well to certain types of directory design, which are covered later in this chapter.

➤ Inherited rights can be blocked. The IRF is designed to block rights assigned at a higher level in directories that have rights actually or potentially flowing into them from those directories. Hopefully, you will not need the IRF, because a well-designed directory structure should not require you to block rights. If you are faced with a situation in which it would be too difficult to redesign your directory structure—or when your needs suddenly change (requiring that you block some rights)—you can use the IRF to block inherited rights.

The IRF has no effect on rights explicitly granted to the directory at which its assignments are made. It's designed to block inherited rights only. It cannot block rights assigned at its own level because those rights are not inherited; they are explicit.

➤ The Supervisor right cannot be blocked. The main purpose of the Supervisor right is to give unhindered access to all files and directories so there is always a user who can access data, regardless of how secure it is. If the file and directory systems were made so secure that someone could block the Supervisor right, an employee who was terminated (or who could not be found and had the only password to the company's data) could present a significant problem.

➤ The explicit rights that you apply to a directory are inherited by all files in that directory, its subdirectories, and their files.

➤ Explicitly assigned rights supercede all other rights. New explicitly assigned rights override whatever rights you inherited in a directory (by any means, such as groups you belong to). This is an effective means of blocking inherited rights without using the IRF.

Note: The same rule applies to the Supervisor right when explicit rights are used to block inherited rights. The inherited Supervisor right cannot be blocked by a new explicit rights assignment.

➤ The IRF can only block rights; it cannot grant them. By default, all rights are enabled in the IRF. If you do nothing to the IRF, it allows rights to flow unhindered by its presence. The only time you notice the IRF actually doing anything is when you use it to block rights.

➤ The IRF can be set only to a directory. It affects all inherited rights for all users (except Supervisor rights, which cannot be blocked) at and below the directory to which you make the assignment. This is why you would tend to use the IRF either sparingly or not at all: It does not have the granularity or flexibility that explicitly assigned rights has.

To filter rights with the IRF:

1. Launch NetWare Administrator and navigate to the directory where you want to set or view the IRF.

2. Right-click on the directory and choose Details.

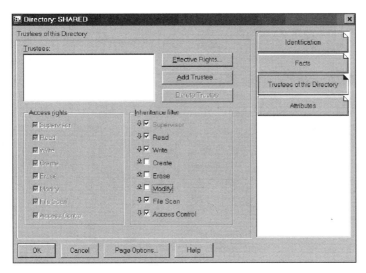

Figure 8.1 The Trustees Of This Directory dialog box.

3. Select the Trustees Of This Directory tab of the property pages. Figure 8.1 shows the Trustees Of This Directory dialog box.

4. The IRF is in the middle of the screen just below the "Inheritance Filter" title. Notice that each of the rights is enabled by default. Click on the boxes you want to filter so that no checkmark appears. Click on OK.

Notice that the Supervisor right is grayed out. As mentioned previously, you cannot block the Supervisor right.

Remember that you cannot assign rights with the IRF; you can only block them.

Trustee Assignments

A *trustee* is an NDS object that has been placed in charge of another NDS object or network resource (such as a file or directory) and appears in the ACL of that file or directory. Every file and every directory has an ACL that lists its trustees and displays the rights that they are assigned. The rights you assign to a trustee determine the operations that the trustee can perform on that file or directory. Figure 8.2 shows the trustees of the Public directory.

> *Note:* *The ACL is sometimes referred to as the trustee list Object Trustee property, and the Object Trustee (ACL) property.*

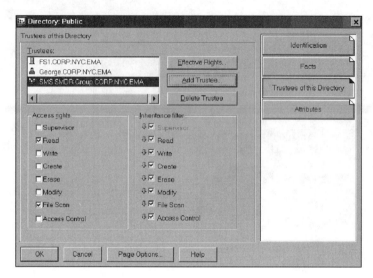

Figure 8.2 Trustee assignments for the Public directory.

When you grant the Access Control right or the Supervisor right, you give the assigned user the power to change assignments in the ACL, thus enabling them to grant any or all file-system rights (with the exception of the Supervisor right) to any trustees. This could present a security problem if the explicit rights you granted the users to files and directories are more restrictive than the Access Control right will ultimately give them the power to exercise. Remember that the Access Control right gives the user the ability to increase his or her own rights.

Typically, rights are thought of as being granted to users. In NDS, you can grant file and directory rights to any NDS object. This feature enables you to grant rights to a container object, which results in every object in that container—and below—inheriting the same rights as the container to which you assigned them. For example, if you want to give an entire organization Read and File Scan rights to a shared data directory, you make the Organization object a trustee of the Public directory and assign Read and File Scan rights to the ACL of the public directory. Now every object in that organization's container has Read and File Scan rights to the Public directory. This applies to all new objects you create in the organization's container and retroactively to all objects that currently exist in the container.

> *Note:*   *Typically, you're better off making trustee assignment to groups when you want to give access to a number of users. Groups are easier to modify and are more flexible to manage than containers.*

User objects can get file-system rights from any of several objects provided two conditions are true:

➤ The object is a trustee.

➤ The object has been assigned file or directory rights.

A user can obtain its rights from five objects:

➤ **User object** You assign rights to a User object when the rights are unique to that user. For example, when you have NetWare Administrator automatically create a home directory for a User object, it assigns RWCEMFA rights to the ACL of that user's home directory. No other object is made a trustee or assigned any rights to that directory.

➤ **Group object** You assign rights to a Group object when a definable collection of users have the same security requirements. You make the group a trustee of the resources that you want the users to access, assign the rights that you want the group to have, and add the user to the group. All users who are listed as members of the group receive the rights that are assigned to the group. Any User object in the Directory tree, regardless of its location, may be added to any group or number of groups in the tree.

➤ **Organizational Role object** The Organizational Role object and the Group object are much the same. The purpose of the Organizational Role object is different in that it's typically outfitted with a security profile for a specific position (such as desk clerk or manager) that changes personnel often. You use the Organizational Role object because the frequent turnover of employees makes it a nuisance to keep redefining users. The Organizational Role object makes your job easier because you define the role once; then add and remove users as they inherit and leave the position. Users added to the Organizational Role object are called *occupants* instead of *members*.

➤ **Container object** You assign trustee rights to a container when it makes more sense to grant rights to all objects in a container. Usually, you do this at higher levels in the NDS tree when you want rights to be more global to an organization or a logical division within an organization. Because containers often represent natural groups of objects within an organization, assigning rights this way (instead of through groups) may best serve your organization's needs. In cases in which your NDS design represents the groups that you would create anyway, you can eliminate the redundancy of creating and managing groups by making your trustee assignments to the containers that represent the groups. Grant rights to a container when all objects in that container and all of its subcontainers require the same rights.

➤ **[Public] trustee** The [Public] trustee is the most unique feature of the NDS tree in that its only purpose is to be a trustee. When you grant rights to the [Public] trustee, you're granting rights to everything connected to the network, whether it's logged in or not. Be cautious when you use this trustee, because it bypasses authentication rules: An object does not need to be logged in to exercise the rights granted to the [Public] trustee.

Note: Another way of receiving rights is through security equivalence. When you make one object's security equivalent to another, the object gains the same rights as the object to which it has been made equivalent.

Understanding Effective Rights

Ultimately, effective rights are the only rights with which you are concerned, because whatever you are trying to achieve through assigning rights ends with the result, called the *effective rights*. These are the rights you actually have at any given time in a file or directory.

As mentioned previously, you can receive rights thorough explicit assignments, inheritance, groups, organizational roles, and security equivalence. Add those rights together and subtract the rights that have been revoked through the IRF and you have effective rights. The rights you have to a given directory or file as a result of all rights granted to you through any means, minus those blocked by the IRF or by explicit assignment, leave you with the rights you can effectively use at any given time.

You must be able to calculate effective rights to design a coherent file and directory structure. To determine a user's effective rights:

1. Determine all (influential) objects from which the user can obtain rights. Check for security equivalencies, groups, organizational roles, and parent containers all the way up the tree to the [Root], [Public] trustee, and the Supervisor right to the Server object that contains the volume on which you're working.

2. Determine what trustee assignments (if any) have been made to these objects at any directory levels above the directory in question.

3. Determine if any rights have been explicitly granted to the file or directory for which you are calculating rights. If there are explicitly assigned rights, these are your effective rights, because explicitly assigned rights override inherited rights. The exception is if you have been given the

Supervisor right at any level, because it permits unrestricted access regardless of other assignments (including rights blocked by the IRF).

4. Determine if any rights are being blocked by the IRF of influential objects at higher levels of the NDS tree.

5. Add all the inherited rights together and subtract the IRF-blocked rights, and you have the effective rights for that directory.

Using NetWare Administrator To View Effective Rights

You can use several NetWare tools to view effective rights, such as the FILER utility, the **NDIR** command, and NetWare Administrator. The most likely tool you'll use is NetWare Administrator. To determine effective rights with NetWare Administrator:

1. Launch NetWare Administrator and browse to the volume and directory whose effective rights you want to view.

2. Highlight the directory and right-click on it.

3. Select Details and click on Trustees Of This Object.

4. Note the Trustees Of The \data Directory. Click on Effective Rights. The Effective Rights dialog box appears.

5. Click the browse button (to the right of the Trustee field). The Select Object dialog box appears.

6. In the Available Objects list, double-click on the object whose effective rights you want to view. The object's effective rights are displayed, as shown in Figure 8.3.

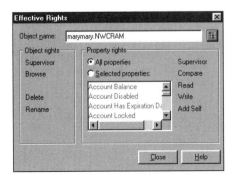

Figure 8.3 The Effective Rights dialog box.

Exercise In Calculating Effective Rights

You must become proficient at calculating effective rights in order to plan an effective directory structure or to troubleshoot a file-system security problem. Again, effective rights are the rights you can actually exercise in a given directory at a given time. You can create a simple chart, like the one in Figure 8.4, to help you calculate effective rights.

For example, for the directory structure shown in Figure 8.4, you must calculate the effective rights at each directory level for Tammy and Samantha. Fill in each level with the appropriate information and calculate the effective rights at the bottom of the grid, as shown in Figure 8.4.

To calculate rights for Tammy, use the following information as you fill in the grid:

➤ She is a trustee of the root directory with R and F rights.

➤ She has an explicit-rights assignment of C at the NYC level.

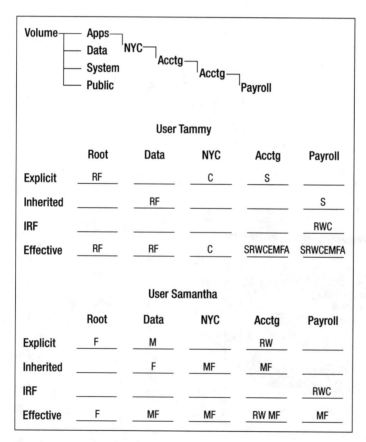

	Root	Data	NYC	Acctg	Payroll
User Tammy					
Explicit	RF		C	S	
Inherited		RF			S
IRF					RWC
Effective	RF	RF	C	SRWCEMFA	SRWCEMFA
User Samantha					
Explicit	F	M		RW	
Inherited		F	MF	MF	
IRF					RWC
Effective	F	MF	MF	RW MF	MF

Figure 8.4 Sample directory structure and effective rights chart.

➤ She has an explicit assignment of S at the Acctg level.

➤ The IRF is set to filter out R, W, and C at the Payroll level.

To calculate rights for Samantha, use the following information as you fill in the grid:

➤ She is a member of the managers group, which is a trustee of the root directory and has the F right.

➤ She is also a member of the audit group, which is a trustee of the data directory with the M right.

➤ She is security equivalent to Bob, who is a member of the warehouse group, which has an explicit trustee assignment of R and W at the Acctg directory.

➤ The IRF is set to filter out R, W, and C at the Payroll directory.

As you can see in our example, we've filled in the rights that Tammy and Samantha have in each directory (note that we calculated the effective rights and notice the IRF assignments to each directory).

File-System Design And Planning

A well-planned file and directory system enables you to spend your time doing more interesting things than resolving rights issues on the network. You must make the rules for file and directory rights work for you instead of against you. Think of trustee rights assignments like water flowing in response to gravity. Rights flow downhill just like water does. If you're managing a river system, you wouldn't want to build and manage a whole bunch of dams. Instead, you would want them strategically placed so you maximize the benefits of gravity without having to build too many dams. Likewise, you should plan your directory structure to make effective use of this principle, and you'll have very few, if any, rights-related network issues.

The power and granularity of NetWare's file and directory security is second to none in the industry. This can give the illusion that you should be using a significant portion of it to be professional. The reason for such a robust suite of tools is to allow you to design the simplest possible security system that still provides the protection you need—without the tools getting in your way.

When planning the file and directory structure, you must take into account a few questions:

➤ What types of data do we have, and how do we want to access them? The answers to this question tend to indicate how the directory structure is best designed.

➤ Who can perform what actions on what data? You plan trustee assignments, IRFs, and file and directory attributes (covered later in this chapter) with the answers this question provokes.

File And Directory Structure Planning

As mentioned previously, you must plan file and directory structure to minimize administration. In general, you place the most-restrictive security assignments near the root of the volume, so you reduce restrictions (and increase rights) as you move lower in the directory structure. This is often referred to as *top-down planning*, and it allows you to design your directory structure to have more-general directory categories at the [Root] level and more-specific categories at lower levels in the directory structure. Figure 8.5 illustrates a typical directory structure.

When planning trustee assignments, you should remember the following points:

➤ Create groups and assign the rights to those groups. Wherever possible, avoid giving directory rights to users. Plan your directory structure and trustee assignments based on a group philosophy.

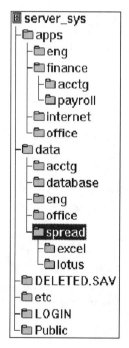

Figure 8.5 A typical directory structure.

➤ Make sure that each trustee has only the required rights to perform the expected actions at a given level.

➤ Begin at the [Root] level and work down the structure, increasing rights as you go.

➤ Plan to block inheritance where inherited rights become excessive at lower levels.

➤ Avoid excessive assignments at higher levels. If you have too many rights at higher levels, you create more potential for needing IRFs at lower levels.

➤ Use the top-down approach, moving from lesser to greater access.

➤ Try to make trustee assignments in the following order:

➤ **[Public]** Security assignments you want anyone to access at any time should be done first. These assignments are naturally the most restrictive, because you want the fewest rights assigned to the [Public] trustee.

➤ **Containers (this includes the [Root] object)** If you can manage your security properly by making assignments to the containers that are already there, you may not need groups at all.

➤ **Groups and organizational roles** If you need several groups and container trustee assignments do not work well, you may manage all your security with groups and/or organizational roles.

➤ **Users** In special situations, you may succumb to making user trustee assignments as the most expedient way to resolve a security issue. (However, it's rarely the best way.)

Securing File And Directory Attributes

You may assign special properties to files and directories that prevent certain actions from being performed on certain files, regardless of what an object's effective rights may be. Other file or directory capabilities—such as migration or compression—may be allowed or prevented by flagging the file or directory with the appropriate attribute. Attributes are assigned directly to the file or directory at a lower level than are trustee assignments. Therefore, attributes do not have the flexibility of being assigned to users. Keep this in mind when planning attribute security.

When you apply attribute security to files and directories, the attributes supersede all other security that a user receives through inheritance, explicit assignments, and security equivalence. Even Admin or Supervisor rights to a file will not allow you to delete the file if it's flagged with the Delete Inhibit (Di) attribute. You must change the attribute to Read/Write (Rw) before you can delete the file. You need to learn the following descriptions of attribute security and their abbreviations. Directory and file attributes are listed with their abbreviations in Table 8.2.

Note: You need the Modify right to change file or directory attributes.

File attributes are listed in Table 8.3.

Table 8.2 Attributes that you apply to both files and directories.	
File or Directory Attribute	**Abbreviation**
Delete Inhibit	Di
Don't Compress	Dc
Don't Migrate	Dm
Hidden	H
Immediate Compress	Ic
Normal	N
Purge	P
Rename Inhibit	Ri
System	Sy

Table 8.3 Attributes that can be applied only to files.	
File Attribute	**Abbreviation**
Archive Needed	A
Can't Compress	Cc
Compressed	Co
Copy Inhibit	Ci
Don't Suballocate	Ds
Execute Only	X
Migrated	M
Read Only	Ro
Read/Write	Rw
Shareable	Sh
Transactional	T

Practice Questions

Question 1

> What are the minimum rights necessary to execute an application? [Choose the two best answers]
>
> ❑ a. Read (R)
>
> ❑ b. Write (W)
>
> ❑ c. Create (C)
>
> ❑ d. File Scan (F)
>
> ❑ e. Access Control (A)

The correct answers to this question are a and d. Read and File Scan are the minimum rights necessary to execute an application. Write, Create, and Access Control are not the minimum rights necessary to execute an application. Therefore, answers b, c, and e are incorrect.

Question 2

> To block the Supervisor, Access Control, and Create rights with the IRF, you must first select the directory in NetWare Administrator, click on the Inherited Rights Filter button, and place a check in the respective boxes where you want those rights to remain enabled.
>
> ○ a. True
>
> ○ b. False

The correct answer to this question is b, false. The IRF cannot block the Supervisor right. You have to know that the IRF cannot block the Supervisor right to know that the statement is completely false, which is why this is a trick question.

Question 3

> Which of the following actions can you perform with the Modify right?
>
> ○ a. Modify the IRF.
>
> ○ b. Change a Read Only file attribute to Read/Write for a specific trustee.
>
> ○ c. Change a Read Only file attribute to Read/Write for files and directories of which you're a trustee.
>
> ○ d. Modify trustee assignments made by the Administrator object.

The correct answer to this question is c. You can change a Read Only file attribute to Read/Write for files and directories of which you're a trustee. Note that you can also use the Modify right to rename a file or directory. You cannot modify the IRF, change attributes for other trustees, or change trustee assignments made by other users with the Modify right. Therefore, answers a, b, and d are incorrect.

Question 4

> Which actions can you perform if you have security equivalence to another user?
>
> ○ a. You can perform the same actions as the other user with the exception of the Supervisor right.
>
> ○ b. You can perform the same actions as the object to which you're made security equivalent.
>
> ○ c. You can perform none of the actions of the object you're security equivalent to, except assigning security equivalence to other objects.
>
> ○ d. You can perform the same actions as the object to which you're security equivalent, except those actions restricted by rights blocked in the IRF.

The correct answer is b. You can perform the same actions as the object to which you're made security equivalent. There are no exceptions or restrictions to security equivalence. Therefore, answers a, c, and d are incorrect.

Question 5

Which file and directory concepts allow a User object to receive rights in a directory that has no trustees listed in its ACL? [Choose the two best answers]

- ❏ a. Security equivalence
- ❏ b. Trustee security
- ❏ c. Inheritance
- ❏ d. Trusteeship

The correct answers are a and c. Security equivalence and inheritance allow a User object to receive rights in a directory that has no trustees listed in its ACL. Trustee security is meaningless in this context, and trusteeship has nothing to do with indirectly acquired rights. Therefore, answers b and d are incorrect.

Question 6

What is the minimum right necessary to change trustee assignments or to modify the space available to a user in a specific directory?

- ○ a. Modify
- ○ b. Supervisor
- ○ c. Access Control
- ○ d. Read and File Scan
- ○ e. Create

The correct answer to this question is c. The Access Control right is the minimum right necessary to change trustee assignments or to modify the space available to a user in a specific directory. The Supervisor right is not the *minimum* right required; however, it would allow you to perform those tasks. Therefore, answer b is incorrect. The Modify, Read, File Scan, and the Create rights are all insufficient. Therefore, answers a, d, and e are incorrect.

Question 7

> What is the minimum right or rights necessary to make new files and directories?
>
> ○ a. Write
>
> ○ b. Create
>
> ○ c. Read and Write
>
> ○ d. Read, Write, and Create

The correct answer to this question is b. The only right necessary to make new files and subdirectories is Create. Therefore, answers a, c, and d are incorrect.

Question 8

> What are the ways by which an object can receive Supervisor rights to the file system without being made a trustee of any file or directory? [Choose the two best answers]
>
> ❏ a. By being the creator of a Volume object
>
> ❏ b. By being the creator of a Server object
>
> ❏ c. By being the trustee of a Volume object with Supervisor rights to that volume
>
> ❏ d. By being the trustee of a Server object with Supervisor rights to that server

The correct answers to this question are b and d. Supervisor rights to the file and directory system are passed on by virtue of having Supervisor rights to a Server object. No file and directory rights are passed on to another object by being the creator or trustee of a Volume object. Therefore, answers a and c are incorrect.

Question 9

The most secure model for assigning file and directory security should be: Maximum file and directory rights should be placed at as high a level as possible and should be filtered with the IRF where restrictions are necessary.

○ a. True

○ b. False

The correct answer to this question is b, false. *Minimal* file and directory rights should be granted at the higher levels and rights should be added only where necessary. This is the most secure model.

Question 10

Which attributes can be assigned to both files and directories?

○ a. Di, Dc, Dm, H, N, P, Ri, Sy, A

○ b. Di, Dc, H, N, P, Ri, Sy, X, M

○ c. Di, Dc, Dm, H, Ic, N, P, Ri, Sy

○ d. Di, Dc, Dm, H, Ic, N, P, A, M

The correct answer to this question is c. Answers a, b, and d have attributes that may be used only on files included in their list. Therefore, answers a, b, and d are incorrect. Study Tables 8.2 and 8.3 to memorize the capabilities of file and directory attributes.

Need To Know More?

 Novell course 560 manual: *NetWare 5 Administration* (Novell Inc., 1998). As of this writing, this is the only complete documentation for NetWare 5. See Section 7 "Creating and Managing Login Scripts." This manual is available from Novell (1-800-NetWare) or from any authorized Novell training center.

 www.novell.com is Novell's Web site. Choose Products, NetWare 5, and then NetWare 5-3 user demo to order your own live copy of NetWare 5. You may also call 1-800-NetWare to order live demo copies of NetWare 5. Having a NetWare 5 server running is essential to administering a NetWare 5 network.

 Search Novell's Web site "trustee file assignments" in the Novell Knowledgebase; you'll find it in the Technical Support section available under the main menu.

Login Scripts

Terms you'll need to understand:

√ Container login script

√ Profile login script

√ User login script

√ Default login script

√ **MAP** command

√ Search drive

√ Identifier variable

√ Directory Map object

Techniques you'll need to master:

√ Using the **MAP** command to map network drives

√ Designing, creating, debugging, and executing login scripts

√ Describing the four types of login scripts and how they execute

√ Using identifier variables to customize login scripts

√ Creating Directory Map objects

√ Understanding and using login script commands

√ Editing login scripts using the login utility

Login scripts have long been Novell's primary way of configuring workstations to interact with NetWare severs. Lately, however, Microsoft's graphical user interface (GUI) desktop environment and use of profiles has somewhat obscured the straightforward consistency, power, and simplicity of login scripts that have always been available in Novell operating systems.

In this chapter, you'll discover how to make the most of login scripts. You'll learn how to create and use the different types of scripts. Perhaps most important, you'll also learn when—and when not—to use them.

Types Of Login Scripts And Their Contents

To make the most of login scripts, you need to learn the four types of login scripts, their purposes, the commands used in them, the order in which they execute, and the features they include. You need to know the fundamental factors necessary to create powerful login scripts that automate critical environment settings for your end users' desktop systems.

A *login script* is a series of commands and instructions that the Novell operating system uses when users log in to create an initial environment that supports the users' anticipated needs. Every time a user logs in, the login script executes the following instructions: drive mappings, search drive mappings, printer assignments, print capture statements, and messages. The login script also executes other commands that customize the user's environment.

> *Note: Drives mapped at the command prompt are temporary and are lost when the user logs out or logs in again.*

The four types of login scripts are *container, profile, user,* and *default.* They are part of the Novell Directory Services (NDS) design and are executed by the NetWare 5 operating system (if they exist) when a user logs in.

> *Note: Because the default login script always exists, it's executed under certain conditions, which are covered in the following paragraphs.*

Each login script executes in a particular order and produces specific results as each script is discovered (if it exists) and read by the operating system. Each time a user logs in, NDS executes the following steps (see Figure 9.1):

1. The user enters a username and password to be authenticated by NDS.

2. The operating system checks for a container script.

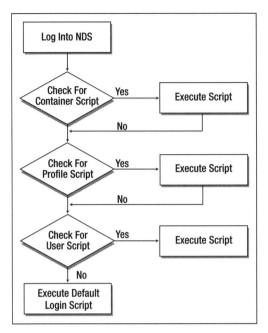

Figure 9.1   The steps NDS follows to execute a login script.

3. If a container script exists, the operating system executes it.

   If a container script does not exist, the operating system checks for a profile script.

4. If a profile script exists, the operating system executes it.

   If a profile script does not exist, the operating system checks for a user script.

5. If a user script exists, it executes and exits all login script procedures.

   If a user script does not exist, the operating system executes the default login script and exits from all login script procedures.

The default login script executes except when the following conditions are true:

➤ When there's a user login script. If a user login script exists (even if it just has a **REMARK** command in it), the default login script is disabled.

➤ When there's a container or profile login script with a **NO_DEFAULT** command in it. (The **NO_DEFAULT** command is covered later in this chapter.)

➤ When there's a container or profile login script with an **EXIT** command in it.

Note: *You must understand how the default login script command works because it can overwrite commands that your other login scripts have executed. This may cause your applications to run improperly or your environment to not function as you expect.*

Container

Novell's convention is to move from the general to the specific when creating login scripts. Therefore, when designing login scripts, you create the container login script(s) first. This sets up the environment for all the users within that container. Then, you identify users who are from different containers but who have identical environment needs; then you create profiles and profile login scripts for those users. Last (if at all), you create individual login scripts for users that have unique needs.

 Remember that you must manage every login script you create. The more scripts you create, the more work you will have to do. On local area networks (LANs), many administrators like to create one large container login script and employ login script commands and identifier variables to set up the environment for all users. This method requires more programming skills, but you can dramatically reduce script management time. Wide area networks (WANs) do not work well with this approach because of traffic problems, but you can still reduce your login scripts to one per geographical location.

Here are some important points to remember about the container login script:

➤ It's always the first login script to execute.

➤ It effects the same login script instructions for every user in the container.

➤ It affects only the User objects in that specific Organization or Organizational Unit container. It does not affect the User objects in subcontainers. In other words, if a user's parent container does not have a login script, no container login script will execute for that user.

➤ It's located in the Login Script property page of the container object.

➤ It's usually created and updated by the network administrator or the container administrator assigned to that container.

Most administrators prefer container login scripts because NetWare Administrator displays the users and groups in every container in such an obvious fashion that the administrator does not have to check each user's Login Script property page, or the access control list (ACL) of each profile to see which users can execute which profile login scripts.

When a user logs into NDS, the only container script that executes for that user is the script located in the parent container of the User object logging in. For example, in Figure 9.2, you see the Acme Organization container, the Research And Development container, and the Marketing container. The following scenarios are possible for the container login scripts in Figure 9.2:

➤ If there's a container login script for the Acme Organization container, it won't execute unless a user you created in that container logs in. The

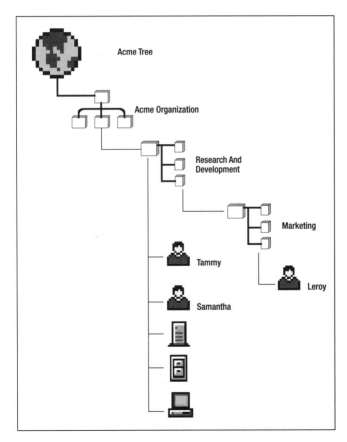

Figure 9.2   Example container login scripts.

login script in the Acme Organization container does not affect users in the Research And Development container.

➤ If Research And Development has a login script, the users Tammy and Samantha will execute that script each time they log into the Acme tree.

➤ If Marketing has no container login script, Leroy won't execute any container scripts even though he's in a subcontainer of Research And Development. (Subcontainers do not inherit login scripts from parent containers.)

When To Create A Container Login Script

You create the container login script in the following conditions:

➤ When you want to send messages and direct them to all users in a container

➤ When you choose to specify a search drive mapping to the \PUBLIC directory instead of leaving it to the default login script

➤ When you assign search drive mappings to shared applications

➤ When you assign network drive mappings to users' home directories

➤ When you are using queue-based printing and you want to capture printer ports and assign them to print queues

➤ When you need to launch applications or menu utilities that are common to all the users in that container

➤ When you choose to employ **IF...THEN...ELSE** statements to provide customized settings that will execute according to the time of day, the week, the month, or group memberships (among other variables) instead of putting them in profile or user login scripts

Profile

You create profile login scripts to provide identical environments for users who reside in different containers or who are a subsets of users within a given container. Understand the purpose of profile login scripts, use them only for that purpose, and use them as sparingly as possible.

Following are some important points to remember about the profile login script:

➤ Each User object has a Profile property field located under its Login Script property page. This property field can contain only one profile name at a time. (Therefore, only one profile script may execute for any given user at any given time.)

➤ It always executes before the user or default login script.

A User object must be a trustee of the Profile object with Read property rights assigned to the login script property of the Profile object; otherwise, the User object won't be able to read the profile's login script, and the profile login script won't execute. (NDS rights are discussed in Chapter 10.)

➤ It always executes immediately after the container login script.

➤ It executes only when the User object has the name of the profile listed in the Profile field of its Login Script property page, and when it has sufficient NDS rights to read the profile's login script property.

➤ It's located in the Login Script property page of the Profile object.

➤ You use it to customize settings for groups of users but not individual users.

➤ You use it to provide login instructions that are unique to a specific group of users who do not reside in the same container.

➤ You use it to set up environments for multiple users.

When To Use Profile Login Scripts

The profile login script is designed primarily to accommodate users who have similar needs but who exist in various containers across the network (or who are a subset of users in a given container). You will typically use a profile login script in the following circumstances:

➤ When you want to assign drive mappings to special data directories or volumes on other servers that contain critical information for users who fit a specific profile but who do not reside in the same container (or, again, who are a subset of users in a given container).

➤ When you want to assign search drive mappings to executable files that a specific group of users needs.

➤ When you have specialized equipment (such as color laser printers, high-graphics equipment, plotters, or die cutters) whose access must be restricted to a subset of certain people from a given group (or groups) of users.

 Make sure instructions in the profile login script do not conflict with the commands in the container login script or the default login script.

User

You create a user login script when you need to provide a set of instructions that are unique for a specific user. You should create a user login script only when there's no other way to customize a user's environment.

You need to remember the following points about the user login script:

➤ It always executes last.

➤ You create it in the Login Script property page of the User object because it's a property of the User object.

➤ You should only put instructions in it that are specific to that user.

➤ You use it to customize settings for individual users.

➤ You use it to set up the environment for a single user.

In a user login script, you use commands that are unique to that user's requirements. Items that you put in a user login script include additional mappings to directories (not found in other scripts), messages or reminders specific to that user, or commands to automatically run executable programs for that user.

 Although you should avoid using the user login script wherever possible, you shouldn't avoid learning about it.

Note: *You can avoid user login scripts altogether by combining identifier variables with IF...THEN...ELSE statements in container or profile login scripts.*

When (Not) To Use User Login Scripts

Do everything in your power to avoid employing user login scripts. Not only will you make your job easier, but you'll make life simpler for the person who inherits your network configuration when you're no longer the network administrator.

You should create user login scripts only in the following situations:

➤ When you assign drive mappings to directories that are specific to a user. This facilitates easier user access in navigating to different directories and subdirectories.

➤ When you want to connect a user to printers (other than those already assigned in the container or profile login script) that are specific to that user's needs each time he or she logs in.

➤ When you want to execute applications or menu utilities every time that user logs in.

 Make sure instructions in the user login script do not overwrite commands executed from the container login script or the profile login script. (Remember, the default login script does not execute when there is a user login script.)

Default

The default login script executes when a user, including the Admin user, without a login script logs in. The first time you log into a freshly installed NetWare server, you need a drive mapping to the \PUBLIC directory, which contains the NetWare command files. Without access to these files, you won't have any functionality or access to the server's hard drive, unless you manually map drives from the \LOGIN directory. The default login script does this all for you so you're up and running immediately with the functionality you need to begin setting up the system.

You need to remember the following points regarding the default login script:

➤ It contains only the minimum commands that are necessary (for example, a drive mapping to \PUBLIC) to let you navigate the system using globally available commands.

➤ It executes when there's no user login script, when the **EXIT** command is in a container or profile login script, or when the **NO_DEFAULT** command is not being used to disable it.

➤ It sets up the necessary commands for the system to function.

➤ It's hard coded into the LOGIN.EXE file in SYS:LOGIN and SYS:PUBLIC and, therefore, cannot be edited.

 This default login script executes for all users who have not been given a user login script. The Admin user is no exception. You can disable the default login script by including the **NO_DEFAULT** command in a container or profile login script that applies to the user for whom you want to disable it. (Identifier variables are covered later in this chapter.) You disable the default login script to eliminate conflicts between the default login script and your other login scripts.

Working With Login Scripts

How well you design your login scripts determines how transparent the network is to your end users; it also determines how much administration you must do to keep your login scripts up to date. Complicated login script schemes usually result in complicated network problems. In the following sections, we cover how to design your login scripts effectively and what your login scripts should contain.

Designing Effective Login Scripts

The key to easy login script management is to use as few login scripts as possible. The following points will help you create an effective login script scheme:

➤ Create all the login script instructions you can in as few container objects as possible.

➤ Design profile login scripts for groups of users who do not reside in the same container but need the same environment settings.

➤ Create any user-specific requirements and use **IF...THEN...ELSE** statements in container or profile login scripts to customize to the needs of individual users.

➤ If you're sure your configuration will work better with user login scripts than it will without them, put user-specific requirements in user login scripts.

Figure 9.3 shows the types of user-configurable login scripts with their respective NDS object types.

Note: The default login script is not user configurable because it is part of the LOGIN.EXE file that executes at login.

You should consider the following questions to best employ login scripts for the benefit of your network users and administrators:

➤ What are your users' needs?

➤ How many users do you have?

➤ What groups or categories can your users be divided into?

➤ How large is your network?

➤ How complex is your network?

➤ What are your users' access requirements for network resources?

➤ How can you make the system easy to administrate?

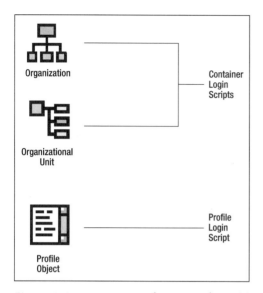

Figure 9.3   Two types of user-configurable NDS login scripts.

Managing The Contents Of Login Scripts

Each type of login script is designed for a particular purpose. Remember the purpose of each type's design, and you'll create effective login scripts. Also, each type of login script is intended to apply to typical sets of tasks. Keep those tasks in mind when designing your login scripts. Above all, remember to limit the number of different scripts that you must manage, and to avoid user scripts completely, if at all possible, and stick to the barest minimum of container and profile scripts, along with the default login script.

The MAP Command

You create login scripts primarily to assign drive letters to the root of volumes or to subdirectories on volumes. In this section, you'll learn how to use the **MAP** command for creating login scripts. Network drives are often very large arrays with deep subdirectory structures that can be difficult to navigate. The whole point of creating a drive mapping is to provide quick access to a specific subdirectory without having to navigate to it whenever you want to access its files.

The **MAP** command ensures that the drive mappings in the login script are restored every time you log in. All versions of DOS and Windows require drive letters to identify a partition on a hard drive. Novell uses names like SYS: and VOL1: to identify volumes that are roughly similar to partitions on hard drives. To give DOS and Windows clients the drive letter they understand,

Novell employs the **MAP** command to assign that drive letter to a Novell volume and/or subdirectory on the volume.

The basic command syntax is:

```
MAP [[option] drive_letter:=[volumename:path]]
```

The following is a brief explanation of each portion of the command syntax:

➤ *option* Any **MAP** option may be used here. (**MAP** options are covered later in this section.)

➤ *drive_letter* Any drive letter from A to Z is an acceptable letter that DOS or Windows and the **MAP** command understands.

➤ *volumename:path* Any actual NetWare [*volume:directory*] name. Either the NDS volume name or the physical volume name is acceptable syntax.

Both the backslash (\) and the forward slash (/) are acceptable when using the **MAP** command. You do not need a slash between the volume name and initial subdirectory. Example: [*volumename*:apps/word] is just as acceptable as [*volumename*:\apps/word] or [*volumename*:/apps/word].

The **MAP** command is used to assign drive letters to volumes, subdirectories, or Directory Map objects. (*Directory Map objects* are NDS objects that point to a directory or volume in the file system; they are covered in more detail in the "Mapping With Directory Map Objects" section later in this chapter.)

You also use the **MAP** command to map search drives. A *search drive* is Novell's implementation of the **PATH** command. A search drive is a drive letter assigned to a directory just like a regular drive mapping. The big difference is that the directory to which you map the drive letter becomes part of the DOS **PATH** statement. In other words, any executable files (such as EXE, BAT, or COM) can now be executed from any location in the directory structure. When a drive mapping is assigned a letter—but is not assigned a search drive—you must navigate to that drive letter before you can activate any executable files in the directory. Once you make that drive assignment a search drive, you can activate any executable files regardless of which directory you are in.

There are four methods used to map drives: You can map drive letters to directories, you can map drive letters to volumes, you can map search drives to directories or volumes, or you can map using Directory Map objects. These methods are covered in detail in the following sections.

Drive Letters Map To Directories

Instead of mapping a drive letter to a NetWare volume and always navigating from the root of that volume, you can map a drive letter directly to a subdirectory on a volume. For example, you can map several drive letters, each to a different directory (to make navigation to those subdirectories easier) using the following series of **MAP** commands:

```
MAP G:=SYS:APPS/GEOPHYS
MAP H:=SYS:APPS
MAP I:=SYS:SYSTEM
MAP ROOT K:=VOLUME2:APPS/DATABASE
```

Many database programs must be run from a root directory. If you create a good file and directory design, chances are your database program will not be located in the root of a volume. Therefore, you'll need to use the **MAP ROOT** command to map a drive letter to the directory so the database program is fooled into thinking it's installed at the root of your volume. The **MAP ROOT** command in the previous example provides a fake root assignment to the subdirectory.

 You can move only lower (not higher) in the directory tree of your file system from the directory your drive letter has been assigned using the **MAP ROOT** command.

Mapping is never permanent, unless you place those mappings in a login script so a consistent set of drives is mapped each time you log in.

> *Note:* Another variation of mapping is Windows' Universal Naming Convention (UNC) drive mapping utility, which you can use to map drives from the Tools option in Windows Explorer. This Microsoft utility maps drives from the Windows interface and has nothing to do with Novell drive mappings. Also, the mappings it produces have no relationship with Novell login scripts. The Windows mapping utility is, in some ways, a weaker implementation of drive mapping in that it can be more susceptible to user corruption than Novell login scripts can. Although it makes it easier for users to map a drive on the fly, it can be more cumbersome for an administrator to manage.

Once you map a drive letter to a directory, you can navigate to it through any DOS or Windows application (such as Windows Explorer or Microsoft Word).

At a DOS prompt, you type the drive letter and a colon (for example, C:) at the prompt, and press the Enter key. In a Windows environment, you click on the drive letter.

Network drives are frequently large drives with deep directory structures. The capability of the **MAP** command to map drives eliminates the burden of memorizing a directory structure and navigating through it to access a particular file or subdirectory.

You map drive letters to frequently used directories (like users' home directories and shared data or application directories) to which you want users to have standardized access. For example, you can map drive L: to the applications directory for everyone in the company. This way, no matter which department you work in or which computer you sit at, you know that L: is the standard drive for applications. You can apply the same scenario using drive O: to a shared data directory containing standard word processing documents for the entire company.

Drive Letters Map To Volumes

You can use the following **MAP** commands to create (or assign) drive letter mappings to the root of NetWare volumes.

To map drive letter G to a physical Volume object, use the command:

```
MAP g:=server/sys:
```

> *Note:* *Case is not important when using the **MAP** command.*

To map drive G: to an existing drive, use the command:

```
MAP g:=y:
```

To delete a drive mapping, use the command:

```
MAP DEL g:
```

To map the next available drive letter (in ascending order from A to Z), use the command:

```
MAP N volumename:
```

All volume names, NDS or physical, end with a colon (:).

You can set the NetWare client to display the login results of your login script(s) as shown in Figure 9.4. The display shows the results of the mappings, errors that occurred, and any other commands (such as capture assignments to printers) in the login script(s).

Novell employs two different methods of identifying volumes:

➤ **Physical volume name** The physical volume name used by the server to identify the volume name is expressed as [*volumename*:]. Legal volume names are composed of numbers from 0 to 9, letters, and the underscore character, and they always end with a colon (:). To express a physical volume name together with the server to which it belongs, you use [*servername/volumename*:], with the server and volume names separated by a slash.

➤ **NDS Volume object name** The NDS volume-naming convention is different from that for the physical volume name. (This is to prevent confusing the two types of volume names.) The physical volume name refers to the actual formatted partition on which the files reside. The

Figure 9.4 The login results as seen in the Results window.

NDS Volume object is an object that points to the physical volume and represents that resource in the NDS tree (in much the same way as a Server object in the NDS tree is different from the actual server it represents).

The physical volume has no NDS security, whereas the NDS Volume object does. You can have more than one NDS Volume object pointing to the same physical volume, but you cannot have more than one physical volume representing itself. The naming convention used to express an NDS volume name is [*servername_volumename*:], with the server name and volume name separated by an underscore and always followed by a colon (:).

Novell tends to promote the NDS object name. Watch for it and make sure you understand the naming conventions of physical volumes and NDS volumes and how they differ from each other.

Once you map a drive to a NetWare volume, you navigate the directory structure with the DOS **CD** command or via Windows Explorer, just as you do a local drive.

Search Drives Map To Directories Or Volumes

Network search drives are drive letters mapped to network directories that are automatically added to the DOS **PATH** statement. In other words, the directory to which a search drive is mapped becomes part of the path. Therefore, you can access executables in that directory from anywhere in the directory structure.

Many Windows applications no longer need the **PATH** statement to access executable files because of the way the applications are designed. Therefore, you'll tend to need fewer search drives than you would have in the days when DOS applications were the norm. However, some applications still need search drives. Windows itself depends on a search drive to its main directory, or it may not function correctly. You should pay particular attention to the use and syntax of mapping search drives so you can prevent application problems.

*Note: When you enter the **PATH** command to find out what search drives exist, it lists only the drive letter. You have to enter the **MAP** command to discover which directories have been mapped to which search drives. Go to a DOS prompt and type "PATH" and then "MAP", and you'll see how the DOS path and NetWare search drives work together.*

Some examples of situations in which you use search drives are:

➤ Applications, batch files, or utilities that are specific to a user and installed in a user's home directory.

➤ A frequently used shared database program that needs to be available at the touch of a key.

➤ Programs consisting of multiple executable files, or overlays, often require search drives to access those files. The NetWare operating system uses a directory of files stored in the \PUBLIC directory, which requires a search drive for the operating system to execute many of its functions.

Note: Search drives work only for executable files. If a directory does not contain any executable files, there's no point in mapping a search drive.

Using The **MAP** Command To Map Search Drives To Volumes Or Directories

When you map a normal network drive, you get a result similar to using the DOS **SUBST** command. When you map a search drive, it's like adding a DOS directory path to the DOS **PATH** command.

Both DOS and Windows operating systems use directories in the **PATH** statement to access executable code. The NetWare operating system also uses search drives to find applications, DLL files, and MSG files.

NetWare is designed to put search drives in the path environment of the local operating system because it knows the local operating system will search the path to discover the executable code for which it's looking.

You use the **MAP** command to assign and insert search drives into the path wherever you choose. This enables you to exercise maximum control over the order in which search drives are searched. The **PATH** command displays the directory paths (in numerical order) that you assign in DOS as drive letters with their subdirectories, separated by semicolons. The **MAP** command displays the drive letter, followed by the NDS volume name and then the path associated with the respective drive letter.

When you map a normal network drive, you have drives usually beginning at D, E, or F, depending on how you have the First Network Drive variable set in the NetWare Client properties. When you use the **MAP N** (map next) command, drives are automatically assigned in alphabetical order beginning with the first network drive. (The default First Network Drive is F). The regular and search drive mappings are depicted in Figure 9.5.

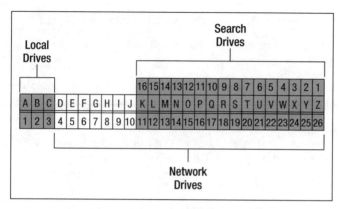

Figure 9.5 Search drive mappings.

When you map a search drive using the **MAP** command, several options are available for customizing your search drive environment. Up to 16 search drives can be mapped, as shown in Figure 9.5. If no search drives are currently mapped and drive Z: is not in use as a regular network drive, then it will be automatically selected to be the first search drive, as shown in Figure 9.5. When you map search drives, the following options are available to customize your search drive order:

➤ You use the **MAP S1** command to map a search drive and make it the first search drive in the path using the highest available drive letter. The syntax is as follows:

```
MAP S1:=VOLNAME:DIRNAME
```

Note: VOLNAME is the name of the volume and DIRNAME is the name of the subdirectory.

The **MAP S1** command maps a search drive in the first position in the search path by overwriting whatever is mapped there.

➤ You use the **MAP S16** command to map the next available search drive to a volume or subdirectory. The syntax is as follows:

```
MAP S16:=VOLNAME:DIRNAME
```

The **MAP S16** command creates a search drive in the next available search position in the path. Consequently, this is also the last available search drive until another one is mapped.

➤ You use the **MAP INS** command to insert a search drive between two other search drives or in the beginning of the path without overwriting other search drives. The syntax is as follows:

```
MAP INS S16:=VOLNAME:DIRNAME
```

➤ You use the **MAP C** command to change (**C** for change) a search drive to a network drive or a network drive to a search drive. The syntax is as follows:

```
MAP C drive_letter:
```

➤ You use the **MAP ROOT** command to create a search drive that is mapped as a root drive. They syntax is as follows:

```
MAP ROOT S1:=VOLNAME:DIRNAME
```

Mapping The Search Drive Order

The order in which you arrange search drives can enhance or degrade the performance of your applications—or even determine whether the applications run properly. To plan the order in which you place your search drives, you need to consider the following factors:

1. When an application makes a request to execute a certain file, the NetWare client passes the request to the operating system to search the user's current directory for the file(s) needed to run the executable.

2. If the operating system does not locate the file(s) it requires, it continues by looking in the directory that is associated with the first search drive, [S1:](search drive 1).

3. If the file is not discovered in the drive assignment for the first search drive, the operating system searches subsequent search drive assignments in numerical order beginning with [S1:] and ending with the last search drive currently assigned.

4. If it does not find the files in any of the search drives, NetWare returns to the current directory, and a "bad command or filename" error message appears on your screen indicating that it did not find the executable you or the application requested.

You can improve your system's performance by assigning the most frequently accessed directories with the highest priority search numbers. S1: is the highest priority, and S16: is the lowest priority.

Mapping With Directory Map Objects

When you make drive mappings like the ones covered so far, you must change all the login scripts that are affected whenever you move a directory location to another subdirectory, volume, or server. You use the Directory Map object to eliminate this problem. When you map drive letters to point to data, you map to a Directory Map object instead of the actual volume or directory. Whenever you move the location of a directory, you just change one pointer in the Directory Map object; you do not need to change any login scripts for the new location to be found by your users or applications.

A major end user advantage of Directory Map objects is that they can map to an object instead of having to know where the associated data is. The end user needs to know only the name of the Directory Map object to assign a drive letter to a data resource.

You map a drive letter to a Directory Map object using the same options as the **MAP** command supports using the following syntax:

```
MAP S16:=directory_map_name
```

Do not place a colon (:) after the name of the Directory Map object or NetWare will think it's a volume name. (Remember Novell's convention for naming volumes is that they always end in a colon.)

Working With Login Scripts

You must plan your login scripts before you create them so you'll have a reference when executing and debugging them. Study the sample login scripts, commands, and identifier variables we cover in the following sections, and you'll have no difficulty producing login scripts that automate your users' environments effectively.

Components Of Login Scripts

Login scripts are composed of two components: commands and identifier variables.

➤ **Login script commands** These are instructions that the operating system knows about and operates on when they are executed within a login script to produce a result. The **MAP** command is a login script command, which was covered in detail earlier in this chapter. **REM** (or **REMARK**) is also a command that tells the operating system to ignore the text following it when it's placed in a line of a login script.

➤ **Login script identifier variables** Identifier variables are placeholders for information that can vary. **LOGIN_NAME** is an identifier variable that holds the place of the login ID of the user logging in to the NDS tree. When a login instruction uses the **LOGIN_NAME** identifier variable, the NetWare operating system replaces the identifier variable with the login ID of the person logging in.

If you use the following command, when a user with a login name of BOBJ logs in, the operating system returns the result of mapping drive F: to the \USERS\BOB subdirectory:

```
MAP F:=DATA:USERS/%LOGIN_NAME
```

All types of login scripts use the same commands and identifier variables, and they work the same way regardless of the type of login script. The following example of a login script demonstrates the use and correct syntax of login script commands and identifier variables:

```
REMARK This is an example of a typical login script.

WRITE "Good %GREETING_TIME, %LOGIN_NAME. How are you today?"
WRITE
WRITE
WRITE "You are currently logging in from station number %STATION"
BREAK OFF
MAP DISPLAY OFF

REM The following commands map network drives.
MAP ROOT H:=SERVER1_SYS:APPS
MAP ROOT M:=SERVER2_DATA:USERS
MAP L:=SYS:

REM The following if statement maps a drive to everyone in the
REM "Admins" group.
IF MEMBER OF "ADMINS" THEN MAP ROOT F:=SERVER1_SYS:SYSTEM

REM The following statement maps a drive to the user's home
REM directory.
MAP ROOT K:=%HOME_DIRECTORY
```

```
REM The following section maps two search drives.
MAP ROOT S2:=SERVER2_SYS:PUBLIC
MAP ROOT S3:=SERVER2_SYS:DATABASE
MAP INS S4:=SERVER2_APPS:WP61


REM The following statement is a weekly reminder.
IF NDAY_OF_WEEK = 2 AND HOUR24 = 12 THEN
 WRITE "CRITICAL REMINDER"
 WRITE "Your timesheets must be completed before 2pm."
 WRITE "You must attend the weekly four o'clock meeting today."
 WRITE "Update your weekly calendars before today's meeting."
 FIRE PHASERS 5
 PAUSE
 FDISPLAY SERVER1_DATA:MESSAGES\WEEKLY.TXT
END


REM The following command disables the default login script.
NO_DEFAULT


REM The following command launches the Commander menu program.
Exit "commandr"
```

All login scripts execute their instructions in the order they are placed in the script, beginning with the topmost instruction. Be sure the instructions within a script do not overwrite the results produced by a previous line.

The following list provides you with descriptions of login script commands and identifier variables. Learn what they mean and determine how you can use them to use login scripts to your best advantage:

➤ **#** This command is an external command identifier. It causes an executable command to execute and then returns control back to the operating system so the login script will continue.

➤ **BREAK** This command permits or denies the user from interrupting the login script with the DOS **BREAK** command.

➤ **FDISPLAY** This command displays the content of a file by filtering out unprintable characters.

➤ **FIRE PHASERS** This is a noise-producing command that emits a primitive sound from the speaker of your PC. A value after this command will tell your PC how many times to emit the sound.

➤ **IF...THEN** This command is used to create conditional statements in which a condition must be met for the command to execute. (If you use the **ELSE** command with the **IF...THEN** command, the **ELSE** command must be entered on a separate line.)

➤ **INCLUDE** This command will include and execute a DOS text file written in login script format, or another login script in another container, profile, or user.

➤ **MAP** This command is used to make drive assignments in login scripts. It's the most frequently used command and, therefore, the most important login script command.

➤ **MAP DISPLAY** This command enables or prevents **MAP** commands from being displayed on the screen. It's followed by the condition **ON** or **OFF**. For example, **MAP DISPLAY ON**.

➤ **NO_DEFAULT** This command prevents the default login script from executing.

➤ **PAUSE** This command stops the login script from continuing and waits for user input to continue.

➤ **REM (or REMARK)** This command tells the operating system to ignore text that appears on the remainder of the line containing this command. The command must have a space after it to function properly. It can be used abbreviated (as **REM**) or spelled out (**REMARK**). Other variations that function the same as this command are a semicolon (;) or an asterisk (*).

➤ **WRITE** This command displays the text that follows and is surrounded by quotes.

You need to learn the following identifier variables to produce significant results from login script commands:

➤ **GREETING_TIME** This identifier variable collects the time of day and displays the result as afternoon, morning, or evening.

➤ **HOME_DIRECTORY** This identifier variable collects the home directory location from the User object home directory value and returns it for the operating system to process in the login script.

➤ **HOUR24** This identifier variable returns the hour of the day based on a 24-hour clock.

➤ **LOGIN_NAME** This identifier variable collects the login name of the user who is logging in and returns it to the operating system to include in the command it's executing.

➤ NDAY_OF_WEEK This identifier variable checks the date and returns the day of the week, beginning with "1" for Sunday.

➤ STATION This identifier variable identifies and displays the workstation connection number.

The Login Utility

The login utility allows you to edit login scripts. To use the login utility to edit login scripts, you must understand the Script page and the Variables window.

➤ **Script page** In this page, you can choose alternate login scripts instead of using the default ones you have been assigned. You can also use a profile script in addition to the one assigned to your username. You can also run a profile script.

➤ **Variables window** In this window, you can enter values for variables that can be referenced in any login script. This command allows you to decide what those variables are going to represent each time you log in.

From the login screen, you can disable scripts from running at all, decide whether to display scripts, decide whether to close the displayed results automatically, or choose a different script altogether. End users may be prevented from operating these options by turning them off in the properties of the client in the Windows network dialog box.

Practice Questions

Question 1

What happens after the profile login script executes? [Choose the two best answers]

- ❏ a.   The default login script executes if no user login script exists.
- ❏ b.   The container login script executes.
- ❏ c.   The user login script executes if no default login script exists.
- ❏ d.   The user login script (if one exists) executes.
- ❏ e.   The template login script executes.

The correct answers to this question are a and d. The container login script executes first, the default login script always exists, and there's no such script as a "template login script." Therefore, answers b, c, and e are incorrect.

Question 2

To disable the template login script, you use the command **NO_ TEMPLATE** in the container login script.

- ◯ a.   True
- ◯ b.   False

The correct answer to this question is b, false. There is no such command as **NO_TEMPLATE**, and there is no such thing as a template login script.

Question 3

> Which of the following are valid login script types? [Choose the two best answers]
>
> ❑ a. Organization
>
> ❑ b. Container
>
> ❑ c. Organizational Unit
>
> ❑ d. User

The correct answers to this question are b and d. Although Organization and Organizational Unit objects are containers, they are not valid login script types. Therefore, answers a and c are incorrect.

Question 4

> Which of the following conditions must be met in order to execute a profile login script? [Choose the two best answers]
>
> ❑ a. The profile must be a trustee of the user.
>
> ❑ b. The trustee must be named in the Profile object.
>
> ❑ c. The user must be a trustee of the Profile object.
>
> ❑ d. The user must have sufficient NDS rights to execute the script.

The correct answers are c and d. The profile does not need to be a trustee of the user, and the trustee cannot be named in the Profile object. Therefore, answers a and b are incorrect.

Question 5

> The right to have a container login script execute for a user _____.
>
> ○ a. flows down the tree
>
> ○ b. belongs to all users in the container with the script
>
> ○ c. belongs to all users in all subcontainers of the container with the script
>
> ○ d. belongs to users who have been made a trustee of the container

The correct answer is b. The right to have a script execute does not flow anywhere; it belongs to all users in the container with the script. Therefore, a container script in one container does not execute in other containers, and being a trustee of a container does not have any effect on whether the script executes. Therefore, answers a, c, and d are incorrect.

Question 6

> The correct syntax to map a drive to an NDS volume with a physical name of sys: is_____.
>
> ○ a. **map s:=server_sys**
>
> ○ b. **MAP S:=SERVER_SYS**
>
> ○ c. **map s:=server/sys**
>
> ○ d. **Map s:=server\SYS:**

The correct answer to this question is d. The first three answers are using illegal volume names. There are no colons after them.

Question 7

> Which of the following are identifier variables? [Choose the three best answers]
>
> ❑ a. **LOGIN_NAME**
> ❑ b. **HOME_DIRECTORY**
> ❑ c. **HOUR_24**
> ❑ d. **GREETING_TIME**

The correct answers to this question are a, b, and d. **HOUR24** should not have an underscore. Therefore, answer c is incorrect.

Question 8

> Which of the following is not a valid login script command?
>
> ○ a. **REM**
> ○ b. **WRITE**
> ○ c. **MAP_DISPLAY**
> ○ d. **BREAK**

The correct answer to this question is c. The **MAP DISPLAY** command should not have an underscore. Answers a, b, and d are valid login script commands, and are, therefore, incorrect.

Question 9

> The user login script always executes last.
>
> ○ a. True
> ○ b. False

The correct answer to this question is a, true. If a user login script exists, the default login script does not execute. Therefore, the user login script will execute last. If there is no user login script, it cannot execute.

Need To Know More?

 Dwww.novell.com/documentation is the source for any and all information pertaining to NetWare. Search for "login scripts" in the NetWare 5 online documentation.

 http://support.novell.com/servlet/Knowledgebase is Novell's Knowledgebase for Technical Information Document (TID) document number 1203151—Troubleshooting Login Scripts.

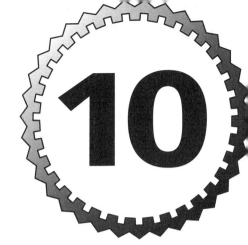

NDS Security

Terms you'll need to understand:

√ Effective rights

√ Inherited Rights Filter (IRF)

√ Object rights

√ All Property rights

√ Selected Property rights

√ Trustee

√ [Root] trustee

√ [Public] trustee

Techniques you'll need to master:

√ Determining a trustee's effective rights

√ Using an Inherited Rights Filter (IRF) to filter out specific rights

√ Troubleshooting incorrectly secured objects and resources in the NDS tree

In Chapter 8, you learned how to manage the file-system security. Now, you'll learn about another important part of the NetWare operating system—Novell Directory Services (NDS) security—and how it's different from and similar to file-system security.

As you'll soon see, NDS security is one of the most important tasks that you must master to be an effective NetWare administrator. Because NDS security controls the entire NDS tree, users rely on it for access to the resources they need, such as volumes, servers, printers, and applications. (Normally, rights must be given to an object before it can gain access to other objects.) By the time you finish this chapter, you'll be able to determine rights and effective rights for objects, block inherited rights, and control access to any given NDS object.

NDS Security

As mentioned previously, NDS security is an extremely crucial part of your network. NDS security gives your users the right to access your NDS resources while simultaneously blocking unauthorized users from doing the same. Because almost every component of a NetWare network exists in the NDS tree—and the information contained within NDS is used to control access to most resources—NDS is the main way to control network resources.

Not only does NDS security specify which users can access the objects and information in the NDS, it also controls what those users do with this information. For example, let's say a user needs to log into the network using a login script, access a volume, view objects in the NDS tree, and print to a specific printer. Before a user can perform any of these tasks, you need to give him or her the appropriate NDS rights with NetWare Administrator.

Although file-system security is different and separate from NDS security, many of the functions are similar. The following section compares the two security systems.

File-System And NDS Security Comparison

As mentioned in the previous section, file-system security and NDS security are two separate entities, and many rival operating systems cannot separate the administration tasks. For example, you cannot have one administrator control the properties of some users while having another administrator control the properties of different users. These security systems—and the entire NDS tree—are constructed so you can assign different tasks to different administrators. You can also have one administrator manage all the users and groups, while having another control all file-system rights.

Several properties apply to both file-system security and NDS security:

➤ Effective rights

➤ Inheritance

➤ Inherited Rights Filter (IRF)

➤ Rights

➤ Trustees

Before a user can be given rights to an object, he or she must be made a trustee of that object. Only then can the user be assigned the desired rights. This is done the same way as it is for file-system security.

Of course, NDS security differs from file-system security in a variety of ways, including:

➤ Whereas file-system security has one set of rights, NDS security has two sets: object and property rights.

➤ Rights, as a rule, do not "flow" from NDS to the file system. There's one case, however, in which the rights flow from the NDS to the file system.

➤ An IRF can be used to block both the Supervisor object right and the Supervisor property right.

NDS Objects Access Control

Assigning access rights to users protects network resources and services. Before you can protect your network services and resources, you must understand the following services:

➤ Object trustees

➤ Object rights

➤ Property rights

➤ Selected Property rights as compared to All Property rights

Object Trustees

An *object trustee* is defined as an NDS object that is granted trustee rights to another object by being placed in that object's access control list (ACL). (Remember that each NDS object maintains a list of objects that have access to it, and this list is known as the ACL.) To assign an object rights to another object, simply click on the object to be assigned the rights, and drag it on top of the object to which the right is being granted (see Figure 10.1). Once this task is

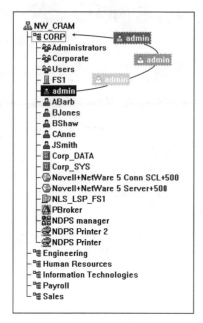

Figure 10.1 Placing an object into another's ACL.

complete, the Trustees Of Administration dialog box appears (as shown in Figure 10.2), which is where you'll set the various rights (covered later in the chapter).

An *object trustee* is defined as an NDS object that is granted trustee rights to another object by being placed in that object's access control list.

Figure 10.2 The NDS object Trustees Of Administration dialog box.

Once you give an object access rights to another object by placing it in the second object's ACL, the first object can manipulate the second object. For example, by placing the Admin User object in the Corp Organizational Unit object's ACL, Admin will have the right to manipulate Corp. Trustees can also be given the right to access and modify information about that object.

Not every NDS object can be made a trustee of another object. The following list contains all objects that can be made trustees. Except for the User object, these objects can immediately grant access to multiple users when they are made an object trustee:

➤ User object

➤ Group object

➤ [Root] object

➤ [Public] trustee

➤ Organizational Role object

➤ Container and parent container objects

 User objects will also receive rights granted to them if they have been given the security equivalence of another User object. It's easier to control access by granting rights to groups of users rather than to individual users. This way, any new User object that is added into the NDS tree and assigned to a group will automatically receive the rights assigned to the group. This happens instantly, and the administrator doesn't have to do anything extra.

The [Root] object and [Public] trustee are special cases. If they are made a trustee of another object, all users in the NDS tree are granted access to the object. For this reason, it's extremely important that you fully understand these implications. If you grant access to either [Root] or [Public] accidentally, you may find that all users have access to the objects. These special cases are explained in the following sections.

The [Root] Trustee

When you install NetWare, the [Root] object is created automatically at the topmost level of the NDS tree. You cannot delete, rename, or move the [Root] object. By default, any user that logs into the network is automatically granted the rights assigned to the [Root] object. The following steps walk you through assigning access to the [Root] object:

1. Right-click on the object to which you would like to assign [Root] as a trustee.

2. Choose the Trustees Of This Object option from the resulting pop-up menu (see Figure 10.3).

3. The Trustees Of *object* window appears (where *object* is replaced by the name of the selected object).

4. Click on the Add Trustee button.

5. Select the [Root] object from the available objects list and click on OK. [Root] has now been added as a trustee. You can now select the different rights you want to assign to the object (see Figure 10.4).

 In most organizations, you don't want to make all objects in the NDS tree available to all users. For this reason, you should avoid using the [Root] trustee for granting access to objects in the tree.

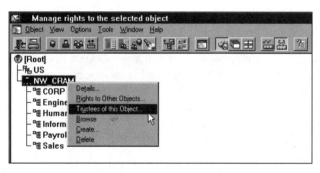

Figure 10.3   Adding the [Root] object as a trustee.

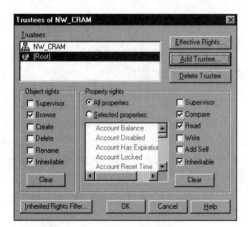

Figure 10.4   [Root] has been added as a trustee.

The [Public] Trustee

Another special NDS component is the [Public] trustee. The [Public] trustee operates as a directorywide Group object (that is, an object that can be used anywhere in the NDS). When you first install NetWare, [Public] is granted trustee rights to [Root] and can therefore browse all objects in the NDS tree. Because of this, all users (because they are automatically part of the [Public] group) can browse the NDS tree. [Public] is automatically made a trustee of all the objects in the NDS tree, as seen in Figure 10.5.

Every object in the NDS tree has security equivalence to [Public]. This gives all users the right to view any other object while they are logging in. Any rights assigned to [Public] are therefore assigned to all objects in the tree.

 Be careful when changing the access rights to [Public]. Because [Public] is a trustee to all the objects in the NDS tree, any extra rights that you assign will grant all users and objects rights to every object in the tree. If you are not careful, you'll find that you have granted the users too many rights.

Object Rights

Once you add a trustee to an object, you can grant it object rights, which control access to the object itself without granting access to the object's properties. Object rights also control what the trustee can do with the object, including deleting, renaming, and browsing the object.

To view and modify the object rights, you can either right-click on the object and choose Trustees Of This Object from the menu, or you can highlight the object and choose Trustees Of This Object from the Objects menu. Once you choose to view the trustees of the object, the Trustees Of *object* window appears.

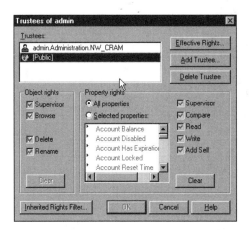

Figure 10.5   [Public] in the object trustee rights.

The object rights that you can assign to a trustee are as follows and shown in Figure 10.6:

➤ **Supervisor (S)** The Supervisor right grants the trustee all the available access rights, including Browse, Create, Delete, and Rename. By assigning this right, you also grant the trustee access to all the property rights.

➤ **Browse (B)** The Browse right allows the trustee to view the object in the NDS tree. If this right is not assigned, the trustee will not see the object when it looks at the NDS tree in either NetWare Administrator or NETADMIN.

➤ **Create (C)** The Create right gives the trustee the ability to create objects below this object in the NDS tree. Because only container objects can contain other objects, this object right can be granted only on a container object and not on a leaf object. If you look at the object rights on a leaf object, you'll notice that this option is grayed out, indicating that it's not available.

Note: The Create right also allows the user to salvage a delete file.

➤ **Delete (D)** The Delete right grants the trustee the ability to delete the object from the NDS tree.

➤ **Inheritable (I)** The Inheritable right is new to NetWare 5. It allows an object trustee of a container to inherit the object rights assigned to that object. It then grants the object trustee these same rights to objects and subcontainers within that container. This object right is granted by

Figure 10.6 The object rights.

default. As with the Create object right, Inheritable is available only on container objects and will be grayed out for leaf objects.

➤ **Rename (R)** The Rename right enables the trustee to rename the NDS object in the NDS tree.

A handy mnemonic to remember the object rights is "Some Bob Cats Danced In (the) Rain."

Property Rights

Property rights are the second type of rights that you can grant to object trustees. These rights allow you to grant information about the property to assigned trustees. They also allow you to control the NDS object's properties, including the ability to view and search for property information.

The property rights are actually on the same window as the object rights. The object rights are on the left of the window and the property rights are on the right (see Figure 10.7).

Each object has many different property values that can be assigned to it. (These values can include the object's account balance, email address, department, login script, telephone number, as well as many others.) If you use other network operating systems, such as Windows NT, you'll notice that NetWare gives you considerably more properties that can be assigned to objects.

Because you're able to control which users can modify individual property values, you are given a capability that very few other network operating systems

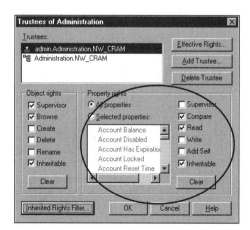

Figure 10.7 The property rights.

have: the ability to designate administrator roles. Most network operating systems use an "all-or-none" approach. Using Windows NT as an example, you can grant a user administrator access, but you cannot easily limit the power the user has. Administrator, by default, has full control over the Windows NT environment. You do not have the ability to take permissions away from one administrator while maintaining them for another. NetWare, on the other hand, gives you that functionality. By assigning specific property rights to an individual, you are, in effect, creating an administrator with limited power. For example, you can assign the Password Management property of all User objects to a single individual. This individual will then be allowed to modify user passwords but will not have the ability to change any other properties of those objects. This is beneficial in large organizations in which a single administrator cannot possibly manage the entire network and the work needs to be divided among multiple administrators.

The property rights are as follows:

➤ **Supervisor (S)** As with the Supervisor object right, assigning this property right grants all property rights to the trustee.

➤ **Compare (C)** Assigning the Compare right grants the ability to compare a property value between two (or more) objects. For example, if a trustee has the Compare right to several User objects, then it can check to see if the two User objects have the same telephone number or work in the same department.

Because the Compare right can be granted on a property-by-property basis, the trustee will not be able to view the value of the property. The trustee would be able just to compare them and get a true or false response to the comparison. For example, a trustee can check to see if the department property for the users BSmith and MJones is Payroll. The only response that the trustee will get is "true" (they are in the same department) or "false" (they are not in the same department). For the trustee to be able to view the property value, it must be granted the Read right.

➤ **Read (R)** The Read right enables a trustee to view the selected property value of the object. Granting the Read right to a trustee automatically grants the Compare right as well.

➤ **Write (W)** The Write right enables the trustee to modify, add, change, and delete property values. When you assign the Write right, the Add/ Remove Self right is added automatically.

➤ **Add/Remove Self (A)** The Add/Remove Self right allows the trustee to add or remove itself from the property.

➤ **Inheritable (I)** This property is the same as that for the object rights.

 A mnemonic you can use to remember these property rights is "Some Companies Really Want An Intranet."

Assigning Property Rights

As you may have noticed in Figure 10.7, you have two options when configuring the property rights: You can choose either to assign rights to All Properties or to Selected Properties. These two options give you a lot of flexibility in controlling property rights.

The All Properties Option

The All Properties option allows you to automatically grant or deny access to all of the object's properties simultaneously. Property rights that are granted through this option affect every property of the object. If, for example, you were to give a user the Read right to All Properties of the object, then that user would be able to view all the properties of that object.

The Selected Properties Option

The Selected Properties option allows you to selectively assign rights to different objects. These rights are independent of each other. For example, if you grant a user the Compare right for the E-Mail Address property and the Read right to the Employee Number property, that user is able to compare the E-Mail Address property of one object with that of another object to which the user has rights. However, the user will be unable to view the value stored in the E-Mail Address property. With the Employee Number property, however, not only will the user be able to compare his or her value to that of another object's Employee Number property, but the user will also be able to view the property's value.

This feature of NetWare is incredibly powerful. It allows you to control not only what can be done to the object, but also which of its many properties can be modified and by whom. As mentioned before, this feature is rare in network operating systems and is one of the things that make Novell's NDS stand above its competitors.

What happens if you were to grant rights to a trustee in both the All Properties and the Selected Properties options? The answer is simple, but one that you need to know. As a rule, the rights that are granted through the Selected Properties option take precedence over the rights that are granted through the All Properties option.

For example, refer to Figure 10.8 (the All Properties option and the Selected Properties option). You grant one of your administrators (BSmith) the right to compare all the properties in your Organizational Unit (Human Resources). You also grant him the right to read the telephone numbers of the User objects contained therein. If he were to attempt to view the email address of one of the users, he would be denied access. He could, however, compare the email addresses of several of the users with success. Remember that he will be informed only if the email addresses are duplicate or not. He will not be told the values of the email addresses are. With the telephone numbers, he will be able to not only compare them among the User objects, but will also be able to view the numbers of each of the users. This happens because the Read right on the User objects overwrites the Compare right. Although BSmith can only compare the rest of the object properties, he is allowed to read the telephone numbers of the objects.

NDS Object Rights Determination

Just as it does with the file-system rights, NDS uses right inheritance in its determination of object rights. Inheritance is used because it minimizes the amount of administration overhead needed to configure NDS object security. By assigning rights at a container level, you let the rights flow down to the

Figure 10.8   The All Properties (left) and Selected Properties (right) options.

objects (both container and leaf) that reside within the container. This inheritance flow is possible because of the hierarchical nature of NDS. Think of NDS as a hill. If you were to stand on the hill and drop marbles on the slope, they would roll down toward the bottom of the hill. This is similar to how the NDS rights work. You assign them at the top, and they roll (or flow) down to the lower levels.

Let's take a look at how rights flow down the NDS hierarchy when we assign a trustee to a container object. Refer to Figure 10.9 as we follow the steps:

1. You assign the Admin User object as a trustee of the NW_Cram organization with full rights [SBCDRI].

   Note: Novell typically uses the first letter of the rights when referring to multiple rights rather than spelling them out repeatedly. Therefore, S=Supervisor, B=Browse, C=Create, D=Delete, R=Rename, and I=Inheritable.

2. The rights flow through to the Dallas Organizational Unit, granting the Admin user the [SBCDRI] rights.

3. Next, [SBCDRI] rights are inherited by the Payroll Organizational Unit.

4. Finally, the user BSmith, the Management group, and the FS1 NetWare server get the [SBDR] rights. The Create right does not flow down to these objects because it is available only on container objects. Because these objects cannot contain other objects, there's no need for the Create right to be assigned.

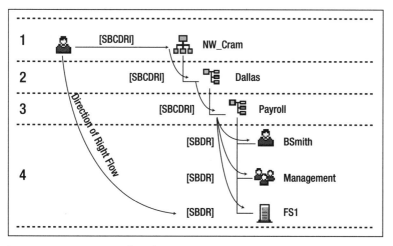

Figure 10.9   NDS right inheritance.

Controlling the "Flow" Of Inherited Rights

Sometimes, you'll want to block the flow of the inherited rights. You may want a user to act as a trustee with the Create right in a parent container, but you do not want the user to be able to create objects in a child container. You can accomplish this in one of two ways: You can block rights using an Inherited Rights Filter (IRF), or you can make a new trustee assignment at the child object in the NDS tree and grant it new rights.

Using An IRF To Block Inherited Rights

As you've learned, NetWare 5 uses IRFs in both the file system and in the NDS tree. The role of the IRF is to filter out the inheritance in the NDS tree. You would place an IRF on objects in the NDS tree to block the inheritance of both object and property rights. Remember that property rights have two options: All Properties and Selected Properties. You can place the IRF on either of these two options.

Previous versions of NetWare did not allow you to place IRFs on the Selected Properties option. Therefore, only the All Properties options could be inherited. The ability to inherit selected properties (as long as the Inheritable property right is granted) is new to NetWare 5.

Note: *By default, NetWare does not grant the Inheritable property right to the Selected Properties option.*

 There's an important difference in how IRF blocks the Supervisor right between the file system and NDS. In NDS, an IRF can be used to block the Supervisor object right. In the file system, however, an IRF system cannot be used to block the Supervisor object right.

Blocking Inherited Rights Using New Trustee Assignments

If you refer back to Chapter 8, you'll recall that the rights flow from directories to subdirectories. To grant a subdirectory different rights than the rights it inherited from the higher directories, you create a new trustee assignment at the lower level.

NDS security works in much the same way. You can override an object right that has been granted at a higher level in the NDS tree by creating an explicit trustee assignment at the lower level. This new trustee assignment changes the trustee's rights at that level.

To restrict the Inheritable right that is granted by default to all properties when rights are established in the All Properties option, you must create a new trustee assignment in a location lower in the NDS tree. Lower objects in the NDS tree, however, inherit only those rights that are assigned through the Selected Properties option if an explicit trustee assignment is created. Once you create this trustee assignment, you can block the inheritance of selected property objects lower in the NDS tree by creating a new trustee assignment that removes the Inheritable right.

 Rights conferred through the Selected Properties option cancel any rights assigned in the All Properties option. For example, if you grant the user BSmith the Read right for all properties of an object—and then grant him the Write right for a selected property—BSmith will be granted the Write right to the selected properties and the Read right to the rest.

Calculating Effective Rights For Objects

When you manage NDS security, you must be able to determine which rights the users will be granted at different levels of the NDS tree. These are known as *effective rights*. The user's effective rights to an object in the NDS tree are found through the combination of rights that are given from the following rights minus the IRFs rights:

➤ [Public] trustee rights

➤ [Root] rights

➤ Container security equivalencies

➤ Explicit rights

➤ Group memberships

➤ Inherited rights from a parent container

➤ Organizational roles

NetWare Administrator gives you two ways to determine a user's effective rights to an object in the NDS tree. You can right-click on the User object that you would like the effective rights for, then choose Rights To Other Objects from the menu. The alternative is to right-click on the NDS object for which you would like to determine the user's effective rights, and choose the Trustees Of This Object option from the drop-down menu.

How To Configure NDS Security

When you implement NDS security, you need to follow some guidelines to ensure that your services and resources are secure and that your users are still able to access the resources they need.

Usually, most users will not need more than the default rights that are assigned to them in the NDS tree. Only the users who are required to manage and modify the NDS objects need more rights assigned to them than the default ones. If you assign too many—or overly powerful—rights, you'll find that you are practically inviting unauthorized access to your network.

Novell recommends that you follow these guidelines to minimize the possibility of assigning incorrect NDS security to objects and resources:

➤ Avoid the All Properties option.

➤ Be careful with the Write property right.

➤ Filter the Supervisor right.

➤ Use the default rights to start.

➤ Use the Selected Properties option.

➤ Use the Supervisor right effect on property rights.

➤ Use the Supervisor right on a Server object.

Avoid The All Properties Option

By assigning rights in the All Properties option to users, you grant them the right to view private information about other users and resources on the network.

The easiest way to grant properties rights is through the All Properties option. You simply grant access rights to a single option, and it automatically grants these rights to all the possible rights, and there are many of them. However, doing this opens all the property information of your object to trustees. Some information will be stored in these objects that even administrators do not need access to. For example, although an administrator may need to view and modify a User object's password or full name, he or she does not necessarily need the right to view that user's date of birth, home address, or Social Security number.

Be Careful With The Write Property Right

You need to be very careful when granting the Write right to the Object Trustee (ACL) property of any object in the NDS tree. When you do this, you give the trustee the right to assign anyone—including itself—all rights including the Supervisor right. (This is another reason to be careful when assigning rights with the All Properties option.)

If you grant the Write right to a trustee, it can breach the NDS security by assigning the Supervisor right for the object to any user.

Filter The Supervisor Right

Be careful when filtering (using IRF) the Supervisor right in a particular section of NDS. If you are not careful, you may find yourself unable to manage an object. For example, you might filter out the Supervisor right on a container and grant a container administrator the only Supervisor right to the object. After time, you delete the container administrator. That section of the NDS tree will no longer be accessible because no existing trustee has the Supervisor right.

Use The Default Rights To Start

Novell has designed the default NDS security to meet the needs of most users. Use Novell's experience for your NDS security implementation. Remember that these default rights give users access to the resources they need without granting them access to ones that they don't. Once this task is complete, you can assign more rights to the users who require them, such as container and user administrators.

Use The Selected Properties

By assigning more-specific property rights through the Selected Properties option, you can avoid some of the security problems that were covered in the previous section. The Selected Properties option is the most efficient way to assign property rights to objects.

 Remember that rights assigned in the Selected Properties option will override ones assigned in the All Properties option.

Use The Supervisor Right On A Server Object

Although a Server object is defined as a leaf object, it still contains volumes. By granting a trustee the Supervisor right, you give the trustee the file-system rights to all volumes on the server. This action will also grant the trustee the Supervisor rights to any volumes that are linked to the Server object.

This is the only instance in which the NDS security rights are inherited by the file system.

Use The Supervisor Right Effect On Property Rights

As covered previously, you might want to grant some container administrators all the object rights except for Supervisor, and then grant them the Supervisor rights using the Selected Properties option. Granting rights in this manner ensures that the container administrators have access only to the properties they need.

Troubleshooting NDS Security

As with most troubleshooting techniques, troubleshooting NDS security requires you to understand how NDS applies its security rules and to follow certain steps to rule out possible problems.

Most NetWare NDS security troubleshooting falls into one of two categories. Either users cannot access objects in the NDS tree that they should be able to, or users can access NDS objects and the objects' properties that they should not be able to. In both these situations, you need to find out why these users can or can't perform these functions.

The troubleshooting procedure for these conditions should begin with a question, such as, "Why can't the user access the Engineering printer?" or "Why is the user able to modify the Organization object properties?"

Because these are the most common NDS security problems, we'll discuss each in detail and define some criteria to check to solve the problem quickly and effectively.

No Resource Access

If a user is not being granted specific rights to a specific NDS container, there are several things that could be wrong. The following lists some things you should check:

➤ Check the User object to make sure the user has been assigned the appropriate rights.

➤ Check Group objects to see if the user has been made a member of a group that has been denied access.

➤ Check Organizational Unit objects to find out if the user has been made an occupant of an Organizational Role object that has had its right(s) revoked.

➤ Check the user's Security Equal To page to see if the user has been granted security equivalence to a particular object.

➤ Check the container to figure out if the container has been assigned rights, in addition to the user (or group).

➤ Check to see if an IRF has been placed on the container.

Note: If an IRF has been placed on the container, make an explicit trustee to the container. If not, check the parent container for IRFs and make explicit assignments.

Unauthorized Resource Access

When a user has access to resources that he or she should not have access to, it's up to you, as the administrator, to determine how these rights are being granted. You can do this by determining the effective rights or determining where the rights are being granted.

Effective Rights Determination

Novell has given you a powerful tool to simplify how you can determine a user's effective rights: NetWare Administrator. To find a user's effective rights through NetWare Administrator, follow these steps:

1. Click once on the resource that you would like to check.

2. Right-click on the object, and select the Trustees Of This Object option from the menu.

3. Click on the Effective Rights button. The Effective Rights dialog box appears.

4. To the right of the Object Name field, click on the browse button.

5. Browse until you find the desired User object, and click on it. Click on OK. The Effective Rights dialog box appears listing the rights of the selected object.

6. Click on the Close button.

Note: The short way to do this is to select the object in the Trustee field of the Trustees Of Object dialog box and then click on Effective Rights.

Where Are Rights Being Granted?

Once you determine where the user's rights are (as discussed in the previous section), you can determine how the user is receiving the rights by checking each object in the NDS tree (using NetWare Administrator) and checking the explicit trustee assignments and the inherited rights for the following:

➤ The [Root] object

➤ The [Public] trustee

➤ The User object

➤ The user's group memberships

➤ The user's Organizational Role object

➤ The security equivalencies given to the user, if any

➤ All containers that the user resides in

Practice Questions

Question 1

What are the six object rights? [Choose the six best answers]

❑ a. Inheritable

❑ b. Create

❑ c. Supervisor

❑ d. Rename

❑ e. Add/Remove Self

❑ f. Delete

❑ g. Compare

❑ h. Browse

The correct answers are a, b, c, d, f, and h. The correct object property rights are Supervisor, Browse, Create, Delete, Inheritable, and Rename. A handy mnemonic to remember these is "Some Bob Cats Danced In (the) Rain." The Add/Remove Self and Compare rights are property rights. Therefore, answers e and g are incorrect.

Question 2

A trustee is granted the Read right to all properties using the All Properties option. The same trustee is then granted the Write right to the Employee Number property under the Selected Properties option. What will his effective right be on the Employee Number property?

○ a. He will be granted the Read right because the most-restrictive right is granted.

○ b. He will be granted the Write right because the least-restrictive right is granted.

○ c. He will be granted the Read right because the rights assigned through the All Properties option override those assigned in the Selected Properties option.

○ d. He will be granted the Write right because the rights assigned through the Selected Properties option override those assigned in the All Properties option.

The correct answer is d. The property right assigned under the Selected Properties option always take precedence over those assigned through the All Properties option. NetWare security does not rely on the least- or most-restrictive rights to control access. The trick to this question lies in answer b. Although it's correct that the trustee will be granted the Write right, he will not be granted this right because it is the least restrictive. Instead, he will be granted the right because it was granted in the Selected Properties option. Therefore, answers a, b, and c are incorrect.

Question 3

> You grant the user Joanne the Create right to the organization NW_Cram. Will she have the Create right to the Organizational Unit Payroll within NW_Cram (OU=Payroll.O=NW_Cram)? Assume that no IRFs exist, the Inheritable right has been granted, and that no other rights were assigned at OU=Payroll.
>
> ○ a. Yes, she will.
>
> ○ b. No, she will not.

The correct answer is a. Three instances could cause Joanne to not have the Create right: if an IRF is placed at OU=Payroll to filter out the Create right; if the Inheritable right is not granted at the O=NW_Cram; and if Joanne was assigned a different right at the Organizational Unit Payroll. Therefore, answer b is incorrect.

Question 4

> Which object rights are available on only container objects and not on leaf objects? [Choose the two best answers]
>
> ❏ a. Supervisor
>
> ❏ b. Browse
>
> ❏ c. Create
>
> ❏ d. Delete
>
> ❏ e. Rename
>
> ❏ f. Inheritable

The correct answers are c and f. Because you cannot create other objects within a leaf object and because these "nonexistent" objects cannot therefore inherit rights, only the Create and the Inheritable rights are available on a container object. Therefore, answers a, b, d, and e are incorrect.

Question 5

> What are the six property rights? [Choose the six best answers]
>
> ❑ a. Inheritable
>
> ❑ b. Create
>
> ❑ c. Supervisor
>
> ❑ d. Rename
>
> ❑ e. Add/Remove Self
>
> ❑ f. Write
>
> ❑ g. Compare
>
> ❑ h. Read

The correct answers are a, c, e, f, g, and h. The six property rights are Supervisor, Compare, Read, Write, Add/Remove Self, and Inheritable. A mnemonic you can use to remember these property rights is "Some Companies Really Want An Intranet." The Create and Rename rights are object rights. Therefore, answers b and d are incorrect.

Question 6

> Inheritance in the file system differs from that in the NDS by being able to block the Supervisor right.
>
> ○ a. True
>
> ○ b. False

The correct answer is b, false. In NDS security, an IRF can block the Supervisor right, whereas file-system security cannot.

Question 7

If you grant the user Joanne the Write right to the Department property of the Organization NW_Cram (O=NW_Cram), will she also be granted the Write right to the Department property in the Organizational Unit Payroll (OU=Payroll.O=NW_Cram)? Assume that the Inheritable right has not been granted along with the Write right, and that the Write right has not been assigned through the All Properties option.

○ a. Yes, she will.

○ b. No, she will not.

The correct answer is b. She will not be granted the Write right unless one of two tasks was completed: The Inheritable right was granted as well at the Organization NW_Cram, or the Write right was assigned to all properties through the All Properties option. If one of these two things had been done, then she would be granted the Write right at the lower level. Therefore, answer a is incorrect.

Need To Know More?

 For more information on NDS security, check out the NetWare 5 online documentation with keyword searches on "security," "trustee," "object rights," "property rights," and "inheritance."

 www.novell.com/documentation/en/nw/nw/docui/index.html is where you can find the is the NetWare 5 documentation on the Web.

Using Z.E.N.works Application Launcher

Terms you'll need to understand:

√ Z.E.N.works

√ Application Launcher

√ Application object

√ Forced run

√ Push distribution

√ Pull distribution

√ Application Explorer

√ Application Object Template (AOT)

√ Application Object Text Template (AXT)

Techniques you'll need to master:

√ Creating Application objects

√ Describing the benefits of Application Launcher

√ Distributing applications with Application Launcher

√ Managing applications with Application Launcher

√ Load balancing applications with Application Launcher

√ Creating Application objects with an Application Object Template (AOT)

Since networks were first implemented, managers, information system (IS) professionals, and users have all complained about the time, the cost, and the delays involved in supporting networks. Installing new applications, bug fixes, and repairing existing applications have burdened IS professionals and support staff with countless trips to individual workstations. These workstations may be spread among several floors of large buildings and, in many cases, multiple buildings. Novell has created Z.E.N.works (Zero Effort Networks) Application Launcher to address these issues.

In this chapter, you'll learn the theory behind Application Launcher and then discover how to implement it. You'll examine the benefits of employing Application Launcher and then learn about its components. Finally, you'll learn how to use Application Launcher to distribute and manage your applications.

> *Note: Application Launcher is also called the Novell Application Launcher and is sometimes abbreviated as NAL.*

Overview: The Application Launcher

In this section, we'll examine Application Launcher, which has actually been available since NetWare 4.x. However, the version of Application Launcher that ships with NetWare 5 is the most robust version to date. It features Application objects that repair their own corrupted or deleted files with the click of a mouse button and roaming profiles that don't burden your network with onerous amounts of traffic. It also allows the instant deployment of upgrades, patches, service packs, or new applications.

Application Launcher Benefits

Application Launcher allows you to distribute application software to your networked workstations without visiting each workstation.

Ordinarily, when you design an application-deployment strategy for a network, you must consider whether to install the applications directly on users' workstations or as shared applications on the network. This decision often involves the following types of dilemmas:

➤ If you install the application on each user's machine, you must visit each workstation to upgrade the application and to provide each user with the necessary support.

➤ If you install the application as a shared network application, you must manage the user's environment by making numerous trips to his or her workstation to create shortcuts to the application, install upgrades or patches, investigate and ensure proper drive mapping, and deal with corrupted or deleted files.

Application Launcher gives you the advantages of both methods without the hassle of having to visit individual workstations to perform those tasks.

Application Launcher Benefits The Administrator

The major benefits of using Application Launcher are centralized maintenance and control of applications, single-point application administration, and any combination of push-and-pull distribution technology.

Centralized Application Maintenance

Application Launcher enables you to determine the architecture of each workstation and specify precisely which applications the users can and cannot access. For example, you specify a minimum hardware requirement (such as available hard-drive space or a minimum amount of RAM) that tells Application Launcher to ignore computers that don't meet the minimum requirement. Therefore, Application Launcher won't deploy applications to workstations that don't meet the specifications you've defined.

If you accidentally or intentionally delete a program file (or files) from an application that was deployed by Application Launcher, you simply right-click on that application's icon and select Verify from the menu. All files, Registry settings, drive mappings, and configuration settings are immediately restored. This restore feature also works on a corrupted file.

Centralized Application Controls

The main benefit of centralized control is reduced downtime for users, reduced costs for application management, timely deployment of updates, and reduced time spent troubleshooting each workstation—all of which contribute to reduced total costs.

Through Application Launcher, you manage the installation, upgrade, deployment, and availability of applications. You decide who has access to any application at any time, and you even have the power to force the termination of an application and to send generic or customized warning messages informing the user of the impending termination of his or her application.

Administering Applications From a Single Point Of Control

You use Application Launcher to create an Application object in the Novell Directory Services (NDS) tree for each application you want to deploy. Because NDS is an enterprisewide database of all network resources, when you grant users the right to access Application objects you have created, the users automatically receive location-independent access to those applications.

You configure the settings and properties that are necessary to run the application in the property pages of the Application object. The major application properties you configure are as follows:

➤ The name of the icon that represents the application

➤ The path (either the drive mapping or universal naming convention, or UNC, path) to the application's executable file

➤ The settings for INI files or Registry entries necessary to configure the program

➤ The printer captures that are needed to redirect print jobs from the application

➤ The program files, command-line parameters, and working directory necessary for the program to run properly

➤ Drive mappings to program data

You use the Group and container objects in NetWare Administrator to grant application access to multiple users who have identical requirements, and you manage access to the applications centrally as you would any other NDS resource. You also benefit from knowing your applications are secure from unwanted intrusion, because access is being granted within the highly secure NDS environment.

Deploying Applications: Push Or Pull?

You have two options to deploy applications:

➤ **Push** Application installations, upgrades, bug fixes, and service packs are deployed to the users without their request or intervention. *Push distribution* is triggered automatically by an event such as the user logging in. This event is called a *forced run*, and you select it in the Forced Run property of the Application object. Push distribution is best used to apply critical patches, client updates, or operating-system patches.

➤ **Pull** Users receive an icon that they must click on to install new software. When the users click on the icon, one of the following events is triggered:

    ➤ An installation program executes and loads software on the user's workstation while making required configuration updates.

    ➤ Application objects are automatically created to accomplish both of the preceding actions.

    ➤ The application launches and automatically makes necessary updates to the workstation.

 Application Launcher is designed to deploy and maintain only application programs and their necessary files. It does not track, restore, or manage data files.

Application Launcher Benefits The User

Four major benefits that significantly enhance productivity for your end users include roaming profile support, load balancing for applications, location-independent application access, and fault tolerance for application availability:

➤ **Roaming profile support** Your applications are available to you regardless of the workstation from which you log in, because Application Launcher detects your profile and downloads the components you need to run your applications from the workstation's desktop you're using.

➤ **Load balancing for applications** When a large number of users are accessing the same application on a server that is overloaded, Application Launcher maintains an acceptable level of performance by launching another copy of the application from an alternate server that is not as busy. Your end users are never aware of this background operation.

➤ **Fault tolerance for application availability** If an application is unavailable from the server you usually access it from, Application Launcher launches the application from an alternate server. Again, your end users are never aware this operation is taking place.

➤ **Location-independent application access to applications** Normally, you need to know on which server an application is loaded to access it. With Application Launcher, you can access applications without knowing where they are located. As long as there's an Application object in the NDS tree that represents the application, you can access it with the click of a mouse button. You do not need to map drives or remember the drive where the application is because the drive mappings are maintained within the Application object.

Application Launcher Components

You must learn the components of Application Launcher to understand how to use it most efficiently to accomplish your network administration duties. Application Launcher has two components for administrative functions and two components for performing user functions. (Each of the components is discussed in detail in the following sections.)

The administrative components are the Application Launcher Snap-In and SnAppShot. The Application Launcher Snap-In allows you to use NetWare Administrator for creating network-launchable applications. SnAppShot is used for taking "before and after" pictures of your system's configuration.

The user components are the Application Launcher Window (NAL.EXE), which provides users access to networked applications and Application Explorer (NALEXPLD.EXE), which deploys applications to various desktop components. It's an option you can use instead of the Application Launcher Window.

Understanding The Application Launcher Snap-In Module

Application Launcher is an extension to the existing NDS database. It's a snap-in module that modifies NDS to recognize and interact with Application objects. Application Launcher adds property pages to existing container, User, and Group objects to enable them to interoperate with Application objects. Therefore, you use NetWare Administrator to perform the following actions on Application objects:

➤ You create, view, and configure Application objects the same as any other NDS objects.

➤ You deploy Windows 3.x, Windows 95/98, and Windows NT applications to users' workstations connected to the network.

➤ You manage applications through the property pages of the Application objects and through the property pages of User, Group, and container objects.

Note: When you modify the users in a container or group, that container or group receives the results of those modifications. When you modify the properties of a user, only that user receives the results of the modification even though he or she resides in a container or belongs to a group.

When you install the Application Launcher Snap-In module, the following items are added to the Tools menu in NetWare Administrator:

➤ AOT/AXT File tools:

➤ AOT → AXT

➤ AXT → AOT

➤ Export Application Object

➤ Generate new GUIDs

➤ Migrate Application Objects

➤ Show Inherited Applications

➤ Search and Replace

➤ Sync Distribution GUIDs

Understanding The SnAppShot Utility

Application Launcher's SnAppShot utility provides state-of-the-art software-distribution capabilities. You use the SnAppShot utility to perform the following sequence of functions:

1. Take a snapshot of the configuration of your machine before installing the application on the machine.

2. After taking the snapshot, SnAppShot prompts you to install the application you want to distribute to your workstations.

3. After you install your application, you take another snapshot of your workstation to record the changes made by the installation.

4. SnAppShot then generates an Application Object Template (AOT) that is essentially a map of the changes from the first snapshot to the second.

The AOT is a template that contains all of the application dependencies required to install and run the application whose installation you mapped with SnAppShot. You can use the AOT to create Application objects or you can convert it to an Application Object Text File (AXT) and use the AXT to create Application objects.

The advantage of using AXTs is that they can be edited in any text editor. The advantage of AOTs is that they are binary files, so they run much faster. When you use an AXT file, you must be meticulous about following correct syntax, because AXT files are sensitive to user-generated inaccuracies.

Note: *You use NetWare Administrator to read an AOT.*

Understanding The Application Launcher Workstation Window

NAL.EXE is the executable file that you run at a workstation to display the applications that Application Launcher will deliver to the user. You execute NAL.EXE from any workstation, and the file detects the operating system you're using and then runs the appropriate executable for that operating system. NAL.EXE supports Windows 3.x, Windows 95/98, and Windows NT. When NAL.EXE launches the appropriate executable, the Application Launcher window appears, as shown in Figure 11.1.

The NAL.EXE file detects which operating system is running and then runs the proper executable program to display the Application Launcher window of applications in the operating system. NAL.EXE terminates automatically when the proper executable for your operating system is executed.

A major advantage of having NAL.EXE determine your operating system is that you can place a single command in a login script and the correct executable will run no matter from which operating system your user logs in (assuming the operating system is Windows 3.x, Windows 95/98, or Windows NT).

NAL.EXE updates the necessary files on your workstation before executing the correct Application Launcher window for your operating system. NAL.EXE detects the appropriate window or system directory and copies its files to it.

Understanding The Application Explorer Utility

Some administrators or users may prefer more flexibility when organizing their applications. Application Explorer (which is run using NALEXPLD.EXE) is designed to deploy applications to the following desktop components:

➤ **Start menu** It can assign application shortcuts to the Start menu.

➤ **System Tray** It can put applications in the System Tray.

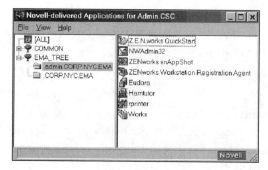

Figure 11.1 The Application Launcher window.

➤ **Workstation desktop** It can put applications on the workstation desktop.

➤ **Windows Explorer** It can install applications in Windows Explorer.

➤ **Application Explorer window** It can put applications in the Application Explorer window (see Figure 11.2).

You cannot run Application Explorer on a Windows 3.x workstation. It can be run on Windows 95/98 or Windows NT workstations only.

Using Application Launcher And SnAppShot

Application Launcher is an application distribution system that's designed to make applications available to end users by placing the applications on the users' desktops. Therefore, you must learn how to use Application Launcher correctly to effectively distribute applications under various conditions.

You use Application Launcher to distribute an application by following a few straightforward steps:

1. Ensure that the user to whom you want to deploy the application has file-system rights to the application's directory.

2. Create the Application object in NetWare Administrator. (The following section, "Simple Application Object Creation," shows how to do this.)

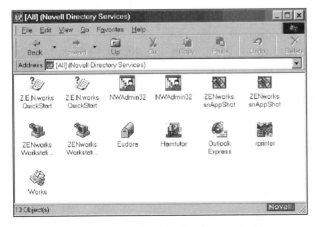

Figure 11.2 The Application Explorer window.

3. Create an association with the end user either directly or though a Group or container object that the user is in.

4. Enable Application Launcher to load at the user's workstation by placing NALEXPLD.EXE or NAL.EXE in a login script or in the user's Startup folder. The User can then launch the application using the Application Launcher window or Application Explorer.

Simple Application Object Creation

The most basic type of Application object is one that requires only a path to the application's executable file and a list of objects (such as User, Group, and container objects) that require access to the application.

To create a simple Application object:

1. Using NetWare Administrator, right-click on the container in which you want the Application object to reside.

2. Select Create. The New Object window appears.

3. Select the Application object and click on OK. The Create Application Object window appears.

4. Click on Create A Simple Application Object (No .AOT/.AXT File).

5. Type an object name and the path to the application; or click on the browse button and navigate to its executable file.

6. Click on Finish. The object is created.

 If, when creating a simple Application object, you use a drive mapping instead of a UNC path in your Path To Executable File, you must ensure that the users also have the drive mapping you're using. Otherwise, the deployment of that application will fail.

Creating Associations To Application Objects

Once you've created an Application object and associated it with the user, it will appear only on the user's desktop. To associate a list of User, Group, or container objects with an Application object, do the following:

1. Right-click on the Application object that you wish to distribute to some users.

2. Select Details to display the property pages for the Application object.

3. Click on the Associations property page to display it.

4. Click on Add to display the Select Object browser window.

5. Select the User, Group, or container objects to which you want to grant application access. Click on OK. You're returned to the Application object's property pages.

6. Click on OK to complete the association.

Note: If you associate an Application object with a container, all the users below that container will also receive the application. This applies to any new User or Group objects you create below that container. If you prefer to keep your associations under stricter control, create associations with groups or individual users.

Using SnAppShot To Create Application Object Templates

If your application will not run by just creating a path to its executable, you must create the Application object from a template. Typically, these applications update several settings (application dependencies) at your workstation, and someone or something has to tell the Application Launcher how to create them. Application Launcher also restores settings from an AOT when a user deletes needed application files or when files are corrupt.

Creating an AOT is rather simple. You use the SnAppShot administrator utility and follow these steps. First, you tell SnAppShot what to inspect as it creates a map of the workstation before you install the application. Then, you install the application and have SnAppShot inspect the changes made by the installation. SnAppShot then creates the AOT.

Preparing For SnAppShot Discovery

The first step in creating an AOT is the discovery process. To take a snapshot of a workstation's preinstallation configuration, follow these steps:

You must begin with a workstation that is representative of the workstations to which you plan to deploy the application(s). The workstation must have only the Windows operating system and the Novell Client installed. You do not want any applications on the system.

1. From the desired workstation, run SNAPSHOT.EXE (located in the \PUBLIC\SNAPSHOT directory). The Novell Application Launcher SnAppShot screen appears.

   Note: It's recommended that you first test the snapshot process in a test environment before implementing it in a production environment.

2. Enter the appropriate information in the dialog boxes requiring an Application object name and an application icon title.

3. Click on Next. A screen appears requesting the path to store FIL files (which are used later to create the AOT file). Use the default path or type in one of your own. Remember to use a unique directory for each Application object you create. You also have the option to browse to an existing path. If the directory does not exist, SnAppShot prompts you to create it.

NDS uses the application name you choose as the default Application object name. Therefore, you must avoid such characters as the period (.), plus sign (+), or equal sign (=). If you do use those characters, NDS won't create the object.

4. Click on Next. You're prompted to provide a path and to specify a file name for SnAppShot to create the AOT file.

5. Click on Next. You're prompted to supply the drive letters of the drives you want SnAppShot to create.

6. Click on Next. You're given the opportunity to review the preferences you selected in the previous screens.

7. Click on Next. SnAppShot begins its discovery process. When it's finished, a dialog screen appears.

8. Click on Run Application Install and provide the location of the setup file or executable that begins the program installation. (The following section, "Installing The Application," shows how to do this.) When you've completed the install, SnAppShot prompts you for the directory in which you want the program installed. If you do not want to specify a target installation directory, leave this field blank.

9. Click on Next to run the final phase of SnAppShot's discovery. When the discovery is complete, SnAppShot displays a dialog screen with a summary of what it accomplished in its discovery and reminds you of the location of the AOT file.

10. Click on Finish to return to your workstation's desktop. The AOT file has been created, and you're ready to create an Application object from an AOT.

Depending on the options you chose in the discovery process, you may also be prompted for such information as:

➤ The location of your workstation's AUTOEXEC.BAT and CONFIG.SYS files.

➤ The scope of discovery you wish SnAppShot to perform.

➤ The directories you want SnAppShot to exclude from the discovery process. (This action saves time.)

Installing The Application

During preinstallation, SnAppShot takes a picture of your workstation's Registry settings, icon groups, and INI files, and prompts you to begin the application setup. To do this, you execute the following steps:

1. Click on the Run Setup button. The Run Setup dialog screen prompts you for the applications setup file.

2. Supply the setup program file for the application you want to install, and click on Open.

3. Follow the instructions to install the application.

You have the option to ignore the Run Setup button and install the application any way you choose; you can even manually copy the application's files and make changes to the Registry or INI files.

Typically, a Windows-based program requires you to reboot the system to complete the installation. If you know that additional configuration is done after the system reboots, you must run SnAppShot after the installation process is complete (which means after you reboot the system).

If you chose to reboot the workstation, SnAppShot restarts when the operating system comes back up, and resumes right where it left off. Even if you close SnAppShot at this point and start it again later, it still resumes where it left off.

Using A Template (AOT or AXT) To Create An Application Object

Using a template to create an Application object for a complex application is much the same as creating a simple Application object. To create an Application object from a template, you do the following:

1. From NetWare Administrator, right-click on the container where you want to put the Application object. Select Create to display the New Object dialog box.

2. Select Application and click on OK. The Create Application Object dialog box appears.

3. Select Create An Application Object With An .AOT/.AXT File and click on Next.

4. A dialog box will prompt you for the path to the AOT/AXT file. Enter the path and click on Next. A dialog box prompts you to customize the object by filling in the appropriate information.

5. Click on Next. Another dialog screen appears with review information. If you select the option to view details after creation, the Application object dialog box appears.

6. Click on Finish to return to NetWare Administrator.

Note: Be sure to create the appropriate associations using the Associations property page of the Application object or your application will not be available to any users.

Displaying The Application Launcher Window And Application Explorer On Workstations

To deploy applications to your users' workstations, you must run NAL.EXE or NALEXPLD.EXE at the workstation. You have three ways of accomplishing this:

➤ You can put a shortcut icon on the users' desktops pointing to NAL.EXE or NALEXPLD.EXE so the users can run the files manually.

➤ You can put a shortcut in the Startup sections of your users' Taskbars (Windows 95/98 and Windows NT only) and run NAL.EXE or NALEXPLD.EXE automatically when the desktop operating system loads. (If no connection to the network is available, an error message will be displayed.)

➤ You can put NAL.EXE or NALEXPLD.EXE in a login script so it will execute only when a user logs in to the network. (This is usually the preferred method because no errors are generated and no user actions are required.)

The syntax to put NAL.EXE in a login script is:

```
@\\servername\SYS\PUBLIC\NAL.EXE
```

The at symbol (@) signals the NetWare operating system to process the command as an external login script command and run it concurrently with the processing of the login script. If you substitute the number symbol (#) for the @ symbol, the login script will stop executing until NAL.EXE is loaded and then continue with the next login script command.

Application Management Using Application Launcher

Managing applications is cumbersome when you oversee a network full of desktop computer systems and you need to run to each one to fix a problem or install an upgrade. In the first section of this chapter, you examined the benefits of using Application Launcher and discovered its components. In this section, you'll learn how to manage applications with Application Launcher.

You use Application Launcher to perform the following application management tasks:

➤ Create or modify an application's identity.

➤ Create or modify an application's environment.

➤ Filter applications so they only install and/or run on workstations whose architecture supports the applications' hardware requirements.

➤ Create or modify distribution schedules.

Creating An Application's Identity

Application Launcher provides the Identification property page (see Figure 11.3) to specify or modify the following items:

➤ The icon (changing it to something other than the default icon).

➤ The icon title for your application.

➤ The path to the application's executable file.

➤ The application to run once only. (This is especially useful for updates, patches, bug fixes, and upgrades. Additionally, you can use the Force Run option for the installation, which prevents the user from refusing the installation.)

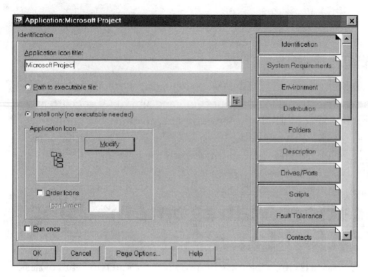

Figure 11.3   The Application Identification property page.

Creating An Application's Environment

Applications have different requirements in order to run properly. Some require alternate working directories than the ones from which they are executed. Some require additional switches to manifest certain properties that are unique to your situation. You may want to load an application but have it run minimized until the user needs it. All of these options are environment-related options that you set in the Environment property page of an Application object (see Figure 11.4).

You set the following parameters in the Environment property page:

➤ You enter command-line startup parameters for executable files with special switches.

➤ You specify the working directory when the application requires a specific directory to run properly.

➤ You determine (if applicable) whether Windows NT will run 16-bit applications in a shared or separate memory space.

➤ You decide whether to have the program default to Minimized, Maximized, or Normal when it starts up.

➤ You enable or disable error logging and decide the file name of the error log and its location. (You use this feature to help troubleshoot Application object failures.)

➤ You can tell Application Launcher to clean up network resources, such as captured ports and mapped drives.

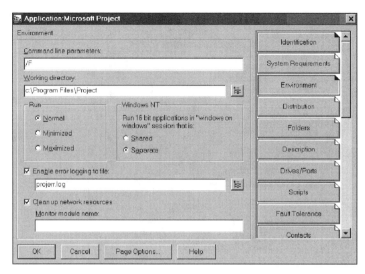

Figure 11.4   The Environment property page.

➤ You specify applications to use a wrapper executable. Wrapper executables detect the operating system you're using and select the proper executable for that system.

The System Requirements Property Page

Application Launcher uses the same icon regardless of the operating system (Windows 3.x, Windows 95/98, or Windows NT) it's required to support. Instead of different icons, Application Launcher provides a System Requirements property page to specify all the operating systems on which the application can run (see Figure 11.5).

You also use the System Requirements property page to specify additional criteria, such as the amount of free disk space or minimum RAM required to run the application. An application will not load on your workstation if it falls short of the required specifications.

 If you do not select the Windows platforms that the application should support, the Application object will not be available to anyone. The application remains hidden until a platform is selected.

The following fields are supported in the System Requirements property page:

➤ The version(s) of operating system(s) on which you want the application to be available. Some operating-system versions support certain applications

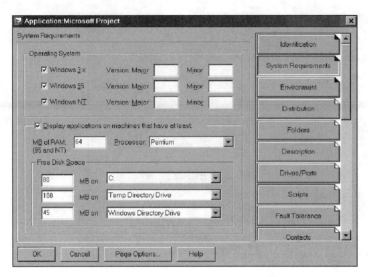

Figure 11.5 The System Requirements property page.

poorly or not at all. In this case, you reduce problems by making sure that that particular operating system does not receive those applications.

➤ Minimum processor requirement. You may find that certain processors are inadequate for running processor-intensive applications. If this is the case, you can prevent an application from being available to computers that don't meet the minimum processor requirements. You can select from 386, 486, and Pentium. You cannot specify the speed of processor.

Note: Windows 3.x does not return values for Pentium processors. It sees a Pentium processor as a 486. Therefore, if you select Pentium processors only for a specific application, Application Launcher will still allow that application to run on 486 machines if they are running Windows 3.x.

➤ The minimum RAM requirement to operate a specific application on a workstation. This field is functional only for Windows 95/98 and Windows NT workstations. You determine the value for this field by calculating the minimum total amount of workstation memory installed on a machine.

You can have Application Launcher determine the amount of free disk space required to install an application. If the minimum space you specify is not available, the application won't be installed. You can have Application Launcher check the amount of free space on several different drives and the amount of space available for temp directories, the Windows system directory, and the Windows directory. Fields you leave blank are ignored.

Note: Application Launcher adds drive space values together when you choose more than one setting on the same drive. If you require 10MB for the temp directory and 20MB for the Windows system directory (and both directories are on the same drive), Application Launcher looks for a minimum of 30MB on that drive before allowing the application to install.

When To Distribute Applications

When you deploy an application, bug fix, service pack, or software upgrade, you can generate a lot of network traffic if several hundred people are accessing the new deployment at the same time. You may want to prevent an application from being deployed on a Friday or over the weekend when limited tech support will be available. You use the Schedule property page of an Application object to specify when it will be deployed. The Schedule property page also allows you to spread the deployment out over a period of time, so it becomes available to users gradually over a couple of hours or even days.

Fault Tolerance And Load Balancing

You set up fault tolerance by assigning primary and alternate locations from which to deliver the application. If a user attempts to access an application and Application Launcher cannot locate it, Application Launcher redirects the request to an alternate copy of the application. Again, this is performed in the background, leaving the user unaware of the operation. The Fault Tolerance property page of an Application object is shown in Figure 11.6.

You use load balancing when you want to provide quicker access to applications by distributing access to them over multiple servers. During peak traffic times, such as first thing in the morning, you can minimize the bottleneck of large numbers of users accessing the same application on the same server at the same time.

Application load balancing works differently than server load balancing (which balances a server's load based on CPU utilization). When you plan to use Application Launcher for load balancing, consider the following:

➤ Do not enable load balancing between servers across wide area network (WAN) links. Enable load balancing only for servers on the same side of any WAN links.

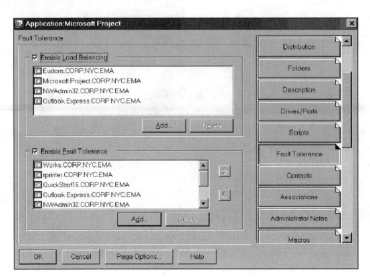

Figure 11.6 The Fault Tolerance property page of an Application object.

➤ Do not consider server CPU utilization as a factor to determine load balancing, because Application Launcher load balancing determines it using a random number in its algorithm.

➤ Be sure to assign file-system rights on each server so the users can access the applications.

Practice Questions

Question 1

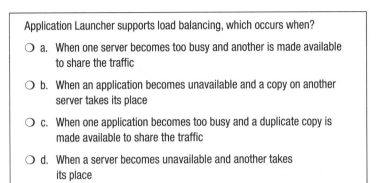

Application Launcher supports load balancing, which occurs when?

- ○ a. When one server becomes too busy and another is made available to share the traffic

- ○ b. When an application becomes unavailable and a copy on another server takes its place

- ○ c. When one application becomes too busy and a duplicate copy is made available to share the traffic

- ○ d. When a server becomes unavailable and another takes its place

The correct answer to this question is d. Application Launcher supports application load balancing, which does not include server load balancing, or making another copy of an application available when one becomes unavailable. Therefore a, b, and c are incorrect.

Question 2

An AXT file, when used to configure a login script to deploy NAL.EXE, can be edited with a text editor.

- ○ a. True

- ○ b. False

The correct answer to this question is b, false. An AXT file is not used to configure login scripts, which is why this is a trick question.

Question 3

Application fault tolerance is used to provide redundancy. If a server goes down and an application fails, the user still has access to it.

○ a. True

○ b. False

The correct answer to this question is a, true. With application fault tolerance, if a server goes down, the user still has access to the application.

Question 4

Which of the following are benefits of using Application Launcher? [Choose the two best answers]

❑ a. Reduced cost of network ownership

❑ b. Reduced licensing costs

❑ c. Reduced support costs for doing software upgrades

❑ d. Reduced server downtime

The correct answers to this question are a and c. Licensing costs and server downtime are not affected by Application Launcher. Therefore, answers b and d are incorrect.

Question 5

The correct command-line parameter for executing NAL.EXE concurrently from a login script is:

○ a. #*servername*\sys\public\NAL.EXE /c

○ b. #*servername*\sys\public\NAL.EXE /con

○ c. @*servername*\sys\public\NAL.EXE /x

○ d. @*servername*\sys\public\NAL.EXE

The correct answer to this question is d. NAL.EXE uses the @ symbol to execute concurrently; it does not use command-line switches to execute concurrently. Therefore, answers a, b, and c are incorrect.

Question 6

Application Launcher supports which of the following workstation operating systems? [Choose the three best answers]

- ❏ a. DOS 6.x
- ❏ b. Windows 3.x
- ❏ c. Windows 95
- ❏ d. Windows NT

The correct answers are b, c, and d. DOS is not supported by Application Launcher. Therefore, answer a is incorrect.

Question 7

Which of the following statements is true of NALEXPLD.EXE?

- ○ a. NALEXPLD.EXE is not a valid Application Launcher file.
- ○ b. NALEXPLD.EXE is used to launch the Application Launcher window.
- ○ c. NALEXPLD.EXE is used to launch the Application Explorer.
- ○ d. NALEXPLD.EXE is used to launch NAL.EXE under Windows NT.

The correct answer to this question is c. NALEXPLD.EXE is a valid file that is used to launch Application Explorer. It's not an Application Launcher file or used to launch Application Launcher. Therefore, answers a and b are incorrect. NALEXPLD.EXE is not used to launch NAL.EXE under Windows NT. Therefore, answer d is incorrect.

Question 8

The SnAppShot utility is used to _____ and _____. [Choose the two best answers]

❑ a. take a picture of a workstation before installing an application

❑ b. create Application objects

❑ c. create Application Template objects

❑ d. create application text files

The correct answers to this question are a and c. NetWare Administrator is used to create Application objects and there are no such things as application text files. Therefore, answers b and d are incorrect.

Need To Know More?

 Search the Help menu in the NetWare Administrator utility. In the Z.E.N.works Contents section, you'll find several topics related to this chapter under the subheading "Understanding Application and Distribution Management."

 www.support.novell.com/servlet/Knowledgebase offers TIDs related to the topics covered in this chapter. At Novell's support Knowledgebase Web site, search for the following:

➤ **2942062** Z.E.N.works Application Launcher 2.5

➤ **2944632** Z.E.N.works, NAL Application/Icon Ordering

Application Management Using Z.E.N.works

Terms you'll need to understand:

√ Z.E.N.works Policies

√ Container Policy Packages

√ User Policy Packages

√ Workstation Policy Packages

√ Workstation registration agent

√ Workstation registration

√ Workstation Import Policy

√ User System Policy

√ Workstation System Policy

√ Desktop Preference Policy

Techniques you'll need to master:

√ Understanding the workstation registration process, both manual and automatic

√ Importing workstations into the NDS tree and controlling their locations and names

√ Understanding how to apply and control both User and Workstation System Policies

Another time-consuming task you'll undertake as a system administrator is managing workstations. Normally, the system administrator must move from workstation to workstation to modify workstation configurations. Z.E.N.works helps change this.

In this chapter, we'll look at some of the features and benefits of Novell's Z.E.N.works as a network management tool. In Chapter 13, we'll examine, in detail, another powerful feature of Z.E.N.works: The ability to control workstations remotely.

Z.E.N.works Advantages

Z.E.N.works (Zero Effort Networks) is a network-management tool that helps reduce the costs and some of the complexities of managing a large number of Windows-based workstations. As with many of the tools that ship with NetWare 5, Z.E.N.works integrates well with the Novell Directory Services (NDS) tree. Using the tools familiar to them, network administrators can manage Windows-based workstations as if they were NDS objects.

Similar to the way that you now group users into User Group objects to ease administration tasks, Z.E.N.works allows you to group workstations into Workstation Group objects. Once you do this, you can set up rules for the group of workstations, and thereby apply the changes to all the workstations in that group.

As an example, let's say you have several engineers in the Engineering Department, and you want to be able to manage all of the engineers' workstations in the same manner. You can create a Workstation Group object in NDS, call it "Engineering", and make each of the engineering workstations a member of that Workstation Group. When you (or the Engineering Department management) decide to change the desktop configuration of all the engineering workstations, you can simply change the Z.E.N.works Policy and apply it to the Engineering Workstation Group object. The policy changes will be replicated to all the workstations in the group.

Maintenance Schedule

To manage your workstations properly with Z.E.N.works, you need to define a schedule that updates the workstation information stored in the NDS tree. If you do not keep this information current, Z.E.N.works cannot properly locate and manage the workstations.

> *Note: By creating and maintaining a Z.E.N.works maintenance schedule, you can ensure that your network's workstations are displayed properly when you view the NDS tree with NetWare Administrator.*

You need to update the NDS workstation information whenever you replace a network board on a workstation, add a workstation to the network, remove a workstation from the network, or move a workstation from one location to another. To update this information using Z.E.N.works, follow these steps:

1. Create new workstation registrations.

2. Update existing Workstation objects in the NDS tree.

3. Delete unused Workstation objects in the NDS tree.

4. Import the new workstations.

The schedule you choose depends on how often you make modifications to the physical network. If your network does not change often, you don't need to create a schedule that uses Z.E.N.works frequently to update the NDS tree. However, if you have a networking environment that evolves and grows on a regular basis, you should create a schedule that is followed regularly.

Whenever you modify the physical network, you should use NetWare Administrator and Z.E.N.works to synchronize all the workstations in NDS, and you should follow these guidelines:

➤ When you add workstations to the network, allow sufficient time for users to log into the network. Then, you can use NetWare Administrator and Z.E.N.works to import the workstations into NDS.

➤ When you move workstations from one location to another, allow sufficient time for users to log into the network. Because the workstations are already registered in the NDS tree, their information will be updated.

➤ When you remove a workstation from your network, use NetWare Administrator and Z.E.N.works to remove the workstation from the NDS tree.

➤ When you replace a network board on one (or more) of your workstation(s), allow sufficient time for your users to log into the network. Because the workstations already exist as objects in NDS, their configuration information will be updated.

 Immediately after installing Z.E.N.works, set up a schedule to update the workstations. You must follow this schedule until every workstation that needs to be represented by an object in the NDS tree is registered.

> A workstation will not be represented as an object in the NDS tree until a user logs into the network from that workstation— only then does the workstation appear in the NDS tree. Depending on the size of your network, it may take several days or longer for all the workstations to be represented in the NDS tree.

Z.E.N.works Policies

When you install Z.E.N.works, new object types are included. One of these objects is known as a *Policy Package*. Policy Packages are NDS objects that allow you to create and maintain Workstation objects in the NDS tree. Each of these Policy Packages is made up of a number of policies that are followed when you manage individual workstations.

Each Policy Package becomes an NDS object that can be associated to User, Group, Workstation Group, or container objects in the NDS tree. Once you create this association, the policies in the Policy Package will be applied to all the objects in the association.

Before you can successfully manage workstations using Z.E.N.works, you must know the various types of Policy Packages—and their policies—that are available to you. These are covered in the following sections.

Z.E.N.works Policy Package Objects

You can define one of seven different Policy Package objects, as shown in the Create Policy Package dialog box in Figure 12.1. Which Policy Package object you choose depends on the policies you need to apply, as well as on the operating system of the workstations.

The seven Policy Packages can be further divided into three subcategories: Container Package, User Package, and Workstation Package. The Container

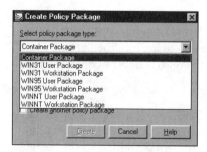

Figure 12.1   The Create Policy Package dialog box.

Package applies only to containers, whereas the User and Workstation Packages are specific to the version of Windows that the user or workstation is currently using or running.

Table 12.1 lists the Policy Package objects that you can create and the type of NDS objects that can be associated with them.

Note: Users logging in from a workstation running Windows 98 and a workstation running Windows 98 use the Windows 95 User Package and the Windows 95 Workstation Package, respectively.

You have the ability to enable, disable, or modify any policy in any Policy Package. This gives you to power to modify policies so they meet your workstation management requirements.

Because of limitations in the Registry on Windows 3.1 workstations, you are limited in your choice of policies to apply to these workstations. Because of their more-advanced Registries, Windows 95/98 and Windows NT workstations allow you considerably more flexibility in applying policies.

In the following sections, we'll detail each of the Policy Package object types: Container Policy Packages, User Policy Packages, and Workstation Policy Packages.

Table 12.1   The Policy Package types and their associated NDS objects.

Policy Package Object	Associated Objects
Container Package	Containers
Windows 3.1 User Package	Users, User Groups, or containers
Windows 95 User Package	Users, User Groups, or containers
Windows NT User Package	Users, User Groups, or containers
Windows 3.1 Workstation Package	Workstations, Workstation Groups, or containers
Windows 95 Workstation Package	Workstations, Workstation Groups, or containers
Windows NT Workstation Package	Workstations, Workstation Groups, or containers

Container Policy Packages

Only containers can be associated with Container Policy Packages. When you apply a Container Policy Package to a container, the policies in that package affect all the objects in the container.

The default policy that exists in the Container Policy Package is called the *search container* (see Figure 12.2). Use the Search Policy to decide which policies (from the other Policy Packages) are going to affect the contents of this container.

Policy Package association flows down the NDS tree, not unlike NDS object rights. The search begins at your selected container and flows up the tree. Once an object is checked for its associations, the Search Policy moves up the tree, searching for other policies. It continues to move up the NDS tree until it reaches the [Root] object.

> *Note: By default, the search order will check the object, followed by the Group object and then the container object (until the [Root] object is reached). You can, however, reorder this search flow or limit it to one or two locations in the NDS tree.*

A common question that administrators new to Package Policies ask is, "What reason would I have to apply a Search Policy on containers?" The best way to answer this is to explain some possible ways that applying a Search Policy can help you.

Once you apply User and Workstation Policies, you can use a Search Policy to determine which Policy Packages are being applied to which objects. This will

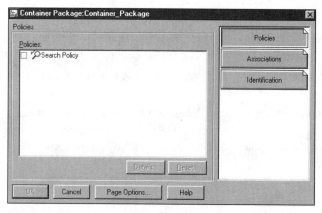

Figure 12.2   The default Container Policy dialog box with the Search Policy.

help you with both troubleshooting policy-related problems and finding policies that have been applied where they should not have (which jeopardizes your security).

 You can avoid unnecessary network traffic by limiting a search to a particular NDS container.

User Policy Packages

User Policy Packages let you control which policies are applied to a user as he or she logs into the system. You can set up controls based on the operating system of the workstation from which the user is logging in. Windows 3.1, Windows 95/98, and Windows NT all support the Policy Packages.

If a user logs into the network from workstations running different operating systems—Windows 95 and Windows NT, for example—the user will get the controls that have been associated to that Policy Package.

You have the option to associate these policies (and, therefore, their controls) with container, User Group, and User objects. By creating a User Policy Package, you can control what resources users can access, according to their membership to objects in the NDS tree.

Novell NetWare with Z.E.N.works will monitor the associations that you create. If you attempt to create multiple User Policy Packages for the same operating system within the same container, the system will alert you of this conflict.

Figure 12.3 illustrates the User Policy Package for the Windows NT operating system platform.

Workstation Policy Packages

As with User Policy Packages, Workstation Policy Packages can be associated with containers. They can also be associated with Workstation Group and Workstation objects, and these policies define which controls are applied to the workstation. When you create policies, they only apply to the policy that matches the operating system. For example, if you create a Windows 95 Policy Package, as well as a Windows NT Policy Package, and then you assign a Windows NT workstation to it, it will only get the controls as defined in the Windows NT Policy Package—the Windows 95 Policy Package will be ignored.

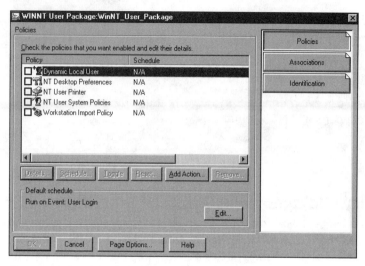

Figure 12.3 A User Policy Package dialog box.

Because the controls defined in the Workstation Policy Package are dependent on the operating system installed on the workstations, it will not matter which user logs in from that workstation. Figure 12.4 shows the dialog box for the Windows NT Workstation Policy Package.

Types Of Z.E.N.works Policies

Remember that the Policy Package object is not much more than a fancy container that holds policies. Once you create the package, you can enable and

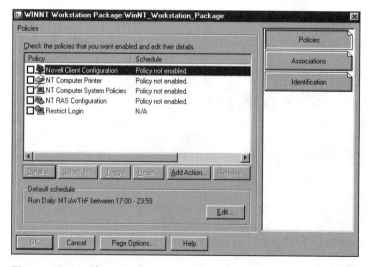

Figure 12.4 The Windows NT Workstation Policy Package dialog box.

configure the individual policies it contains. Once a policy has been enabled and you have associated it with other objects in the NDS tree, its properties will be given to the users and workstations to which the policy applies.

As long as the workstations have an updated version of the NetWare Client (it must have the Z.E.N.works component), you can control the workstation or user desktop settings, as well as the printer configuration and availability. You can also provide remote help using the Z.E.N.works remote control feature. The enabled policies take effect only when the workstations they are to be associated with are imported into the NDS tree.

> *Note:* *Once they are enabled, each of the Z.E.N.works Policies will appear in the NDS tree as individual objects. You can then configure each of the policies individually. Some objects in Workstation and User objects are named the same but apply to different NDS objects.*

Tables 12.2, 12.3, and 12.4 outline the different Z.E.N.works Policies and their descriptions.

Table 12.2   Policy in the Container Policy Package.

Z.E.N.works Policy	Description
Search	This policy can be used to search the NDS tree for policies that are associated with containers and objects.

Table 12.3   Policies in the User Policy Package.

Z.E.N.works Policy	Platform	Description
95 Desktop Preferences	Windows 95/98	Can be used to control the user's desktop environment, including backgrounds, screen savers, and color schemes.
95 User System Policies	Windows 95/98	Allows you to set system policies according to which user is logged into the network. For example, you can control which options appear on the Windows 95/98 Start menu (such as the Run or Find commands) and which options are available on the desktop (for example, you can hide the Network Neighborhood).
Dynamic Local User	Windows NT	Uses NDS to manage user access to the Windows NT workstations.

(continued)

Table 12.3   Policies in the User Policy Package (continued).

Z.E.N.works Policy	Platform	Description
Help Desk	All platforms	Determines the choices provided in the Help Desk user interface and provides information about the support contact or department, such as a current name, phone number, and email address. This policy must be enabled if you use the Help Requester application (covered in Chapter 13).
NT Desktop Preferences	Windows NT	Used to control the user's desktop settings.
NT User Printer	Windows NT	Similar to the Workstation Printer policies in the Workstation Policy Package, but is used to assign and install a printer (with its printer driver) to a User object, rather than to a Workstation object.
NT User System Policies	Windows NT	Used to restrict which commands and applications the user has access to on the desktop and Start menu.
Remote Control	All platforms	Allows you to control whether a remote control session can be established with a user who is logged into the network.
Workstation Import	All platforms	Allows you to configure how workstations are named when they are imported into the NDS tree and where in the tree they should be created. (See the section "Registering And Importing Workstations" later in this chapter.)

Table 12.4   Policies in the Workstation Policy Package.

Z.E.N.works Policy	Platform	Description
3.x Computer System	Windows 3.x	Allows you to control which files are down-loaded to the workstation(s) when they are logged into the network. You can manage either ASCII files (such as those with .BAT and .INI extensions) or binary files (such as those with .EXE and .COM extensions).

(continued)

Table 12.4   Policies in the Workstation Policy Package (continued).

Z.E.N.works Policy	Platform	Description
95 Computer Printer	Windows 95/98	Allows you to automatically select a printer and a printer driver for the workstation to use. The printer will be installed automatically.
95 Computer System	Windows 95/98	Allows you to control which applications will be automatically placed on the workstation's desktop. This policy is independent of which user is logged into the workstation.
95 RAS Configuration	Windows 95/98	Allows you to automatically control the workstation's Dial-Up Networking configuration.
NT Computer Printer	Windows NT	Allows you to automatically install printers and their associated printer drivers.
NT Computer System	Windows NT	Allows you to control which applications are pushed to the desktop. This policy is dependent on the type of workstation rather than on the user who is logged into the network.
Novell Client Config	Windows 95/98 and NT	Allows you to control some of the settings for the Novell Client application. You can control the protocol settings (IPX and TCP/IP), login and capture information, and services that might be installed on the network (such as SNMP or IP gateway).
Remote Control	All platforms	Allows you to specify whether remote control can be used on the workstations that use this Policy Package. You can control some of the settings used when taking control of a remote workstation.
Restrict Login	Windows 95/98 and NT	Allows you to set guidelines to restrict the workstation's access to the network. For example, you can control the login times for the workstation using this policy.
Workstation Inventory	Windows 95/98 and NT	Allows you to update the NDS tree so it can inventory the hardware present on the workstations.

NDS Design Considerations

You'll find that, with many of the systems administrator tasks you'll face, knowing how to complete a task and knowing how to complete it *well* (or properly) are two different things. To help you design User and Workstation Policies properly, we'll present (and answer) three different questions:

➤ Which Policy Packages should you create in the NDS tree?

➤ How should you associate NDS objects with the Policy Packages?

➤ How do you customize the policies contained within the Policy Packages?

The following sections cover each of these questions and give you some guidelines as to how to answer them.

Which Policy Packages Should You Create?

The answer to this question depends on several criteria: the size of your current network, the operating-system platforms used on your network, and whether you need multiple Policy Packages to be applied to a container of the same type.

When you are creating Policy Packages, follow these three guidelines:

➤ Create the Container Packages as high up the NDS tree as you can without passing the container that is a location in the organization. (For example, if your organization has an office in Boston and one in Chicago, do not place the Container Policy Package for Boston at a higher level than Boston.)

➤ Create the User Packages in the same container as that of the users associated with the User Policy Packages you created.

➤ Create the Workstation Packages in the same container as that of the workstations associated with the Workstation Policy Package.

How Should You Associate NDS Objects?

When you create an association between a Policy Package and an NDS object, make sure you take into account the order these policies will be applied to the object. Policies are applied to NDS objects in much the same way as NDS rights are applied to objects.

If you were to create a Container Policy Package and then create a User or Workstation Policy Package for a user or workstation located inside the container, the User or Workstation Policies would take precedence over the Container Policies. If we compare this to NDS rights, the rights assigned to a leaf object take precedence over those assigned to the container in which the leaf object is located.

 Whenever possible, associate policies with container objects rather than with individual users or workstations. By associating policies with the container, you automatically associate all the objects that reside within that container. These objects will automatically get the policies associated with the container.

How Do You Customize The Policies?

When you configure policies to work with your network, remember that your network may be affected by the way that you choose to implement the policies. For example, if you have a large network and you import all of your workstations into the NDS tree as objects, you can quickly increase the number of NDS objects you need to maintain.

 Novell recommends that you limit the objects in each container to fewer than 1,500. This keeps your NDS from becoming too difficult and resource intensive to control.

Registering And Importing Workstations

Now that you have an understanding of what Policy Packages are and what they accomplish, it's time to start pulling everything together. Before we can start to apply Workstation Policy Packages to our networking infrastructure, we must complete a task called *registering and importing* workstations.

You cannot create objects in the NDS tree that will represent your workstations until you execute a program, called a *registration agent*, on each of your workstations. Once the registration agent runs, it registers the workstation that it represents and allows you to create the objects that will represent the workstation.

To simplify matters, Z.E.N.works includes a registration agent that automatically registers the workstation it's running on as long as the following two conditions are true:

➤ The workstation is running the Novell Client 32 that has the Z.E.N.works functionality.

➤ The workstation is used to log into the Novell network.

Once the workstation has logged into the network, the registration agent sends four different properties to the NDS:

➤ The workstation's registration time

➤ The workstation's network address, also known as the Media Access Control (MAC) address or the hardware address

➤ The last server to which the workstation was connected

➤ The last user who used this workstation to log into the network

> *Note: If you have a large network, it may take some time for all the workstations to register with NDS. Once the workstations have been registered, you can import them into NDS.*

Table 12.5 lists the file names that are associated with the registration agent on different operating systems.

Once all the workstations have been registered, you can begin to import them into NDS. Before you do this, however, you must configure a Workstation Import Policy. To create and configure this Workstation Import Policy, you must complete the following tasks:

1. Create a User Policy Package for each operating system (Windows 3.x, Windows 95/98, and/or Windows NT) installed on your workstation.

2. Configure the Workstation Import Policy so it creates Workstation objects using the naming convention that you assign it and in the correct container in the NDS tree.

Table 12.5 The workstation registration agent.

File Name	Platform
WSREG32.EXE	The 32-bit version of the registration agent. Used for Windows 95/98 and Windows NT workstations.
WSREG16.EXE	The 16-bit version of the registration agent. Used for DOS and Windows 3.x workstations.
WSREG32.DLL	Used for all Windows workstations, but only when the Desktop Management component of Z.E.N.works is used.

Registering Workstations

To make things easier, as a systems administrator you should configure the workstations so they register themselves automatically. You can do this in three ways (all of which are discussed in detail in the following sections):

➤ If the Desktop Management component of Z.E.N.works is not being used, you should use the Application Launcher to register your workstations automatically.

➤ If you have Windows 95/98 or Windows NT and all the Z.E.N.works components installed on the workstations, you should use the Z.E.N.works Scheduler.

➤ If you want to automatically register DOS workstations—or neither the Desktop Management component of Z.E.N.works nor the Application Launcher are installed—you should register the workstations using login scripts.

Using The Application Launcher

If you recall in Chapter 11, you learned how to use the Z.E.N.works Application Launcher to control which applications are available to the users and which applications are executed when a user logs into the network. To use the Application Launcher to automatically register the workstation in NDS, simply create an Application object for each executable (.EXE) file required (see Table 12.5). Then associate this newly created Application object with its container, User, or User Group objects in the NDS tree.

Now, when users log into the network, the workstation registration agent will run (as defined in the Application Launcher), and the workstations will be registered according to the correct policy.

Using The Z.E.N.works Scheduler

Assuming your workstations have the Novell Client for Z.E.N.works installed and configured, a component called the Z.E.N.works Scheduler automatically registers the workstation in NDS according to a preconfigured schedule. The Scheduler will automatically run the first time a user logs into the network using the workstation.

> *Note: The Z.E.N.works Scheduler will run only on workstations running Windows 95/98 or Windows NT. This is because it relies on the Z.E.N.works Desktop Management component, which is available only on these platforms.*

If the Scheduler is running on your workstation, the system tray (located in the bottom-right corner of your desktop) will contain an icon. You can look at the Scheduler's configuration by either double-clicking on the icon, or by right-clicking and selecting the Display Schedule option from the menu. Once you do this, the Scheduler dialog box appears and allows you to view your workstation registration schedule, as seen in Figure 12.5.

You can add, remove, or disable actions by clicking on the corresponding button. You can force the action to initiate immediately by clicking on the Run Now button. If you want to make modifications to an existing action, simply highlight it and click on the Properties button. The Action Properties dialog box (shown in Figure 12.6) will appear, and you'll be able modify the action's properties.

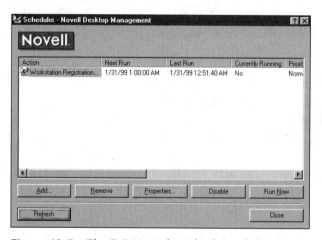

Figure 12.5   The Z.E.N.works Scheduler dialog box.

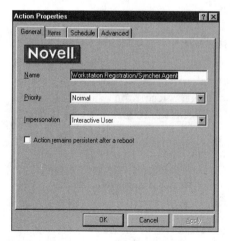

Figure 12.6   The Action Properties dialog box.

Using Login Scripts

If your workstations do not have the ability to run either the Application Launcher or Desktop Management from Z.E.N.works (or if you chose not to install these components), all is not lost. You can still ensure that workstation registration is completed on a fairly regular schedule by creating a container-based login script. When the users log in, the login script will execute and run the appropriate executable file for that workstation registration agent (see Figure 12.7).

Following is a sample login script. The script checks the platform that the workstation is running and executes the corresponding registration agent:

```
IF "%PLATFORM%" = "WIN" THEN begin
#wsreg16.exe
end

IF "%PLATFORM%" = "W95" THEN begin
#wsreg32.exe
end

IF "%PLATFORM%" = "WNT" THEN begin
#wsreg32.exe
end
```

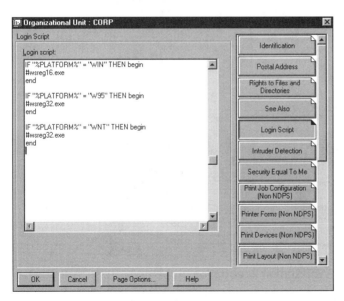

Figure 12.7 Creating a login script for a container.

Workstation Registration Verification

You can confirm that a workstation has been registered with NDS in two ways. The first method uses a log file that is created on the workstation when the workstation is registered, and the second method uses one of the property pages of the NDS object within the NetWare Administrator program.

The log file is stored in the root directory of the workstation. If you have a Windows 95/98 or Windows NT workstation, the log file is named WSREG32.LOG. If, on the other hand, your workstation has Windows 3.1 installed, the log file is called WSREG16.LOG. (The information stored in both files is almost identical.) The log file stores both successful and unsuccessful registrations with NDS.

The second method allows you to view the workstations that have registered with NDS by viewing the container's Details property page using the NetWare Administrator program. To access this property page, right-click on the container object, select Details from the menu, and click on the Workstation Registration button. Any workstations that have been registered with the NDS (but not imported) will appear in the Workstation Registration property page, as seen in Figure 12.8.

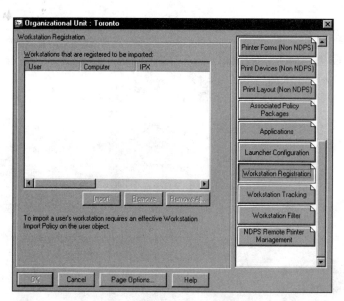

Figure 12.8 The Workstation Registration property page.

Importing Workstations Into The NetWare NDS Tree

Registering a workstation in NDS does not make it an object; for that to occur, you must import the workstation. Unlike the registration procedure, the workstation import procedure is not automated. Instead, you have to reimport the workstations on a regular basis. Because this process is manual, if you do not complete it regularly, you'll soon find that the workstation information in the NDS tree is outdated or wrong.

You can configure an Application object and have the Application Launcher run it on a regular basis. You can also create an action using the Scheduler. Both of these methods will automate the task of importing workstations into the NDS tree.

The following steps illustrate how you would manually import workstations using NetWare Administrator:

1. Right-click on the container object where you would like the workstations to be imported to as objects. Select Create, and choose Policy Package.

2. Create a User Policy Package that will match the operating system of your workstations.

3. Implement the Workstation Import Policy. To enable the Workstation Import Policy, click on the checkbox to the left of the policy. To configure it, simply click on the Details button. The Workstation Import Policy dialog box appears, as shown in Figure 12.9.

In this screen, you can set two options:

➤ You can configure the location in which the Workstation objects will be created. Click on the Workstation Location tab to the right of the window and enter the necessary information in the fields provided.

➤ You can also configure the naming convention that will be used when the workstation is imported. Click on the Workstation Naming tab to the right of the window. This name will be given to the Workstation object. By default, the naming convention is the computer name

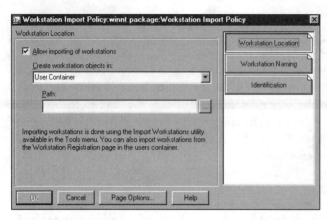

Figure 12.9 The Workstation Import Policy dialog box.

and the network address. You can modify which fields are used in the name and the order in which they are to be applied. You can use either the IPX or IP network address to identify these workstations.

4. Next, you need to associate this Policy Package with a container object. To accomplish this, simply click on the Associations button and select the desired object.

5. Click on OK to finalize the configuration.

6. In NetWare Administrator, choose the Import Workstations option from the Tools menu (see Figure 12.10). Make sure that the container where you would like the workstations imported is still highlighted. This utility will look for the registered workstations and import them into NDS as objects. The policy that you configured in the first five steps will be applied to these workstations, and they will be named and placed accordingly.

7. The Import Workstations dialog box will appear, as shown in Figure 12.11. Notice that the object that you had selected (when you ran the Import Workstations option) appears in the Import Registered Workstations From field. If you made a mistake, you can change it by clicking on the browse button and selecting a new location. When you have the location selected, click on OK.

8. The Import Workstations utility will now import the registered workstations into the location you specified (with the naming convention you selected). The amount of time it takes to import the workstation depends on how many workstations have registered. When the process

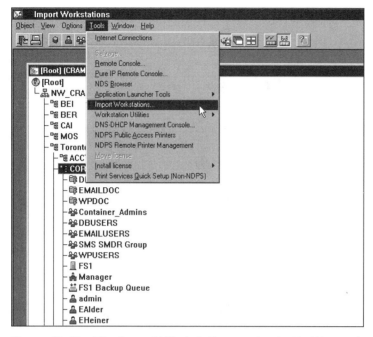

Figure 12.10   The Import Workstations option in NetWare Administrator.

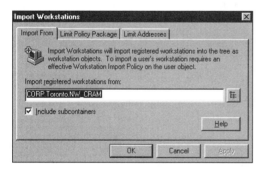

Figure 12.11   The Import Workstations dialog box.

is completed, a dialog box will appear, letting you know how many entries were found, how many were created, and how many were not created (this option appears only if there is a problem in creating one or more Workstation objects). You can view either the error log or the success log (depending on the results of the import). Figure 12.12 illustrates the Completed Workstation Import dialog box as it would appear if an error had occurred.

Figure 12.12   The Completed Workstation Import information screen.

> *Note: The Import Workstations utility creates two log files. One (NERROR.LOG) is used to log workstation import error messages, and the other (NSUCCESS.LOG) is used to log successful workstation imports.*

9. To view the newly imported workstations, you'll need to refresh the NDS tree in NetWare Administrator (or you can collapse and expand the container object).

Configuration Of The Desktop Environment Using Policies

Now that you've imported workstations into the NDS tree, what can you do with them? Chapter 13 covers one of the most powerful features of Z.E.N.works: workstation remote control. In this section, we'll look at another feature that allows us to configure the workstation's (or user's) desktop environment.

You can control the desktop environment by defining either user-specific or workstation-specific controls. You do this by configuring policies in both the User and the Workstation Policy Packages.

You can use these policies to control and customize both the desktop applications and the overall look and feel of the Windows user interface.

Installing And Controlling Desktop Applications

Two policies can be used to customize the desktop applications that will appear on the workstation. One, the User System Policy, is found in the User Policy Packages. The other, the Computer System Policy, is found in the Workstation Policy Packages. Together, they define the applications that will appear on the workstation's desktop.

The User System Policy allows you to control the workstation's desktop on a user-by-user basis. You can limit the tasks a user can accomplish by hiding desktop applications from the user. For example, you can hide the Network Neighborhood icon so users cannot browse network resources, or you can hide the Run command from the Start menu to limit which applications users can execute. The available User System Policies are as follows:

➤ Control Panel

➤ Desktop

➤ Network (Windows 95/98 only)

➤ Shell

➤ System

➤ Windows 95/98 Shell or Windows NT Shell (depending on the operating system)

➤ Windows NT System (Windows NT only)

➤ Zero Administration Kit (ZAK) Policies

The Computer System Policies allow you to control the desktop on a work-station-by-workstation basis. You can control which application will be available on the workstation as it connects to the network, as illustrated in Figure 12.13.

The following Computer System Policies are available:

➤ Network

➤ System

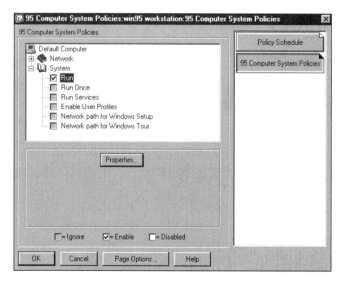

Figure 12.13   The Computer System Policies dialog box.

➤ Windows NT Network Sharing (Windows NT only)

➤ Windows NT Printers (Windows NT only)

➤ Windows NT Remote Access (Windows NT only)

➤ Windows NT Shell (Windows NT only)

➤ Windows NT System (Windows NT only)

➤ Windows NT User Profiles (Windows NT only)

 When selecting options within the policies, remember that each policy has three different options:

➤ A grayed-out box signifies that the option will be ignored.

➤ A checked checkbox signifies that the option is enabled.

➤ An empty checkbox signifies that the option is disabled.

The modifications you make to both the User and Workstation System Policies are effective immediately. However, users who are logged in when the changes take effect will not see the changes until they log out and then back into the network.

Because the configuration information in the User and Workstation System Policies is complementary, it's combined to create the desktop with which the user is presented.

Customizing The Look And Feel Of Windows

When we talk about customizing the look and feel of Windows, we are talking about the active screen saver on the system, the wallpaper, and the color schemes.

Using the User and Workstation Policies, we can customize a companywide standard for the look of the desktop and prevent the users from changing it. Many of the control panels that users can normally modify are available in these policies.

To configure a user interface for your workstations, follow these instructions in the NetWare Administrator program:

1. Select a container object that will hold the User Policy Package, and create a User Policy Package that matches the operating system(s) you have installed on your network.

2. Check the checkbox to the left of 95/98 Desktop Preferences (or NT Desktop Preferences, depending on the operating system), and click on Details.

3. Double-click any of the icons available to you and make modifications as you would a regular Windows Control Panel and click on OK to accept the configuration.

4. Click on the Associations button to associate this Policy Package with a container object where the users reside, and click on OK to finish the configuration.

The following are available for you to configure:

➤ Accessibility Options

➤ Console (Windows NT only)

➤ Display

➤ Keyboard

➤ Mouse

➤ Sounds

Practice Questions

Question 1

What are three situations in which you'll have to update workstation information in the NDS tree? [Choose the three best answers]

❏ a. You rebooted the server.

❏ b. You added, removed, or moved workstations.

❏ c. Two employees in accounting have retired and new employees took their places. You have to update the information because the user information has changed.

❏ d. A network board failed on a workstation and you replaced it.

❏ e. You noticed that a few of the workstations do not appear in the NDS tree.

The correct answers are b, d, and e. The three instances that would force you to update the workstation information in the NDS tree are when you add, remove, or move workstations; when you replace a network board in a workstation; and when workstations do not appear in the NDS tree. The NDS information is stored in a database and does not need to be rebuilt or updated after a server reboot. Therefore, answer a is incorrect. Workstation NDS objects are user independent, and changing the users who operate the workstations will not change the workstation NDS objects. Therefore, answer c is incorrect.

Question 2

You have not installed the Desktop Management component of Z.E.N.works. It's impossible for your workstations to automatically register themselves with the NDS tree.

○ a. True

○ b. False

The correct answer is b, false. You can use the Application Launcher or a login script to automate the registration process. Therefore, answer a is incorrect.

Question 3

> You have several workstations in the Engineering Department. The manager of the Engineering Department would like to control the configuration of each workstation. What would you do to simplify administration so all workstations are managed in the same way? [Choose the best answer]
>
> ○ a.   Create a Workstation Policy Package, configure it, and associate it to each Engineering workstation individually.
>
> ○ b.   Create a User Policy Package, configure it, and associate it with each Engineering user individually.
>
> ○ c.   Create a Workstation Policy Package, configure the policies, create a Workstation Group object, and associate it with the Policy Package. Make each Engineering workstation a member of the Workstation Group.
>
> ○ d.   Create a User Policy Package, configure the policies, create a User Group object, and associate it with the Policy Package. Make each Engineering user a member of the User Group.

The correct answer is c. To simplify the management of a group of workstations, create a Workstation Group object and assign the individual workstations to it. Then assign policies to the Workstation Group object and all of its members inherit these policies. Answer a will solve the problem of maintaining all the Engineering workstations, but it will not simplify their administration. The work involved in creating this solution is inefficient and time consuming. Therefore, answer a is incorrect and the reason why this is a trick question. Creating a User Group and assigning policies to it will not fulfill the requirement, because this solution will not give you the ability to manage the workstations, only the users. Therefore, answers b and d are incorrect.

Question 4

> Which two conditions must be met for workstations to be registered automatically? [Choose the two best answers]
>
> ❏ a. The administrator must log in from each of the workstations using a special registration account.
>
> ❏ b. The NetWare Client software with Z.E.N.works must be installed.
>
> ❏ c. The workstation must be running Windows 95/98.
>
> ❏ d. The workstation must be running Windows NT.
>
> ❏ e. A user must log in from the workstation.

The correct answers are b and e. The NetWare Client software must have the Z.E.N.works component installed on the workstation, and the user must log into the network to activate the registration agent. There is no "special registration account." Therefore, answer a is incorrect. The workstation registration process is platform independent and works with all Windows platforms. Therefore, answers c and d are incorrect.

Question 5

> Which three Policy Package objects can be associated with containers, Workstation, and Workstation Group objects? [Choose the three best answers]
>
> ❏ a. Container Package
>
> ❏ b. Windows 3.1 User Package
>
> ❏ c. Windows 3.1 Workstation Package
>
> ❏ d. Windows 95 User Package
>
> ❏ e. Windows 95 Workstation Package
>
> ❏ f. Windows NT User Package
>
> ❏ g. Windows NT Workstation Package

The correct answers are c, e, and g. Workstation Policy Packages can be associated with container, Workstation, and Workstation Group objects. Container Policy Packages can only be associated with container objects. Therefore, answer a is incorrect. User Policy Packages can be associated with container, User, and User Group objects. Therefore, answers b, d, and f are incorrect.

Need To Know More?

 For more information on Z.E.N.works, check the Z.E.N.works online documentation with keyword searches on "Policy Packages," "Z.E.N.works," "User System Policies," "Computer System Policies," and "NDS Workstation objects."

 Search for "Z.E.N.works" in your favorite search engine for more information.

Remote Access Using Z.E.N.works

Terms you'll need to understand:

√ Remote Control

√ Remote Control Policy

√ User Policy Package

√ Workstation Policy Package

√ Help Requester

√ Help Desk Policy

Techniques you'll need to master:

√ Installing and configuring the Remote Control Policy

√ Taking remote control of a target workstation and making modifications to it

√ Using the Application Launcher to push the Help Requester application to each user's desktop

√ Using the Help Desk Policy to control how users can utilize the Help Requester application

In Chapter 12, we covered the steps for registering and importing workstations into Novell Directory Services (NDS). Now you have the knowledge to control both the desktop and the look and feel of the Windows user interface. In this chapter, you'll learn about some of the most powerful features of Z.E.N.works for NetWare.

One of the most powerful features of Z.E.N.works is its ability to allow you to control a workstation remotely. Why is this a useful tool? Imagine having the ability to make modifications to a workstation located in a different building, or even in a different part of the country. Imagine being able to troubleshoot end-user problems by simply "watching" the user operations. You can even help a user learn new tasks by "showing" the user how to perform them from the comfort of your own workspace.

Overview: Remote Control Access To Workstations

Once you've registered and imported all of your workstations into the NDS tree, you can use Z.E.N.works to establish a session with these workstations to control them from a remote location. Installing the remote control portion of Z.E.N.works is painless and automatic. When you install the Novell Client for Z.E.N.works, it automatically installs the remote control agent (the application that allows remote control sessions to be established). This agent is activated when the workstation logs into the network.

 It's important that you realize that the capabilities for remote control (and the Help Requester application, as we'll see later in this chapter) are available only in the full version of Z.E.N.works version 1.1. If you have the Novell Client software, you probably have the Z.E.N.works Starter Pack. The full Z.E.N.works product includes an NDS-enabled help desk request system, hardware inventory, software, metering, and remote control.

 The advanced features of Z.E.N.works are automatically installed when the Novell Client for Z.E.N.works is installed. No other installation parameters are needed.

The remote control agents use NDS authentication to ensure that the user making the request for remote control is authorized to do so. Therefore, a user cannot take control of a workstation remotely unless he or she has been granted that right to the Workstation object.

Before you can use the Z.E.N.works remote control option, you must complete the following tasks (each of which will be covered in detail in the following sections):

1. Make sure the user being used to remotely control workstations has the required NDS rights.

2. Make sure that the workstation being used meets all the requirements stated previously (that is, it has the NetWare Administrator and the Client for Z.E.N.works installed).

3. Define remote control security for the workstations that you would like to control. You complete this by creating a Remote Control Policy, which exists in both the User and the Workstation Policy Packages. (Having the policy in both packages gives you great flexibility to control not only which workstations can be controlled, but also which users.)

4. Make a connection to the target workstation to be controlled.

5. Control the workstation and complete any modifications or assistance required.

6. Terminate the remote control session.

Remote Control NDS Rights

Before you can remotely control a workstation, you must have certain rights granted to you in the NDS tree. You must have the Write right to the DM:Remote Verification property on the Workstation object, and the Read right to All Properties for the Workstation object—this right is usually granted by default to the [Public] trustee.

Are The Client Requirements Met?

The workstation you wish to control remotely has to meet several different criteria:

➤ The Novell Client installed on the workstation must have the Z.E.N.works components.

➤ The workstation must be registered in the NDS tree.

➤ The workstation must be imported into the NDS tree. (In other words, the workstation must have an object associated with it in the NDS tree.)

The workstation you'll be using to remotely control other work-stations—called the *administrative workstation*—must have NetWare Administrator on it, because NetWare Administrator is what is actually used to remotely control workstations.

Defining A Remote Control Policy

To make sure that no unauthorized access is granted to users to remotely control workstations, you'll want to set up security that controls who has the right to access these remote workstations.

How you configure remote control security depends on the number of users or workstations that need to be configured. If you have only a few users or workstations, you can simply set up the access rights through their object property rights in NDS (using the NetWare Administrator).

However, if you have many users or workstations that need to be given rights to access workstations remotely, it becomes inefficient and time consuming to do this manually. In this situation, you'll want to use the Remote Control Policy in either the User Policy Package or the Workstation Policy Package.

You can create and configure the Remote Control Policy for either users or workstations by following these simple steps:

1. Create either a User or a Workstation Policy Package object in the desired location in the NDS tree.

2. Enable the Remote Control Policy (in the appropriate Policy Package).

3. Configure the security parameters for the Remote Control Policy so it matches your desired configuration.

4. Apply the Remote Control Policy to the desired users or workstations by associating individual User, Workstation, User Group, or Workstation Group objects, or the container object in which the users or workstations reside.

 When Workstation objects are created, the remote control Access right is enabled, which means that, by default, all workstations can be remotely controlled (assuming that the user attempting to control them has the correct rights).

Before can take control of a remote workstation, you need to set some parameters. These parameters can be set in either the Remote Control property page of the individual User or Workstation object, or they can be set in the Remote

Control Policy in either the User Policy Package or the Workstation Policy Package. The following lists the parameters that you can configure:

➤ **Default Protocol To Use For Remote Controlling** This parameter allows you to choose the networking protocol (IP, IPX, and so on) that will be used to remotely control the workstations.

➤ **Enable Remote Control** If this parameter is selected, the workstation can be controlled remotely. Unchecking this option disables remote control of the workstation and disables the rest of the parameters in this table. This parameter is enabled by default.

➤ **Give User Audible Signal When Remote Controlled** If this parameter is selected, an alert will sound on the targeted workstation to inform its user that the workstation is being controlled remotely. This parameter is disabled by default.

➤ **Give User Visible Signal When Remote Controlled** If this parameter is selected, an icon will be displayed on the user's desktop when the workstation is being accessed remotely. This parameter is enabled by default.

➤ **Prompt User For Permission To Remote Control** If this parameter is selected, the user who is logged into the targeted workstation must confirm (agree to) the remote control session. The administrator cannot access the remote station unless the user allows the access. By default, this option is enabled.

In the following two sections, we'll detail the steps needed to set up remote control security on User or Workstation objects and through the Remote Control Policy in the User Policy Package or Workstation Policy Package.

Remote Control Security Through Objects

Follow these steps to set up remote control access to a workstation through either a User or Workstation object:

1. In NetWare Administrator, select the User or Workstation object to which you would like to grant or restrict access.

2. Right-click on the object, and choose Details from the pop-up menu.

3. Click on the Remote Control button on the left side of the object's Details dialog box. The remote control parameters (as listed in the previous section, "Defining A Remote Control Policy") will be displayed in the left side of the dialog box. The Remote Control parameters dialog box for a workstation is displayed in Figure 13.1.

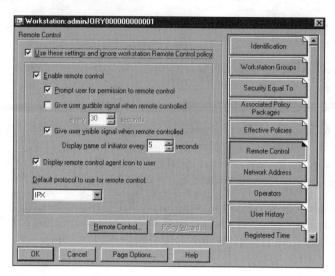

Figure 13.1 The Workstation Remote Control dialog box.

4. To activate the remote control security parameters, enable the Use These Settings And Ignore Workstation Remote Control Policy option. The remote control security settings will now override any settings configured through User or Workstation Policy Packages (which are covered in the following section).

5. To disable the ability for an administrator to take remote control of this workstation, disable the Enable Remote Control option.

6. Choose the remote control security parameters that best fit the standards set for your organization. Choose from requesting permission from the remote user, sounding an alert, or displaying an icon when remote control is taken. You also need to determine the protocol to use to establish the remote control session.

Remote Control Security Through Policy Packages

To configure remote control access for a group of users or workstations, you use a Remote Control Policy. Follow these steps to configure the Remote Control Policy:

1. In NetWare Administrator, create either a User or a Workstation Policy Package. Make sure that the Policy Package matches the operating system your workstations are running. (For example, make sure that you create a Windows NT–specific Policy Package if your workstations are running Windows NT.)

2. Select an existing (or newly created) Policy Package, right-click on it, and select Details from the pop-up menu.

3. Enable the Remote Control Policy by marking the checkbox as active.

4. Once the Remote Control Policy is highlighted, click on the Details button to display the dialog box shown in Figure 13.2.

5. Ensure that Remote Control is selected.

6. To enable remote control access using this Policy Package, check the Enable Remote Control option.

7. As with the configuration for individual users and workstations, choose the notification options that best fit your needs.

8. Associate this policy with a User (or Workstation) object, a User Group (or Workstation Group) object, or a container object.

Making The Connection

You can now remotely control a workstation with problems or one with which a user needs help. Simply select its Workstation object in the NDS tree using NetWare Administrator, and then choose an option from the Tools menu. Once you take remote control of a workstation, its screen and actions will be displayed in a window on your desktop.

Remember, before you can take remote control of a workstation, your administrative workstation (the one that will take remote control of another) must have NetWare Administrator installed, and the target workstation (the one that will get controlled) must have the IPX protocol installed and be running the Novell Client for Z.E.N.works.

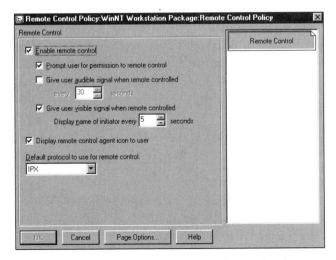

Figure 13.2   The Remote Control Policy dialog box.

Follow these steps to take control of a remote workstation (as long as the remote access security has not disabled remote control):

1. In the NetWare Administrator program, select the Workstation object that is associated with the workstation you wish to remotely control.

2. Choose the Remote Control Workstation option from the Tools menu. A window will display the status of the remote connection.

3. If you configured the remote control security information to request permission from the user to remotely control his or her workstation, a dialog box will appear on the target workstation (as seen in Figure 13.3). The remote control session can continue only if the user clicks on the Yes button. If the user clicks on the No button, then the remote control session will be denied.

 The user has five seconds to respond to this dialog box. If he or she does not respond within this time, you are notified. You then have to attempt the remote connection again, or contact the user to discuss the matter.

4. Once the remote control session is established, a window will appear on your desktop displaying the target workstation's desktop, as seen in Figure 13.4.

Controlling The Remote Workstation

As soon as you can see the target workstation's desktop, you can remotely control it. The window that appears with the target desktop has four extra buttons (five if you're using Windows NT) on the right side of the top bar (to the left of the Minimize and Maximize buttons). These buttons can be used to navigate the remote workstation. Figure 13.5 shows the buttons as they appear on the controlling workstation. The buttons that appear on all systems are:

➤ Start

➤ Application Switcher

➤ System Key Pass Through

➤ Navigation

Note: The extra button you see in the middle (the key) appears only if the controlling workstation is running Windows NT. It simulates the Ctrl+Alt+Del keystroke on the remote system.

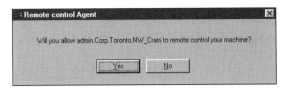

Figure 13.3   The Remote Control Agent permission prompt.

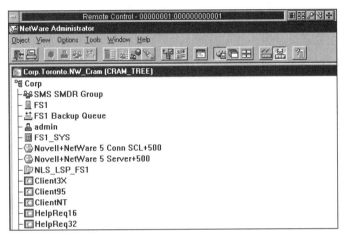

Figure 13.4   The target workstation's desktop as seen on the controlling workstation.

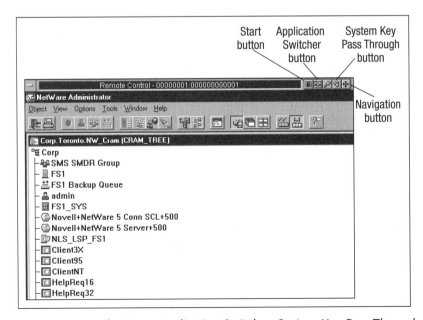

Figure 13.5   The Start, Application Switcher, System Key Pass Through, and Navigation buttons.

Remember to tell users not to use their workstations while you're remotely controlling their workstations, because their keyboard and mouse are still active.

The following sections describe these buttons and their functions. We'll also look at some hot keys that are defined (and can be redefined) to make controlling the target workstation easier.

The Start Button

Clicking on the Start button in the remote control window has the same effect as the user clicking on the Start menu button on his or her desktop. If the remote workstation is a Windows 95/98 or Windows NT 4 workstation, the Start menu will appear. If, however, the remote workstation is running Windows 3.x or Windows NT 3.5, this button will launch the Task List on the target workstation.

The Start button simply sends a Ctrl+Esc key command, which is the keyboard equivalent of clicking on the Start button with the mouse. Once the Start menu (or the Task List, depending on which platform the remote system is running) appears, you can access it in the same way as you would access the Start menu (or Task List) on your own workstation.

The Application Switcher Button

Normally, on a Windows 95/98 or Windows NT workstation, if multiple applications are running, the bottom control bar will have buttons that represent the applications. You can access the open applications by either clicking on these buttons or pressing the Alt+Tab key combination and scrolling through them. When remotely controlling a Windows 95/98 or Windows NT workstation, however, you must use the Application Switcher button. Clicking on the Application Switcher button simply sends the Alt+Tab key command to the target workstation.

The System Key Pass Through Button

One of the limitations of the remote control feature of Z.E.N.works is your inability to directly use the system keys, such as Ctrl and Alt on the target computer. To solve this problem, Novell has included the System Key Pass Through button.

Whenever you want to use system key commands, such as Ctrl+Esc or Alt+ Tab, you can enable the feature. Simply click on the System Key Pass Through button. Any system keys you press on your keyboard will automatically be sent to the target workstation. This feature will be active until you click on the System Key Pass Through button again to disable it.

The Navigation Button

If you have reduced the display window of a remote workstation and you would like to see more of the screen, you can use the Navigation button to navigate around the target workstation's desktop. This feature gives you the ability to have the desktops of several remote workstations on your screen at the same time, without losing the ability to navigate them efficiently.

When you click on the Navigation button, the Area window will appear with a small representation of the target workstation's desktop. Move the red frame in that window to choose the area of the target workstation that will be displayed.

Remote Control Hot Keys

Novell has included several predefined hot keys that will make your remote control sessions easier to manage. These keys can be used to control both your remote control environment and the target workstation's environment.

Table 13.1 lists all the hot keys that can be used to control your remote control environment.

You can view the default hot key combinations by selecting the Hot Keys option from the viewing window's menu. (To access this menu, click on the upper-left corner of the window's title bar.) You can also change the hot key combinations by selecting the field to modify and pressing the new key combination. The Hot Keys dialog box appears in Figure 13.6.

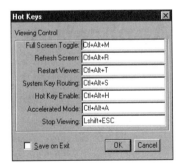

Figure 13.6 The Hot Keys dialog box.

Table 13.1 The remote control hot keys.		
Hot Key	**Option**	**Description**
Ctrl+Alt+A	Accelerated Mode	Increases the refresh rate of the viewing window for the target workstation.
Ctrl+Alt+H	Hot Key Enable	Enables the control options' hot keys on the target workstation.
Ctrl+Alt+M	Full Screen Toggle	Enlarges the viewing windows so they fill your screen. It displays the viewing windows without the window borders.
Ctrl+Alt+R	Refresh Screen	Refreshes the target workstation's screen.
Ctrl+Alt+S	System Key Routing Toggle	Enables the System Key Pass Through option.
Ctrl+Alt+T	Restart Viewer	Reestablishes the remote control session and redisplays the target workstation's screen.
Left-Shift +Esc	Stop Viewing	Closes the remote control session and disconnects from the target workstation.

Terminating The Remote Connection

You can disconnect from the target workstation and close the remote control session in several different ways:

➤ Press the Alt+F4 key combination. (The System Key Pass Through option must be enabled.)

➤ Use the Left-Shift+Esc hot key combination.

➤ In the viewing menu, click on the upper-left corner to access a pull-down menu, and choose Close.

The Help Requester Application

One of the problems most large organizations face when providing help desk services to their users is how to manage all the information. Even getting the calls from the end user to the network administration team can be extremely complex.

Companies have tried having the users email the support staff, fill out special problem notification forms, and complete problem tickets through an intranet-based Web site. The problem with many of these solutions is that there's no consistency between them, and the user has to learn a new tool.

Novell has included a Z.E.N.works component—the Help Requester application—that allows users to request technical support to their workstations, servers, or applications.

Help Requester is designed to work with organizations with an email infrastructure to manage the transfer of support messages. If your organization does not have an existing email system, your users can still launch the application and find contact information.

To make life even easier, you do not have to manually install the applications on each user's workstation. Instead, you can use the Novell Application Launcher to *push* the Help Requester application to a user's desktop when he or she logs into the network. Once you complete this task, the Help Requester application will appear as an icon in the Application Launcher window.

Before you can install and configure Help Requester, you need to complete the following tasks, which are covered in the following sections:

1. Ensure that the users have been granted the correct rights in NDS to access the Help Requester application.

2. Make sure that the software installed on the client workstations meets the requirements of the Help Requester application.

3. Use the Novell Application Launcher to push the Help Requester application to the users' desktops.

4. Configure the Help Desk Policy in a User Policy Package to ensure that the users receive the correct configuration for the Help Requester application.

5. Train your users on the proper way to use Help Requester to report technical problems.

Rights Verification

Before your users can access the Help Requester application, you need to verify that they have the correct rights granted to them. You need to verify two different types of rights: the file-system rights and the NDS rights.

➤ **File-system rights** For users to gain access to both the Application Launcher and the Help Requester application, they require the Read and File Scan file-system rights to the directory in which the applications are installed. By default, they are both installed in the SYS:Public directory.

➤ **NDS rights** Before an administrator can use the Application Launcher to deliver the Help Requester application to the desktop, he or she needs to be assigned the Supervisor Object right to the [Root] object of the NDS tree.

Users require the Read and Compare rights, to the All Properties rights, to access the Application objects (the Help Requester application is one of these objects). Luckily, these rights are automatically granted to any container, User, or User Group objects that you associate with an application.

Software Requirements

The software requirements for the Help Requester application can be divided into two sections:

➤ The network operating system requirements

➤ The client workstation requirements

Client

For the workstation to function properly with the Help Requester application, the following requirements must be met:

➤ The workstation must have the Novell Client that is supplied with Z.E.N.works.

➤ The workstation must connect into the network using the NDS tree (that is, clients running in bindery mode, from NetWare 3.1x, are not compatible).

➤ The workstation that is being used to access the Help Requester application must be registered and installed in the NDS tree.

When the client workstation executes the NetWare Administrator program, you must make sure that the version that ships with Z.E.N.works is the version that is installed.

Network Operating System

The only real requirement for the network operating system is that either NetWare 4.11 or NetWare 5 be installed. Also, to take advantage of an existing email system (to allow users to send help requests via email), you need to run a MAPI-compliant messaging service, such as Novell's GroupWise or Microsoft's Exchange Server.

Distributing The Help Requester Application

To distribute the Help Requester application to the required user so the Application Launcher Window automatically launches and the Help Requester application is available to the user the next time he or she logs in, complete the following tasks:

1. Make sure that the users have rights to access the Network Application Launcher (NAL.EXE).

2. Add one of the following lines to the login script that is associated with the user's container

   `#\\servername\SYS\PUBLIC\NAL.EXE`

   or:

   `@\\servername\SYS\PUBLIC\NAL.EXE`

3. Associate the correct Help Requester objects, HELPREQ16 for Windows 3.x clients and HELPREQ32 for Windows NT and 95/98 clients, with the correct container, User, or User Group objects.

Setting Up The Help Desk Policy

One of the most time-consuming aspects of the Help Requester application is creating and configuring the Help Desk Policy. Using the NetWare Administrator program, you can create a User Policy Package and configure the Help Requester application using the Help Desk application.

The Help Desk Policy does four things:

➤ It checks to see if an email infrastructure exists. If one does, the policy will display a Mail button within the application. This button allows users to email technical support staff.

➤ If an email infrastructure exists, it will configure the messaging server to send and receive email.

➤ It gives subject line topics for Help Requester messages.

➤ It identifies and records the contact's name, phone number, and email address.

Follow these steps to install and configure the Help Desk Policy properly:

1. Using the NetWare Administrator program, create a User Policy Package object (or select an existing one).

2. Right-click on the newly created Policy Package (or the existing one), and choose the Details option from the menu.

3. Enable the Help Desk Policy by clicking on the checkbox to the left of the policy.

4. Click on the Details button to configure the Help Desk Policy.

5. Enter the information for the contact (such as name, email address, and phone number) in the Information property page (see Figure 13.7).

6. In the Configuration property page, you can configure how users can send help requests via an email system (as in Figure 13.8). You can

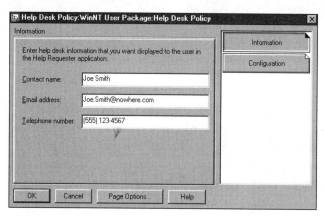

Figure 13.7 The Information property page for the Help Desk Policy.

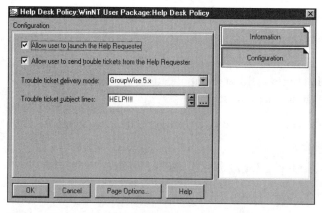

Figure 13.8 The Configuration property page for the Help Desk Policy.

configure this option only if an email infrastructure exists. You can use this page to:

➤ Give permission for the users to launch the Help Requester application and to use it to send email messages.

➤ Choose the delivery mode for the support messages (that is, which email infrastructure to use for the delivery).

➤ Configure the subject line of the support messages.

7. Finally, right-click on the container, User, or User Group object with which you want to associate the Policy Package and choose Details from the pop-up menu.

8. Click on the Associated Policy Packages property page and add the appropriate Policy Package.

Using The Help Requester Application

Your users can now launch the Help Requester application and use the application's Mail, Call, and Info buttons to send support and error messages to the help desk. If you have a MAPI-compliant messaging service and the NetWare Administrator program with the remote control feature of Z.E.N.works configured, you'll have a very powerful help desk system in place.

The Help Requester application (as seen in Figure 13.9) has four different buttons that the users can use to report problems to your help desk system: Mail, Call, Info, and Help. We discuss the buttons that represent features in the following sections.

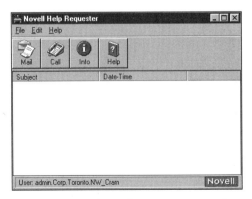

Figure 13.9   The Help Requester application window.

The Mail Feature

The Help Requester application can interface with email (or messaging) systems that you have installed on your network, as long as they are MAPI compliant. (This allows the users to email the help desk from the Help Requester application.)

Users need to follow these simple steps to send email messages to the help desk:

1. Click on the Mail button in the Help Requester application window. The Mail For Help window, shown in Figure 13.10, will appear.

2. From the Subject field's drop-down menu, select a subject that best describes the nature of the message. The entries that appear in the drop-down menu are configured in the Help Desk Policy configuration dialog box.

3. In the Message field, type the message that you would like to be submitted to the help desk.

4. Click on the Send button to send the message.

Once the user has sent the message, it'll appear in the lower part of the Help Requester application windows. The user will be able to monitor all the messages that he or she sent, in the order that they were submitted.

The Call Feature

In some organizations, the email system is used for just that—emailing. Therefore, you may not be able to use the messaging infrastructure for help desk–related messages. In this situation, you can use the Help Requester application's Call feature.

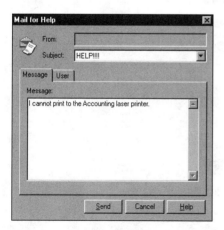

Figure 13.10 The Mail For Help window.

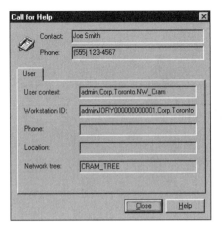

Figure 13.11   The Call For Help window.

When a user has a problem, he or she can click on the Call button, and the Call For Help window will appear (see Figure 13.11). The contact information will appear at the top of the window. In a small organization, this information may probably be just you. In larger organizations, however, this may be the contact numbers for the Technical Support Department.

The rest of the information (in the User tab) can be used to locate the User object in the NDS tree. If you have ever worked at a help desk, you know that users often do not know enough information about their location in the network or their login information to be much help. This feature helps simplify matters. Information of a user's context, workstation ID, phone number, location, and which NDS tree they are located in is presented to them in the User tab of the Call For Help window.

> *Note: The Phone and Location fields appear only if they are configured when the User object is created in the NDS tree.*

The Info Feature
The Info button simply gives the users the same information that appears in the User tab of the Call For Help windows, but with the addition of the contact information as assigned in the Help Desk Policy.

The Help Feature
The Help button simply gives the user a help file that outlines the features and proper usage of the Help Requester application.

Practice Questions

Question 1

> In which of the following is the Remote Control Policy found?
>
> ○ a. The User Policy Package only
>
> ○ b. The Workstation Policy Package only
>
> ○ c. The Container Policy Package only
>
> ○ d. Both the User and the Workstation Policy Packages

The correct answer is d. The Remote Control Policy is found in both the User and the Workstation Policy Packages. Therefore, answers a and b are incorrect. The Container Policy Package has no Remote Control Policy in it. Therefore, answer c is incorrect.

Question 2

> When you disable the Allow User To Send Trouble Tickets From The Help Requester option in the Configuration page of the Help Desk Policy, which of the four buttons in the Help Requester application will not be available?
>
> ○ a. The Mail button
>
> ○ b. The Call button
>
> ○ c. The Info button
>
> ○ d. The Help button

The correct answer is a. Users will only be able to send a trouble ticket (via email) if two criteria are met: A messaging infrastructure must be in place, and the Allow User To Send Trouble Tickets From The Help Requester option must be enabled in the Configuration page of the Help Desk Policy. The other options are still available. Therefore, answers b, c, and d are incorrect. This information is not explicitly stated in the chapter, but you should be able to figure it out; therefore, this is a trick question.

Question 3

> If you attempt to take control of a remote workstation and the user of that workstation denies you access, you can override his or her restriction and still take remote control.
>
> ○ a. True
>
> ○ b. False

The correct answer is b, false. If the user denies you access to remotely control his or her workstation, you cannot override it: The user's choice is final. Therefore, answer a is incorrect.

Question 4

> Which of the following is not a button that appears in the Help Requester application?
>
> ○ a. The Mail button
>
> ○ b. The Call button
>
> ○ c. The Remote button
>
> ○ d. The Help button

The correct answer is c. The Help Requester does not have a Remote button. The four buttons are Mail, Call, Info, and Help. Therefore, answers a, b, and d are incorrect.

Question 5

> In which of the following is the Help Desk Policy found?
>
> ○ a. The User Policy Package only
>
> ○ b. The Workstation Policy Package only
>
> ○ c. Both the User and the Workstation Policy Packages

The correct answer is a. The Help Desk Policy is found only in the User Policy Package. This is because only users (and not workstations) have access to the Help Requester application. Therefore, answers b and c are incorrect.

Need To Know More?

 For more information on Z.E.N.works, check the Z.E.N.works online documentation with keyword searches on "Help Requester," "remote control," "Remote Control Policy," and "Help Desk Policy."

 www.novell.com/documentation/lg/zen/docui/index.html is the online copy of the Z.E.N.works documentation. Search for "Help Requester," "remote control," "Remote Control Policy," and "Help Desk Policy."

Multicontext Resource Management

Terms you'll need to understand:

√ Context

√ Current context

√ Multicontext

√ Common name

√ Distinguished name

√ Alias object

√ Application object

√ Directory Map object

Techniques you'll need to master:

√ Setting the current context in the Novell Client configuration window

√ Using shortcut techniques to enhance user access to resources

√ Using Application and Directory Map objects to enhance multicontext handling of resources

√ Using Group objects for multicontext resource access

√ Understanding the rights that are required to perform the actions necessary to grant authority to NDS objects

In this chapter, you'll learn how to access and manage Novell Directory Services (NDS) objects when your directory tree has multiple containers. If your NDS tree has only one organization container, you probably have only one context that contains all of your organization's objects (assuming you're not using the [Root] object to contain any objects other than your one Organization object). In this case, you won't be required to manage or access objects in other contexts. However, if you have more than one container object with other objects in it, you must ensure that objects in other containers (contexts) can access objects outside their own container.

How Network Administration Is Affected By The Design Of The NDS Tree

An NDS container object contains other objects (such as User, Group, Printer, other container objects, and any other class of NDS objects). Container objects are a class of objects that hold (or contain) other objects. Because you may distribute NDS objects in multiple containers, you need to have a way to identify where an object is so you can access it. An object within a container uses that container's *distinguished name* to define its context. For example, the user Jbob resides in the context:

```
.OU=CORP.OU=OREM.O=ACME
```

The distinguished name determines Jbob's context. Therefore, Jbob's distinguished name is:

```
.CN=Jbob.OU=CORP.OU=OREM.O=ACME
```

To access NDS objects, you must change contexts from one container to another. You accomplish this in DOS using the **CX** command or in Windows by pointing your mouse and clicking on the container to which you want to navigate. Your context within the NDS tree is the container you're in at that moment.

Your NDS tree should be designed so it's both organizational and functional. Where you put your NDS objects determines the approach you use to grant access to objects in one container to objects in another container. For example, the user PeteH needs his monthly expense report to print out on the Accounting Department's printer. PeteH resides in context

```
.OU=CORP.OU=OREM.O=ACME
```

and you want to grant him access to the printer HP_LASER in

```
.OU=ACCTG.OU=OREM.O=ACME
```

You can use multiple methods to do this, and how you design your NDS tree plays a significant part in which method you'll use to access objects in other containers. To have a well-organized and functional NDS tree, you must also consider the methods available to access objects across the tree.

The following three sections cover the areas of administrative responsibility that concern NDS tree design.

Planning The NDS Tree Structure

The NDS database is a tool that allows you to create a tree structure that fits the needs, nature, and workflow of your organization. You plan the tree structure based on a formal or informal model of how your organization's resource distribution should function.

Your plan should produce an efficient tree design that ensures network traffic is minimized, while retaining a fault tolerant database and providing a structure that is easy to administrate without losing sight of the fact that users must be able to easily locate information.

The two most basic tree structure designs are:

➤ **Geographic** A geographic structure uses physical locations as context identifiers. You name containers after cities, districts, states, provinces, countries, and so on (see Figure 14.1).

➤ **Organizational** An organizational structure uses your company's organization chart as context identifiers. In this structure, you name containers after departments and positions (see Figure 14.2).

These two tree structures, or a hybrid of the two, form the basis of all NDS tree design.

 Novell recommends that you do not make your NDS tree design more than six containers deep.

When you design your NDS tree, you need to consider many influential factors. You should consider the size and complexity of your organization when studying three factors that affect your tree design:

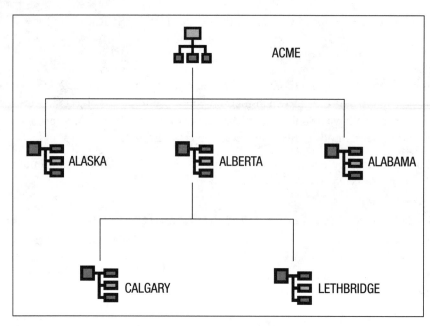

Figure 14.1 Geographic structure of an NDS tree.

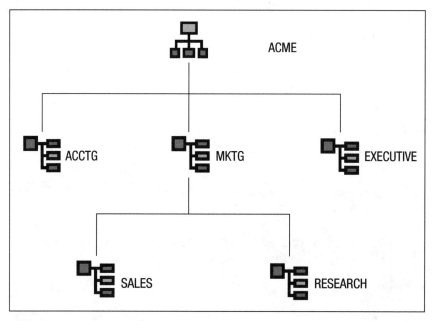

Figure 14.2 Organizational structure of an NDS tree.

➤ **Workgroups** The clusters of people whose positions and departments may vary but whose collaborative efforts share common data and objectives.

➤ **Resource allocation** Resources may be shared by various departments, workgroups, and even other companies.

➤ **Information flows** Your NDS tree design must accommodate your company's internal information infrastructure.

Planning How Users Access Resources

Ideally, a user should have to enter his or her password only at login. You should minimize support difficulties to end users by setting the preferred context at login so users do not have to know or enter their context when they log in. You should also make sure you use the correct naming conventions to access objects in different contexts.

Pre-Login Context Settings

Use the NetWare Client configuration window (shown in Figure 14.3) from Windows 95/98 and Windows NT workstations to set the current context when the Novell Client loads. You must enter the distinguished name of the container that you want to use as your default login context. If you have only

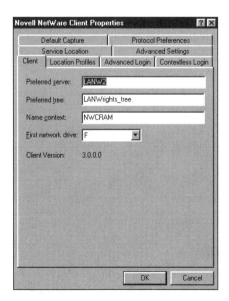

Figure 14.3 The Client configuration window.

one organization container, you can enter the name of the container and NetWare will find it.

Generally, you use the typeless distinguished name to identify the default login context. The typeful distinguished name requires more typing than a typeless distinguished name, and it won't produce a better result in the Client configuration window. (For further discussion of typeless and typeful names, refer to Chapter 3.)

> *Note:* *You can use a relative distinguished name or a distinguished name for the name context, provided you observe the rules for relative distinguished names. (See Chapter 3 for more discussion of relative distinguished and distinguished names.)*

Using The **CONTEXT** Command To Set Your Current Context

Normally, you do not want to train users any more than is necessary to do their job, because they probably already have enough to do. You especially don't want to have to teach them more than they need to know about contexts and distinguished names. Therefore, it's much easier to set the user's current context during the login process. In most cases, this allows the user to avoid using distinguished names to access NDS resources.

You set a user's current context during login by adding the following command to a container, profile, or user login script:

```
CONTEXT distinguished_name
```

A typical example of the **CONTEXT** command usage in a login script would appear as:

```
CONTEXT .ACME.CALGARY.AB
```

Using the login script **CONTEXT** command is not workstation specific. You set it for individual users or for groups.

Accessing Objects By Name

Sometimes the quickest way to access an object after you've logged in is to type its common or distinguished name. To access an object in your current context, you type in its common name. To access an NDS resource in a context outside your current context, you refer to it by its distinguished name.

Common Names

To access an object by its common name, you must be in the same context as that object. NetWare treats a common name as a relative distinguished name and appends the object name to the current context. Appending the common name to the current context provides NetWare with the distinguished name it needs to access the NDS object you requested.

For example, your current context is

```
OU=ACCT.OU=ACME.O=PTLND
```

and you want to access an object called LASER in the ACCT container. You reference the object using the common name LASER, and NetWare internally creates the distinguished name

```
CN=LASER.OU=ACCT.OU=ACME.O=PTLND
```

when it accesses the object LASER.

Therefore, you want to set a user's current context to the container that contains the largest number of resources that he or she is likely to use.

Distinguished Names

You use a typeful distinguished name to distinguish an NDS object from all other NDS objects and to identify its location in the NDS tree. Therefore, when you use a typeful distinguished name, you know the exact location of the object as well as its identity.

When you use a relative distinguished name, your current context determines whether NDS can append your relative name to the context you are in. However, when you use the full typeful distinguished name of an object, you can access any object regardless of the container you're in because your current context is irrelevant.

For example, if you log in with the following command, you'll be logged in regardless of your current context:

```
LOGIN .CN=DBJ123.OU=ACME.O=USA
```

You map a drive with the command:

```
MAP ROOT G:=.CN=APPS.OU=ACME.O=CA
```

The drive is mapped regardless of your current context.

Using Shortcuts To Access Resources

Shortcuts are simple and time-saving ways to access and manage resources. You use Group, Alias, and Application objects to access or manage objects in containers other than your current context.

Using Group Objects

You use Group objects in a multicontext environment because members can be added from any context and can be assigned rights that flow to all members of the group. The location of the Group object in the NDS tree does not matter; the rights you grant to the Group object are immediately available to all members of the Group object.

Often, you'll want to grant global rights to users on your network. In other words, you want certain resources made available to all users in the tree. You designate a group name (such as All or Everyone), add all the users to it, and grant global rights to the group. Doing this allows you to regulate and manage global access to network resources from a single object.

You use Group objects to greatly simplify access to objects from any container in your NDS tree. Suppose you have file servers distributed around the globe with spreadsheet files that are specific to a few engineers located in various cities. You want to give them exclusive access to these files. To do this, you would:

1. Create a Group object and give it a descriptive name.

2. Add the engineers, from their respective contexts, to the Group object.

3. Make the Group object a trustee of each directory on the servers that host the spreadsheet files.

4. Assign directory/file rights to the Group object.

Now the engineers have immediate access to all the files and directories you specified, regardless of where the files are stored or the geographical location of each engineer. You deny or modify access rights for any or all of the engineers by modifying that one Group object.

Using Alias Objects

Alias objects are pointers to objects in other containers (contexts) in the NDS tree. You use an Alias object so a user can access an object that is not in his or her own container (context). Alias objects are best employed when you want users to access objects in other containers without having them actually navigate to those other containers.

An Alias object, as its name implies, points to another object. For a user to alias another object, the user must have certain rights to the actual object. This is an ideal time to use a Group object. You grant the access rights to the Group object and then have the access rights flow to the users through their membership in the Group object.

Alias objects are also particularly useful when you want users from multiple containers to all have access to a resource in a different container. To create an Alias object:

1. Use NetWare Administrator to grant access rights to the object you want to alias. Minimum access rights are:

   ➤ The Create right to the parent container where you want to create the Alias object. (The Browse right, which you need to see the container, is supplied by default from the [Public] object.)

   ➤ The Browse right to the object you want to alias.

2. Right-click on the container in which you want to create your Alias object. Click on Create to view the list of object classes.

3. Select Alias and click on OK. The Create Alias dialog box appears (see Figure 14.4).

4. Give the Alias object a descriptive name, type in the distinguished name of the object you want to alias, and click on Create. (Alternatively, use the browse button next to the aliased object field to navigate to the object, select the object you want to alias, and click on Create.) The object is created, and you're returned to NetWare Administrator.

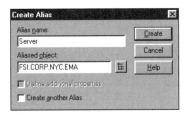

Figure 14.4   The Create Alias dialog box.

Using Application Objects

Application objects and Directory Map objects are similar in that they both represent file-system objects on NetWare volumes. With both, you can provide access to data on volumes that exist in other contexts but that need to be available in multiple containers.

For example, say you have a database application that cannot be installed on multiple servers. You create an Application object and grant access to a group representing users from multiple containers. Now you have the same advantage as if you had installed the application on a server in each of the containers where the application is needed.

Using Directory Map Objects

When users are spread out among several geographical locations, you often need to share files with a large number of users from different containers in your NDS tree. You cannot have duplicate directories on multiple servers, because the confusion of having multiple files of the same type at various stages of being updated results in chaos. It also would become impossible to track the correct versions of the files. Instead, you create a Directory Map object that points to the one set of files that everyone accesses from their unique location.

The only difference between Directory Map and Alias objects is that Alias objects only point to other objects that exist in the NDS tree. Applications and directories are not NDS objects. When you create a Directory Map or Application object, you are actually creating an NDS object that represents that application or directory in the NDS tree.

Resources In A Multicontext Environment

To set up resources in a multicontext environment, you must follow some guidelines to prevent confusion and to provide you with a functional NDS tree. A number of issues arise in regard to NDS security, user accounts and login security, file-system design and security, and printing security. These issues require the following approaches:

➤ **NDS and NDS security** Plan the tree so you can delegate containers to other administrators to manage. Decide whether you should restrict delegated Supervisor object rights to Create, Delete, and Rename (instead of full object rights). Wherever possible, use the default assignments to maintain conventions throughout the tree.

➤ **User accounts and login security** Enable intruder detection for each container to expose any attempts to breach security. Use intruder detection on the Template object in each container. Create Alias objects for users who frequently log in from computers with different workstation-specific contexts.

➤ **File-system design and security** Wherever possible, implement global objects to provide access to files and directories that you want to distribute universally. Remember to consider objects such as Group objects, the [Public] object, and [Root] object for global assignments.

To grant volume rights to users in a different context than the one where the volume exists, you make the object a trustee of the volume and assign the necessary rights. Use the distinguished name of a Volume object to map a network drive to a volume in a different container, or create an Alias object in your current context.

➤ **Multicontext Printer objects** To centralize and simplify printer management, use one print manager to manage your printers in multiple containers. Create public access printers (instead of controlled access printers) for printers that are needed by anyone on the network. Grant specific print roles to objects such as container, Group, or User objects.

Required Access Rights And Actions

You must have certain rights to perform the necessary actions that allow you to use the following resources: Alias, Application, Directory Map, Group, Organizational Role, NDPS Printer, Profile, or Volume objects. The resources with the necessary rights and actions are as follows:

➤ **Alias object** For a user to use an Alias object, you must grant the user access rights to the object that has been made an alias. To do this, you must have authority to grant access rights in the container that contains the object being made an alias.

➤ **Application object** For a user to access an Application object in another container, you must enable appropriate file-system rights to the application and associate the user with the Application object.

For a user to use an Application object, you must have a minimum of the Access Control right to the directory or file. To associate the user with the Application object, you must have the Write property right to the access control list (ACL) property of the Application object and the Write property right to the ACL property of the User object to which you're granting access.

➤ **Directory Map object** To allow a user to access a Directory Map object, you must enable appropriate file-system rights to the directory (and files) and associate the user with the Directory Map object. You must then grant the user the Read property right to the Path property of the Directory Map object.

To grant rights for a user to access files or directories, you must have a minimum of the Access Control right to the directory/files. To grant the user the Read property right to the Path property of the Directory Map object, you must have the Write property right to the ACL property of the Directory Map object.

➤ **Group object** To allow a user to benefit from a Group object, you must add the user to the Group object's Group Membership list.

To add a user to a Group object's membership list, you must have the Write property right to the Member and Object Trustees (ACL) properties.

➤ **Organizational Role object** To enable a user to be an occupant of an Organizational Role object, you must add the user to the Occupant list of that Organizational Role object.

To add a user to the Organizational Role object's Occupant list, you must have Write property rights to the Occupant and Object Trustees (ACL) properties.

➤ **NDPS Printer object** To grant a user access to an NDPS Printer object, you add the user to the User Role list of the NDPS Printer object.

To add a user to the User Role list of an NDPS Printer object, you must be a trustee of the NDPS Printer object. You must also have the Write property right to both the Users and Object Trustees (ACL) property rights of the NDPS Printer object to which you want to add the user.

To grant the Write right to the Users and Object Trustees (ACL) property rights, go to the NDPS Printer object's Trustees Of This Object menu and click on Selected Properties. Then, scroll down to the User object, select it, and select the Write right (or verify that it's already selected). Then, scroll down to the Object Trustees (ACL) property and do the same.

➤ **Profile object** For a Profile object to update a user, you must add the Profile object to the Profile property of the User object. Then you must grant to the User object the Read property right to the Login Script property of the Profile object.

To add a user to the Profile property of a Profile object, you must have the Write property right to the Object Trustees (ACL) property of the Profile object.

➤ **Volume object** To give file system rights to the directory or file in a Volume object, you must have the Supervisor right or the Access Control right.

Login Scripts That Execute In Multiple Containers

A login script executes much like a batch file. It's a series of commands that executes for a user when he or she logs in. Because the login script only executes in the same container as the object in which the login script exists, you must have a way to access objects in other containers during the login process. Container, Profile, and User objects do not recognize objects outside the container in which they exist. As a general rule, you should identify resources that are outside of a login script's current context using distinguished names, instead of using common names or relative distinguished names. Otherwise, your login script may not execute properly. When you reference objects in multiple containers, use distinguished names if you want to consistently reference the same object at login regardless of your current context, and use common names or relative distinguished names if you want to access objects in (or relative to) your workstation's current context at login.

Practice Questions

Question 1

What do you use an Alias object for?

- ○ a. To access other container objects in the NDS tree by pointing to them with relative distinguished names
- ○ b. To access objects in other NDS trees
- ○ c. To provide access to an object in another context by navigating to it
- ○ d. To provide an object that mimics another object by pointing to an object in a different context

The correct answer to this question is d. Many features in NetWare Administrator provide access to other objects. Alias objects do not provide access through navigation, and they do not provide access to objects in other trees. Therefore, answers a, b, and c are incorrect.

Question 2

The recommended minimum number of levels in an NDS tree is six.

- ○ a. True
- ○ b. False

The correct answer to this question is b, false. The recommended *maximum* number of levels in an NDS tree is six. There is no recommended *minimum* number of levels.

Question 3

How can you ensure that the current context is set to be user specific during the login process?

- ○ a. Put the **CONTEXT** command in the login script object.
- ○ b. Enter the name context in the Novell NetWare Client Properties dialog box.
- ○ c. Put the **CONTEXT** command in one of the definable login scripts.
- ○ d. Enter the name context in the Login Properties dialog box.

The correct answer to this question is c. There's no such thing as a login script object, the Name Context setting in the client produces a workstation-specific context, and there's no Login Properties dialog box. Therefore, answers a, b, and d are incorrect.

Question 4

You use the _____ command to set the context in the default login script.

- ○ a. **SET CONTEXT** *distinguished_name*
- ○ b. **@CONTEXT** *common_name*
- ○ c. **#CONTEXT** *distinguished_name*
- ○ d. **SET CONTEXT** *common_name*
- ○ e. None of the above

The correct answer to this question is e. You cannot set the context in the default login script.

Question 5

> What NetWare features allow you to simplify the login process? [Choose the two best answers]
>
> ❑ a. The ability to change contexts
>
> ❑ b. The ability to set current context
>
> ❑ c. The ability to set context before login
>
> ❑ d. The ability to set context during login

The correct answers are c and d. The ability to change contexts does not simplify the login process, nor does the ability to set current context. Therefore, answers a and b are incorrect.

Question 6

> What are the benefits of a well-planned NDS tree design? [Choose the three best answers]
>
> ❑ a. Reduced network traffic
>
> ❑ b. Fault tolerance
>
> ❑ c. Easier management
>
> ❑ d. Enhanced structural integrity

The correct answers to this question are a, b, and c. Enhanced structural integrity is not discussed in NDS tree design and, subsequently, is not a benefit of it. Therefore, answer d is incorrect.

Question 7

> The type of object that you use to access a directory in a different context is
> _____.
>
> ○ a. a Directory object map
> ○ b. a Directory Access object
> ○ c. a Volume Map object
> ○ d. a Directory Map object

The correct answer to this question is d. A Directory object map, a Directory Access object, and a Volume Map object are not object classes. Therefore, answers a, b, and c are incorrect.

Question 8

> An Application object is primarily used to _____.
>
> ○ a. provide location-independent access to User objects
> ○ b. provide location-specific access to applications on other networks
> ○ c. provide an easy way of uninstalling applications
> ○ d. provide access to applications in other contexts

The correct answer to this question is d. Application objects are not concerned with access to User objects, with accessing applications on other networks, and they're not designed to uninstall applications. Therefore, answers a, b, and c are incorrect.

Need To Know More?

 Novell course 575 manual. *NDS Design And Implementation*. Novell Inc., 1998. This manual explains how to provide fault tolerance and decrease NDS network traffic, as well as providing details on planning an NDS tree. This manual is available from Novell (1-800-NetWare) or from any authorized Novell training center.

 For more on planning your NDS tree, search for "NDS" or "NDS tree" in the NetWare 5 online documentation.

 www.support.novell.com is Novell's Support Connection Web site. Go to the Knowledgebase and search on "NDS tree."

Performing
A Simple
NetWare 5
Installation

Terms you'll need to understand:

√ NetWare kernel

√ Server console

√ NetWare Loadable Module (NLM)

√ Disk drivers

√ LAN drivers

√ Name space modules

√ NLM utilities

Techniques you'll need to master:

√ Understanding the various core components of NetWare 5

√ Performing a simple NetWare installation and joining an existing tree

√ Performing a simple NetWare installation and installing a new Novell Directory Service (NDS) tree

Although this book covers the administration and management of Novell NetWare 5, it's also important that you know the NetWare 5 components and be familiar with a simple installation. This chapter deals with just that—the NetWare components and a very simple installation.

> *Note: For a thorough look at the NetWare components and a more advanced NetWare installation, check out the rest of the* Exam Cram *books for the CNE certification.*

The NetWare 5 Components

As with many other operating systems, the installation for NetWare 5 is simple and straightforward. However, to truly understand the actual installation process (and be able to answer the questions asked during the installation), you need to understand NetWare's key components and how they operate.

Unlike Microsoft Windows NT, the computer running the NetWare operating system functions solely as a server: You cannot use it for word processing, spreadsheet or email applications, or Web browsers. The operating system is loaded into the computer's memory and enables the server to provide network services and resources to the users and workstations. The NetWare operating system is made up of three main components: the NetWare kernel, server console, and NetWare Loadable Modules (NLMs). We'll cover each of these briefly in the following sections so you'll have a basic understanding of them.

> *Note: For a more detailed look at these components and their roles in NetWare 5, see* Exam Cram for Advanced NetWare 5 Administration CNE, *also published by Certification Insider Press.*

 To start the NetWare server, you run a program called SERVER.EXE. This file is located in the NetWare server startup directory, which is C:\NWSERVER by default.

NetWare Kernel

The NetWare kernel is the heart of the operating system, and the applications that run on the server use the kernel for their core functions. The NetWare kernel is responsible for memory, process, task, and disk management. If we were to compare an operating system to the human body, the kernel would be the brain. The brain does not complete many of the functions (such as breathing and moving of limbs), but it does control them. Without the kernel, we would have several components working completely independently of each other.

Server Console

To actually control the NetWare server, you issue commands at the server console, which has a command prompt similar to DOS. However, the commands that are executed are not EXE or COM files, but NLMs (which we'll discuss in the following section).

The following is a partial list of some of the tasks that can be performed from the NetWare server console:

➤ Add and remove services

➤ Load and unload device drivers

➤ Load and unload programs

➤ Load and unload protocol drivers

➤ Mount and dismount volumes

➤ Reboot the server

➤ View connected users and workstations

➤ View memory usage

NetWare Loadable Modules (NLMs)

All the major operating systems currently on the market have components that connect (in essence, glue) their components together. In Windows NT, these components are known as *services*; in Unix, they are known as *daemons*; and in DOS or Windows 3.x/9x, they are known as *executable* or *command* files. With the NetWare operating system, they are known as *NLMs*.

NLMs are small applications that reside on the server and give the server added functionality in how it communicates with its components. They allow NetWare to connect its five main components (disk drives, LAN drivers, name space modules, management utilities, and server enhancements).

As with most server-based operating systems, you can usually load and unload these components (NLMs) without disrupting the operation of the server. In some cases, however, unloading an NLM can hinder or even "crash" a server. For example, if you were to remove the NLM that allows NetWare to communicate with its network boards, the server would no longer be able to operate properly. To load an NLM, you would issue the following command

```
LOAD NLM
```

where *NLM* is the module you are loading. To unload it, you would issue this command:

```
UNLOAD NLM
```

 With NetWare 5, the **LOAD** command itself is not necessary; you can just enter the name of the NLM at the prompt and the module will be loaded. In the preceding example, you could simply type in *"NLM"* to load it.

 We stated that NLMs can be easily unloaded. However, some NLMs will load other NLMs, and so on. When unloading these NLMs, you must unload them in the reverse order that you loaded them.

The four main types of NLMs in NetWare are listed in Table 15.1.

Table 15.1	The main NetWare NLMs.	
Name	**Extension**	**Description**
Disk driver	.HAM and .CDM	The disk-driver NLMs act as the translator between the NetWare server and the hardware storage devices. Remember that NLMs can be unloaded without affecting the server's operation, so you can unload the NLM that communicates with the CD-ROM drive while the server is still running. Be aware, however, that if you unload the NLM that communicates with the hard drive on which the SYS volume is located, the server will be shut down.
LAN driver	.LAN	The local area network (LAN) driver NLMs communicate between the server and the network boards that are installed in the server.

(continued)

Table 15.1	The main NetWare NLMs (continued).	
Name	**Extension**	**Description**
		As with the disk-driver NLMs, you can load and unload network board drivers without having to shut the server down, which is a great troubleshooting tool. (Note that if you unload the LAN driver, the network connection will be lost.)
Name space module	.NAM	The name space module NLMs allow NetWare to communicate and share information with non-DOS operating systems and file names. For example, if you store Macintosh files on the system, you need to load the MAC.NAM module.
NLM utilities	.NLM	The NLM utilities add services that are not automatically installed on the server. Most of the NLMs that you load into NetWare are applications and utilities that add functionality to the server.

Installing NetWare 5

Installing NetWare 5 is a fairly simple process, thanks to the NetWare 5 installation program. Although it's a simple program to run (you simply execute it and answer a few questions), it does have some powerful features, such as the automatic detection of hardware, the ability to choose and configure networking protocols, a graphical user interface (GUI) (a new feature of NetWare 5), and version checking of files to ensure that only updated files are copied to the server.

The entire NetWare 5 server installation process can be completed in 16 steps:

1. Meet the hardware requirements as set by Novell.

2. Prepare the network for the installation.

3. Prepare the computer for the installation.

4. Begin the installation.

5. Select the installation type and regional settings.

6. Select the storage adapters to be installed.

7. Select the storage devices and network boards to be installed.

8. Create a NetWare partition and a SYS volume.

9. Give the server a name.

10. Install the file system.

11. Install and configure the network protocols.

12. Choose a time zone.

13. Set up Novell Directory Services (NDS).

14. Install licenses.

15. Choose other networking products to install.

16. Customize the installation.

These 16 steps can be divided into 4 major parts (each of which are discussed in the following sections):

➤ Installation preparations

➤ Starting the installation program

➤ The text screens

➤ The graphics screens

Installation Preparations

Before you begin your NetWare 5 server installation, you should complete the following tasks:

1. Ensure that the server meets or exceeds the hardware levels as recommended by Novell. If you don't meet this criterion, you may find yourself having to abort the installation halfway through. With today's technology (assuming that you're installing NetWare 5 on a relatively new server), the minimum hardware requirements are not really an issue. Novell recommends the following:

   ➤ A Pentium-grade (or better) computer

   ➤ A VGA video card (Super VGA recommended)

   ➤ 550MB of disk space (50MB for the boot partition and 500MB, unpartitioned, for the NetWare partition)

   ➤ 64MB of RAM (128MB recommended for Java-based applications)

   ➤ One or more network boards

   ➤ A CD-ROM drive

2. Create and format a partition, using DOS. Make this partition approximately 50MB. You can use an existing DOS partition (or Windows 95/98) as well.

3. Choose whether you will be installing from the network or from the CD-ROM.

4. Choose a network protocol.

5. Decide whether the server will be installed into a new NDS tree or join an existing one.

Getting Started

To start the installation program, you have to make sure that you can boot to DOS, because the installation program will not run from Windows. Because the installation files are on a CD-ROM, you'll need to load any necessary drivers so you can access the CD-ROM drive.

Once you are in DOS and can access the CD-ROM drive, simply insert the NetWare 5 CD, switch to the drive assigned to the CD-ROM, type "install", and then press the Enter key.

The Text Screens

To complete the text phase of the NetWare 5 server installation, follow these steps:

1. When you execute the installation program, it loads a bare-bones version of NetWare that is used to complete the installation.

2. The next screen presents you with the NetWare license agreement. If you agree with the license agreement, press the F10 key.

3. Next, you're asked if you're performing a new server installation or upgrading an existing server. You can also specify the target installation directory for the server. (The server will be installed in the C:\NWSERVER directory by default.) Press the Enter key to continue.

4. The next screen asks you to choose the country codes and the keyboard type that will be used with this server. Make your configuration choices, highlight the Continue option, and press the Enter key.

5. Now choose the type of mouse that you have installed on your NetWare server:

   ➤ PS/2 (the default option)

   ➤ COM1

➤ COM2

➤ Other

Also, select your display type: VGA or Super VGA (the default option). Highlight the Continue option, and press the Enter key.

 Make sure the display type you choose here can be displayed on your system. If you choose the wrong one, you'll find that you may not be able to continue the installation when the installation program switches to the graphical section. Choose the VGA option to be safe. Doing so will ensure that the graphical section of the installation program will work. You can always change the display settings after the installation is completed.

6. The installation program will now copy the necessary files to the server, detect the storage devices and the network boards, and install the drivers for them.

7. Now, you create the NetWare partition, but you must be very careful because it's difficult to modify these settings after they are set. You can choose the default settings, which will create a single NetWare partition that will take all the unpartitioned space on your hard drive(s) and create a single SYS volume in it. Or, you can modify the partition information so it creates a NetWare partition and SYS volume more to your liking.

8. The installation program will now mount the SYS volume, as well as the CD-ROM drive, and start copying the rest of the necessary files. (These are the files for the graphical portion of the installation.)

The installation program will now switch to its graphical portion.

The Graphical Screens

When the installation program switches to the graphical screen, you know it has installed and executed a Java Virtual Machine (JVM). The installation is completed from within this Java-based screen. To continue with the graphical portion of the installation, follow these steps:

1. The first screen that appears—Server Properties—will ask you to choose a name for your server (see Figure 15.1). The installation program generates a server ID number and assigns it to the server. To continue to the next screen, click on the Next button.

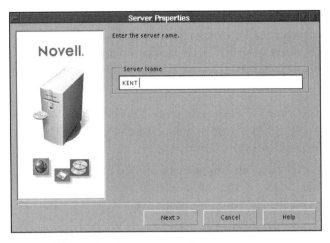

Figure 15.1 The Server Properties screen.

2. You can now add and modify volumes as needed (for example DATA, MAIL, and so on). Click on the Next button to continue.

3. The installation program asks if you would like all the volumes to be automatically mounted when the server starts up. Make your selection and click on the Next button to continue.

4. The installation program now enables you to configure the IP and/or IPX protocols (see Figure 15.2). If you have multiple network boards in your server, you need to configure them individually. To configure a network board, select it in the left window and configure the IP or IPX

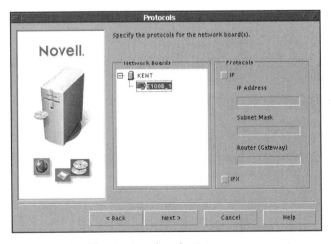

Figure 15.2 The Protocols selection screen.

protocols in the right window. For the IP protocol, you need the IP address, the subnet mask, and the router address (gateway). For the IPX protocol, you simply have to select it; the installation program sets the default frame types of Ethernet_II for TCP/IP and Ethernet 802.2 for IPX/SPX.

5. Choose your server's time zone and whether to use daylight-saving time (DST). Once you have completed your selections, click on the Next button to continue.

6. Choose how you would like NDS to be installed. You can choose to install to an existing NDS tree or to create a new NDS tree. Make your selection and click on the Next button to continue.

7. If you chose to create a new NDS tree, the screen shown in Figure 15.3 appears, and you have to complete the following tasks:

   ➤ Enter a name for the tree.

   ➤ Enter the context in the tree where you would like the server to reside. You can click on the browse button and add organizations and organizational units before proceeding.

   ➤ Enter the Admin name and Admin context. By default, the installation program calls the Admin user "Admin," and places the User object in the same context as that of the server.

   ➤ Enter the password and then confirm it.

   Click on the Next button to continue.

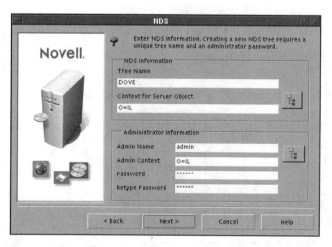

Figure 15.3 The new NDS tree configuration screen.

Note: *The installation program will now ensure that the NDS tree name you selected is unique and is not being used by another network. It then installs NDS onto your server.*

8. Once the installation program installs and configures NDS, it displays a window informing you of the configuration it used to install NDS on the server. You may want to write this information down for future reference. Click on the Next button to continue.

9. A licenses window will now appear. You can either insert a license diskette or choose to install the server without a license file. (You can always add or remove licenses after you complete the installation.) Make your selection and click on the Next button to continue.

10. The Additional Products And Services screen appears (see Figure 15.4). Choose any other products and/or services that you would like installed and click on the Next button.

11. The installation program now displays a screen confirming your installation choices. When you click on the Next button, the installation program will install all the server files and prompt you to reboot the server. The NetWare 5 server is now installed.

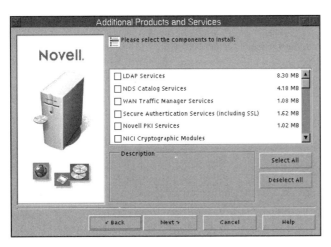

Figure 15.4   The Additional Products And Services screen.

Practice Questions

Question 1

> What is used to control the NetWare server?
>
> ○ a. The kernel
>
> ○ b. The server console
>
> ○ c. DOS
>
> ○ d. NLMs

The correct answer is b. The NetWare server is controlled through the server console. Although the kernel is the inner workings of the server, it's not used to configure the server. Therefore, answer a is incorrect. DOS is used only to start the server. Once the server is started, DOS drops out of the equation. Therefore, answer c is incorrect. NLMs are used to add functionality to the server; they don't control it. Therefore, answer d is incorrect.

Question 2

> Which program is used to execute (start) the NetWare server?
>
> ○ a. NWSERVER.EXE
>
> ○ b. START.EXE
>
> ○ c. NWSRVR.EXE
>
> ○ d. SERVER.EXE

The correct answer is d. The only program that is used to start the NetWare server is called SERVER.EXE and is located in the C:\NWSERVER directory by default. Therefore, answers a, b, and c are incorrect.

Question 3

When configuring the IP protocol during the installation process, what is the frame type that is selected automatically?

○ a. Ethernet_II

○ b. Ethernet_SNAP

○ c. Ethernet 802.2

○ d. Ethernet 802.3

The correct answer is a. The frame type that is specified by the installation wizard is Ethernet_II. Therefore, answers b, c, and d are incorrect.

Question 4

When configuring the IPX protocol during the installation process, what is the frame type that is selected automatically?

○ a. Ethernet_II

○ b. Ethernet_SNAP

○ c. Ethernet 802.2

○ d. Ethernet 802.3

The correct answer is c. The frame type that is specified by the installation wizard is Ethernet 802.2. Therefore, answers a, b, and d are incorrect.

Question 5

What is the name of the program used to install a NetWare server or client?

○ a. INSTALLED

○ b. SETUP

○ c. INSTALL

○ d. CREATE

The correct answer is c. Running INSTALL from the CD will begin a server or client installation. INSTALLED, SETUP, and CREATE are not valid program names. Therefore, answers a, b, and d are incorrect.

Question 6

Which of the following are NLMs in NetWare? [Choose the best answers]

❑ a. Disk drivers

❑ b. LAN drivers

❑ c. Name Space Modules

❑ d. NLM Utilities

All of the answers are examples of NLMs. Therefore, answers a, b, c, and d are all correct.

Need To Know More?

 For more information on installing NetWare 5, check the NetWare 5 online documentation with keyword searches on "installing NetWare," "kernel," "name space," "NetWare Loadable Modules," and "server console."

 www.novell.com/documentation/en/nw5/nw5/nw5docui/ index.html features the NetWare 5 documentation.

Sample Test

In this chapter, we provide pointers to help you develop a successful test-taking strategy, including how to choose proper answers, how to decode ambiguity, how to work within the Novell testing framework, how to decide what you need to memorize, and how to prepare for the test. At the end of the chapter, we include 77 questions on subject matter pertinent to Novell Test 050-639: "NetWare 5 Administration." Good luck!

Questions, Questions, Questions

There should be no doubt in your mind that you're facing a test full of specific and pointed questions. NetWare 5 Administration is a form exam that consists of 77 questions that you can take up to 105 minutes to complete. This means you must study hard so you can answer as many questions as possible correctly, without resorting to guesses.

Note: We expect Novell to change this test to adaptive format eventually. Please see Chapter 1 for more information on adaptive testing.

For this exam, questions belong to one of six basic types:

➤ Multiple-choice questions with a single answer

➤ Multiple-choice questions with multiple answers

➤ Multipart questions with a single answer

➤ Multipart questions with multiple answers

➤ Operate a simulated NetWare console or utility interface

➤ Pick one or more spots on a graphic

Always take the time to read each question at least twice before selecting an answer, and always look for an Exhibit button as you examine each question. Exhibits include graphics information related to a question. An exhibit is usually a screen capture of program output or GUI information that you must examine to analyze the question's contents and formulate an answer. The Exhibit button brings up graphics and charts used to help explain a question, provide additional data, or illustrate page layout or program behavior.

Not every question has only one answer; many questions require multiple answers. Therefore, it's important to read each question carefully, to determine how many answers are necessary or possible, and to look for additional hints or instructions when selecting answers. Such instructions often occur in brackets, immediately following the question itself (as they do for all multiple-choice, multiple-answer questions).

Simulation questions can be a mixed blessing. These task-oriented questions allow you to demonstrate your abilities to complete a certain task or to apply some analysis or management technique. The Net Ware Administrator utility appears particularly often in NetWare 5 simulation questions because it's the nerve center for NetWare administration. This means it's essential for you to spend some time familiarizing yourself with the key administration and management tools in NetWare 5 so you'll be ready when simulations show up in test questions.

Picking Proper Answers

Obviously, the only way to pass any exam is to select enough of the right answers to obtain a passing score. However, Novell's exams are not standardized like the SAT and GRE exams, and they can sometimes be quite a bit more challenging. In some cases, questions can be hard to follow or filled with technical vocabulary, and deciphering them can be difficult. In those cases, you may need to rely on answer-elimination skills. Almost always, at least one answer out of the possible choices for a question can be eliminated immediately because it matches one of these conditions:

➤ The answer does not apply to the situation.

➤ The answer describes a nonexistent issue, an invalid option, or an imaginary state.

➤ The answer may be eliminated because of the question itself.

After you eliminate all answers that are obviously wrong, you can apply your retained knowledge to eliminate further answers. Look for items that sound correct but refer to actions, commands, or features that are not present or not available in the situation that the question describes.

If you're still faced with a blind guess among two or more potentially correct answers, reread the question. Try to picture how each of the possible remaining answers would alter the situation. Be especially sensitive to terminology; sometimes the choice of words ("remove" instead of "disable") can make the difference between a right answer and a wrong one.

Only when you've exhausted your ability to eliminate answers, and you're still unclear about which of the remaining possibilities is correct, should you guess at an answer (or answers). Guessing gives you at least some chance of getting a question right; just don't be too hasty when making a blind guess.

Decoding Ambiguity

Novell exams have a reputation for including straightforward questions. You won't have to worry much about deliberate ambiguity, but you will need a good grasp of the technical vocabulary involved with NetWare and related products to understand what some questions are trying to ask. In our experience with numerous Novell tests, we've learned that mastering the lexicon of Novell's technical terms pays off on every exam. The Novell tests are tough but fair, and they're deliberately made that way.

However, you need to brace yourself for one set of special cases. Novell tests are notorious for their use of double negatives and similar circumlocutions, such as "What item is not used when creating a User object?" Our guess is that Novell includes such Byzantine language in its questions because it wants to make sure its examinees can follow instructions to the letter, no matter how strangely worded those instructions might be. Although this may seem like a form of torture, it's actually good preparation for those circumstances where you have to follow instructions from technical manuals or training materials, which are themselves not quite in the same ballpark as "great literature" or even "plain English." Even though we've been coached repeatedly to be on the lookout for this kind of stuff, it still fools us anyway from time to time. So, you need to be on the lookout yourself and try to learn from our mistakes.

The only way to beat Novell at this game is to be prepared. You'll discover that many exam questions test your knowledge of things that are not directly related to the issue raised by a question. This means that the answers you must choose from, even incorrect ones, are just as much a part of the skill assessment as the question itself. If you don't know something about most aspects of NetWare 5, you may not be able to eliminate obviously wrong answers because they relate to a different area of the operating system than the one that's addressed by the question at hand. In other words, the more you know about NetWare in general, the easier it will be for you to tell a right answer from a wrong one.

Questions often give away their answers, but you have to read carefully to see the clues that point to those answers. Often, subtle hints appear in the question text in such a way that they seem almost irrelevant to the situation. You must realize that each question is a test unto itself and that you need to inspect and successfully navigate each question to pass the exam. Look for small clues, such as the mention of utilities, services, and configuration settings. Little things like these can point at the right answer if properly understood; if missed, they can leave you facing a blind guess.

Because mastering the technical vocabulary is so important to testing well for Novell, be sure to brush up on the key terms presented at the beginning of each chapter. You may also want to read through the Glossary at the end of this book the day before you take the test.

Working Within The Framework

The test questions appear in random order, and many elements or issues that receive mention in one question may also crop up in other questions. It's not uncommon to find that an incorrect answer to one question is the correct answer to another question, or vice versa. Take the time to read every answer to each question, even if you recognize the correct answer to a question immediately. That extra reading may spark a memory or remind you about a feature or function that helps you on another question later in the exam.

Review each question carefully; test developers love to throw in a few tricky questions. Often, important clues are hidden in the wording or special instructions. Do your best to decode ambiguous questions; just be aware that some questions will be open to interpretation.

You might also want to jot some notes on your piece of paper or plastic sheet about questions that contain key information.

Don't be afraid to take notes on what you see in various questions. Sometimes, what you record from one question—especially if it isn't as familiar as it should be or reminds you of the name or use of some utility or interface details—can help you with other questions later in the test.

Deciding What To Memorize

The amount of memorization you must undertake for an exam depends on how well you remember what you've read and how well you know the software by heart. If you're a visual thinker, and you can see drop-down menus and dialog boxes in your head, you won't need to memorize as much as someone who's less visually oriented. The tests will stretch your recollection of NetWare 5 concepts, tools, and technologies.

At a minimum, you'll want to memorize the following types of information:

➤ The various components of NetWare 5

➤ The tasks you'll be responsible for as a NetWare Administrator

➤ The various NDS objects

➤ An overview of the NetWare 5 Java console's layout and functions

➤ The concepts and configuration of Novell Distributed Print Services (NDPS)

➤ The characteristics of the various types of NetWare security

➤ Using Z.E.N.works to manage workstations and client software

If you work your way through this book and try to exercise the various capabilities of NetWare 5 that are covered throughout, you should have little or no difficulty mastering this material. Also, don't forget that The Cram Sheet at the front of the book is designed to capture the material that's most important to memorize; use this to guide your studies as well. Finally, don't forget to obtain and use Novell's test objectives for Course 560 as part of your planning and preparation process.

Preparing For The Test

The best way to prepare for the test—after you've studied—is to take at least one practice exam. We've included one in this chapter for that reason; the test questions are located in the pages that follow. (Unlike the preceding chapters in this book, the answers don't follow the questions immediately; you'll have to flip to Chapter 17 to review the answers separately.)

Give yourself no more than 105 minutes to take the exam, keep yourself on the honor system, and don't look at earlier text in the book or jump ahead to the answer key. When your time is up, or you've finished the questions, you can check your work in Chapter 17. Pay special attention to the explanations for the incorrect answers; these can also help to reinforce your knowledge of the material. Knowing how to recognize correct answers is good, but understanding why incorrect answers are wrong can be equally valuable.

Taking The Test

Relax. Once you're sitting in front of the testing computer, there's nothing more you can do to increase your knowledge or preparation. Take a deep breath, stretch, and start reading that first question.

There's no need to rush; you have plenty of time. If you can't figure out the answer to a question after a few minutes, though, you may want to guess and move on to leave more time for remaining unanswered questions. Remember that both easy and difficult questions are intermixed throughout the test in random order. Because you're taking a form test, you should watch your time carefully: Try to be one-quarter of the way done (20 questions) in at least 26 minutes, halfway done (39 questions) in at least 52 minutes, and three-quarters done (58 questions) in 78 minutes.

Set a maximum time limit for questions and watch your time on long or complex questions. If you hit your time limit, you need to guess and move on. Don't deprive yourself of the opportunity to see more questions by taking too long to puzzle over answers, unless you think you can figure out the correct answer. Otherwise, you're limiting your opportunities to pass.

That's it for pointers. Here are some questions for you to practice on.

Question 1

What are two characteristics of a NetWare server? [Choose the two best answers]

❑ a. It has a preemptive multitasking operating system.

❑ b. It can act as a server and workstation at the same time.

❑ c. It is used to store the NetWare file system.

❑ d. Access to file server resources is done through a client.

Question 2

Which of the following duties is not typical of the responsibilities of a NetWare administrator?

○ a. Installing clients on workstations

○ b. Installing NetWare 5 on file servers

○ c. Repairing workstation PCs

○ d. Setting up network printing

Question 3

Which of the following is not a characteristic of the NDS design?

○ a. No resource on a NetWare 5 network may be accessed except through NDS.

○ b. NetWare 5 can run without NDS if it's run as a standalone server.

○ c. All NetWare 5 servers on any given multiserver network contain NDS.

○ d. All NetWare 5 servers on any given multiserver network have access to any part of the NDS tree.

Question 4

Which of the following statements are false regarding NDS objects? [Choose the best answers]

❑ a. They all have definable properties and values.

❑ b. They may all be named using 84 characters or fewer.

❑ c. Three types of container objects are required to create an NDS tree.

❑ d. All container objects may contain leaf objects.

Question 5

What is the typeful distinguished name for the following typeless distinguished name?

`.Bsmith.Engineering.NewYork.Widgets`

○ a. CN=Bsmith

○ b. .OU=Engineering.OU=NewYork.O=Widgets

○ c. OU=Engineering.OU=NewYork.O=Widgets

○ d. .CN=Bsmith.OU=Engineering.OU=NewYork.O=Widgets

Question 6

Which of the following describes "current context" accurately? [Choose the best answer]

○ a. The location of the [Root] object relative to your current location

○ b. The name assigned to your current object in the NDS tree

○ c. The location of your cursor in NetWare Administrator

○ d. Your current location relative to the [Root] object

Question 7

Which of the following are incorrect examples of the typeful distinguished name for the user Jjonas, located in the HR organiza- tional unit of the Sprockets organization? [Choose the three best answers]

❑ a. Jjonas.HR.Sprockets

❑ b. U=Jjonas.OU=HR.O=Sprockets

❑ c. N=Jjonas.OU=HR.O=Sprockets

❑ d. CN=Jjonas.OU=HR.O=Sprockets

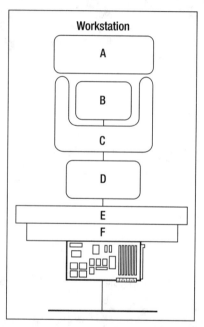

Figure 16.1 Use this figure for Questions 8 through 11.

Question 8

In Figure 16.1, which component should appear in section B?

○ a. TCP/IP and IPX protocols

○ b LAN driver

○ c. Application

○ d. Novell Client software

○ e. Operating system

Question 9

In Figure 16.1, which component should appear in section E?

○ a. TCP/IP and IPX protocols

○ b. LAN driver

○ c. Application

○ d. Novell Client software

○ e. Operating system

Question 10

In Figure 16.1, which component should appear in section D?

○ a. TCP/IP and IPX protocols

○ b. LAN driver

○ c. Application

○ d. Novell Client software

○ e. Operating system

Question 11

In Figure 16.1, which component should appear in section A?

○ a. TCP/IP and IPX protocols

○ b. LAN driver

○ c. Application

○ d. Novell Client software

○ e. Operating system

Question 12

What is the most fundamental object in the NDS tree?

○ a. [Root]

○ b. [Public]

○ c. User

○ d. Country

Question 13

Which of the following are true concerning User objects? [Choose the three best answers]

❑ a. You can create a User object only in NetWare Administrator.

❑ b. You cannot create a User object without an entry in the last name field.

❑ c. You can assign User objects absolute access to any object and its properties in the NDS tree.

❑ d. To have access to a printer on the network, you must have a Printer object associated with your User object.

Question 14

You can run the ConsoleOne utility from a workstation if you have Java loaded on your workstation.

○ a. True

○ b. False

Question 15

Which of the following statements accurately describe the Template object? [Choose the three best answers]

❑ a. You may alter the properties of many User objects at the same time by making the changes to the Template object.

❑ b. You use the Template object to create multiple users from a database of usernames.

❑ c. You use the Template object to manage the property fields of large groups of users.

❑ d. You can modify objects created and assigned to a Template object by making changes to the Template object.

Question 16

Currently, which object cannot be created in ConsoleOne?

○ a. User

○ b. Group

○ c. Country

○ d. Organizational Unit

○ e. Organization

Question 17

Which of the following items is not a valid component of the NetWare licensing system?

○ a. Server license container

○ b. User license

○ c. License Certificate object

○ d. Server license

○ e. Container license

Question 18

To create a Template object in ConsoleOne, which of the following mandatory fields do you need to fill in?

○ a. Define Additional Properties

○ b. Members

○ c. Template Name

○ d. None of the above

Question 19

Which of the following are not valid gateways for NetWare 5 NDPS? [Choose the two best answers]

❑ a. IBM gateway

❑ b. Hewlett-Packard gateway

❑ c. Novell gateway

❑ d. Xerox gateway

❑ e. Microsoft gateway

Question 20

Which of the following are true concerning a public access printer? [Choose the three best answers]

- ❑ a. It has no security.
- ❑ b. It was not available in NetWare 4.11.
- ❑ c. It's an NDS object.
- ❑ d. It's a Printer Agent.

Question 21

Which of the following statements describe the NDPS Manager? [Choose the three best answers]

- ❑ a. It's a place to store Printer Agents.
- ❑ b. It determines who can access Printer Agents.
- ❑ c. It's used to improve maintenance.
- ❑ d. You use it to create Printer Agents.

Question 22

You want to create an NDPS printer queue. Which of the following conditions must first be met?

- ○ a. You must be logged into the network and have NetWare Administrator running in Create mode.
- ○ b. You must be in the container object in which you want the queue created.
- ○ c. You must have a valid container license installed in NDS and assigned to a server.
- ○ d. You must have the proper rights to create the object.
- ○ e. None of the above.

Question 23

Which of the following are not components of the NetWare file system? [Choose the two best answers]

❑ a. File

❑ b. CD-ROM

❑ c. Disk drive

❑ d. Subdirectory

❑ e. Directory

❑ f. Volume

Question 24

Legacy applications that are not aware of the NetWare file system cannot access applications on a NetWare server unless _____.

○ a. Windows Explorer is running on the workstation

○ b. the **MAP** command is used to make the application available

○ c. the IPX protocol is bound to the application interface

○ d. a drive letter is made available through the **CAPTURE** command

Question 25

You must salvage a file that existed within a directory you deleted. Where will you find the file?

○ a. In the recycle bin

○ b. Nowhere; once you delete a directory, the files are not recoverable

○ c. In the parent directory of the deleted directory

○ d. In the DELETED.SAV directory at the root of the volume where the directory existed

Question 26

You are required to restrict volume space for the "operations" directory on your file server. Which utility would you use to perform this task?

- ○ a. FILER
- ○ b. NetWare Administrator
- ○ c. FLAG
- ○ d. Windows Explorer

Question 27

What are the minimum rights necessary to execute an application? [Choose the best answer]

- ○ a. R
- ○ b. F
- ○ c. RF
- ○ d. W
- ○ e. A

Question 28

If you have security equivalence to another user, which of the following can you do? [Choose the best answer]

- ○ a. You can perform the same actions as the object you are security equivalent to, plus any additional rights you have been assigned by other means.
- ○ b. You can perform the same actions as the object to which you're made security equivalent.
- ○ c. You can perform none of the actions of the object you're security equivalent to, except assigning security equivalence to other objects.
- ○ d. You can perform the same actions as the object to which you're security equivalent, except those actions restricted by rights blocked in the IRF.

Question 29

Which file and directory concept allows a User object to receive rights in a directory that has no trustees listed in its ACL?

- ○ a. Explicitly assigned trustee rights
- ○ b. Trustee security
- ○ c. Inheritance
- ○ d. Trusteeship

Question 30

What are the two ways an object can receive Supervisor rights to the file system without being made a trustee of any file or directory? [Choose the two best answers]

- ❑ a. By being the creator of a Server object
- ❑ b. By being the trustee of a Server object with Supervisor rights to that server
- ❑ c. By being the creator of a Volume object
- ❑ d. By being the trustee of a Volume object with Supervisor rights to that volume

Question 31

What is the most secure model for assigning file and directory security?

- ○ a. Assign maximum file and directory rights at the higher levels and fewer rights at the lower levels.
- ○ b. Assign fewer file and directory rights at the higher levels with increasing rights at the lower levels.
- ○ c. Distribute rights as they are needed.
- ○ d. Allow the users to determine the rights they require.

Question 32

Which of the following is the most commonly used login script for mapping network drives?

○ a. Profile

○ b. Container

○ c. Default

○ d. User

Question 33

A profile login script will only execute under which of the following conditions? [Choose the three best answers]

❑ a. The User object must have Read right to the login property of the Profile object.

❑ b. The User object must have Read right to the login directory on the Profile object.

❑ c. The User object must be a trustee of the Profile object.

❑ d. The User object must have the Profile object selected in its login script property page.

Question 34

In what order do login scripts execute? [Choose the two best answers]

❑ a. Default, container, user profile

❑ b. Container, profile, user

❑ c. Container, profile, default

❑ d. Container, profile, user, default

Question 35

The correct syntax to map a drive to an NDS volume with a physical name of vol3: is _____.

○ a. **map s:=server/sys**

○ b. **Map s:=server\VOL3:**

○ c. **map s:=server_vol3 :**

○ d. **MAP S:=SERVER_VOL3 :**

Question 36

The default login script always executes last.

○ a. True

○ b. False

Question 37

Which of the following are not object rights? [Choose the two best answers]

❏ a. Inheritable

❏ b. Add/Remove Self

❏ c. Create

❏ d. Browse

❏ e. Delete

❏ f. Supervisor

❏ g. Rename

❏ h. Compare

Question 38

When you create a user's home directory in NetWare Administrator, which of the following rights does the directory automatically receive? [Choose the four best answers]

❑ a. File Scan

❑ b. Read

❑ c. Erase

❑ d. Create

❑ e. Supervisor

❑ f. Modify

Question 39

The file-system inheritance rules are different from the NDS in that you can block the Supervisor right in NDS but cannot in the file-system rights.

○ a. True

○ b. False

Question 40

A trustee is granted the Read right to all properties using the All Properties option. The same trustee is then granted the Write right to the Employee Number property under the Selected Properties option. What will the trustee's effective right be on the Employee Number property?

○ a. He will be granted the Read and Write rights.

○ b. He will be granted the Write right because the rights assigned through the Selected Properties option override those assigned in the All Properties option.

○ c. He will be granted the Read right because the rights assigned through the All Properties option override those assigned in the Selected Properties option.

○ d. He will be granted no rights because the two cancel each other out.

Question 41

You grant the user Joanne the Create right to the organization NW_Cram. Assuming she has no explicit assignments at the Payroll container, will she have the Create right to the Organizational Unit object Payroll within NW_Cram (OU=Payroll.O=NW_Cram)? [Choose the best answer]

○ a. She will if the Inheritable right at the NW_Cram level has not been deselected.

○ b. She will if no IRF is blocking the Create right.

○ c. She will if both a and b are true.

○ d. She will regardless of the effect of a or b.

Question 42

Application Launcher supports load balancing. When does load balancing occur?

○ a. When an application becomes unavailable on one server and a copy on another server takes its place

○ b. When a server becomes unavailable and another takes its place

○ c. When one server becomes too busy and another is made available to share other applications

○ d. When Application Launcher makes a duplicate copy to share the traffic when one application becomes too busy

Question 43

An AXT file, when used to configure a Template object to deploy NAL.EXE, can be edited with a text editor.

○ a. True

○ b. False

Question 44

Which of the following are benefits of using Application Launcher? [Choose the two best answers]

❑ a. Reduced NDS partitioning requirements

❑ b. Reduced licensing costs

❑ c. Reduced cost of network ownership

❑ d. Reduced support costs for performing software upgrades

Question 45

The correct command-line parameter for executing NAL.EXE consecutively from a login script is:

○ a. #\\fs2\sys\public\NAL.EXE/con

○ b. @\\fs2\sys\public\NAL.EXE/x

○ c. #\\fs2\sys\public\NAL.EXE

○ d. @\\fs2\sys\public\NAL.EXE

Question 46

Application Launcher supports DOS if which of the following conditions is true?

○ a. You have the 32-bit NetWare Client installed correctly.

○ b. You remove any Windows references from the FAT.

○ c. No conditions are necessary, because DOS has always been supported.

○ d. There are no conditions that will enable Application Launcher to run in DOS.

Question 47

The SnAppShot utility is not used to _____, _____, or _____. [Choose the three best answers]

❏ a. take a picture of a workstation while installing an application

❏ b. create application text files

❏ c. create Application objects

❏ d. create Application Template objects

Question 48

What is an Alias object used for?

○ a. To access objects in other contexts without navigating to them

○ b. To access objects in other NDS trees without navigating to them

○ c. To access other container objects in the NDS tree by pointing to them with relative distinguished names

○ d. Both a and b

Question 49

Novell's recommended maximum number of levels in an NDS tree is six.

○ a. True

○ b. False

Question 50

How can you ensure the current context is set to be workstation specific during the login process? [Choose the best answer]

○ a. Put the **CONTEXT** command in the login script object.

○ b. Set the name context in the Novell NetWare Client Properties dialog box.

○ c. Put the **CONTEXT** command in one of the definable login scripts.

○ d. Set the name context in the Login Properties dialog box.

Question 51

Which command is used to set the context in the default login script?

○ a. **#CONTEXT** *distinguished_name*

○ b. **SET CONTEXT** *distinguished_name*

○ c. **SET CONTEXT** *common_name*

○ d. **@CONTEXT** *common_name*

○ e. None of the above

Question 52

Which NetWare feature helps you simplify the login process? [Choose the best answer]

○ a. The ability to set global context

○ b. The ability to set current context

○ c. The ability to change contexts

○ d. The ability to set context before login

Question 53

What is not a benefit of a well-planned NDS tree design?

- ○ a. It provides enhanced structural integrity.
- ○ b. It's easier to manage.
- ○ c. It provides fault tolerance.
- ○ d. It decreases network traffic.

Question 54

You want to access a directory located in a different context. Which type of object would you use?

- ○ a. Volume Map object
- ○ b. Directory Map object
- ○ c. Directory Access object
- ○ d. Directory object map

Question 55

An Application object is not used to _____, _____, or _____. [Choose the three best answers]

- ❏ a. provide location-independent access to User objects
- ❏ b. provide location-specific access to applications on other networks
- ❏ c. provide an easy way of uninstalling applications
- ❏ d. provide access to applications in other contexts

Question 56

Which of the following three situations would require you to update Workstation object information? [Choose the three best answers]

❏ a. Two accounting employees left the company and new employees have replaced them. You must update the user information because it has changed.

❏ b. You added, removed, or moved workstations.

❏ c. You replaced a failed network board on a workstation.

❏ d. You rebooted the server.

❏ e. You noticed that a few of the workstations do not appear in the NDS tree.

Question 57

The manager of the Personnel Department wants to control the configuration of every workstation in the department. As the administrator, it's your job to figure out how to do this. How do you simplify administration and centralize control of the workstations?

○ a. Create and configure a Workstation Policy Package and associate it to each workstation in the department.

○ b. Create and configure a User Policy Package and associate it with the users in the department.

○ c. Create and configure a Workstation Policy Package; create a Group object and make the employees members; and then associate the Group object with the Policy Package.

○ d. Create and configure a User Policy Package, create a Template object, add the employees, and then associate the Template object with the Policy Package.

Question 58

Which of the following components are peripheral devices? [Choose the three best answers]

❑ a. External CD-ROM drive

❑ b. Network board

❑ c. Laser printer

❑ d. PCMCIA card

Question 59

Which of the following is not a NetWare service or resource?

○ a. Novell Storage Services

○ b. Application Explorer

○ c. Storage Management Services

○ d. Novell Intranet Access Server

Question 60

In NDS, there are more than three classes of leaf objects.

○ a. True

○ b. False

Question 61

The Country object is not a required object.

○ a. True

○ b. False

Question 62

Which of the following statements about the [Root] object are correct? [Choose the two best answers]

❑ a. It's a container object that contains the entire NDS tree.

❑ b. It can be replicated using a third-party utility.

❑ c. It cannot be created or deleted.

❑ d. It can be renamed only when the tree is reinstalled.

Question 63

Which type of objects cannot be created in an Organization object? [Choose the three best answers]

❑ a. Organization

❑ b. Organizational Unit

❑ c. [Root]

❑ d. Country

❑ e. Leaf

Question 64

Workstations register automatically under which conditions? [Choose the two best answers]

❑ a. A user must log in from the workstation.

❑ b. The workstation component of Z.E.N.works must be installed.

❑ c. The workstation must be running Windows 95 or Windows NT.

❑ d. The administrator must log in from each workstation using a registration account.

Question 65

Of the Policy Package objects listed, which three can be associated with container, Workstation, and Workstation Group objects? [Choose the three best answers]

❑ a. Container Package

❑ b. Windows 3.1 Workstation Package

❑ c. Windows 95 Workstation Package

❑ d. Windows NT Workstation Package

❑ e. Windows 3.1 User Package

❑ f. Windows 95 User Package

❑ g. Windows NT User Package

Question 66

If you have not installed the Desktop Management component of Z.E.N.works, can your workstations still register automatically with the NDS tree?

○ a. Yes

○ b. No

Question 67

The Remote Control Policy is found in each of the following, except _____ and _____. [Choose the two best answers]

❑ a. the User Policy Package

❑ b. the Workstation Policy Package

❑ c. the Container Policy Package

❑ d. the Template Policy Package

Question 68

When you prevent users from sending trouble tickets using the Configuration page of the Help Desk policy, which one of the four features available in the Help Requester Application will be unusable?

○ a. The Info button

○ b. The Call button

○ c. The Mail button

○ d. The Help button

Question 69

Assuming the remote control feature is configured and functional, who or what ultimately determines whether you can take control of a user's workstation?

○ a. The user

○ b. The administrator

○ c. The NetWare operating system

○ d. The help desk rules

Question 70

Of the buttons listed, which ones appear in the Help Requester application? [Choose the three best answers]

❑ a. The Help button

❑ b. The Remote button

❑ c. The Call button

❑ d. The Mail button

❑ e. The Create button

❑ f. The Insert button

Question 71

Where can you find the Help Desk Policy?

○ a. In the Workstation Policy Package only

○ b. In the User Policy Package only

○ c. In both the User and the Workstation Policy Packages

○ d. In neither the Workstation nor User Policy Packages

Question 72

Once the NetWare operating system is running, how do you run NetWare applications and utilities?

○ a. You load EXE files from ACONSOLE

○ b. You load NLM files from JCONSOLE

○ c. You load EXE files from RCONSOLE

○ d. You load NLM files from the server console

Question 73

From the DOS boot partition, what default directory and executable launches the NetWare 5 server?

○ a. C:\NWSERVER\NWSERVER.EXE

○ b. C:\NWSERVER\SERVER.EXE

○ c. C:\NW5SVR\SERVER.EXE

○ d. C:\NW5SVR\NWSERVER.EXE

Question 74

What is NetWare's default IP communication frame type?

○ a. Ethernet_802.3

○ b. Ethernet_802.2

○ c. Ethernet_II

○ d. Ethernet_SNAP

Question 75

What is NetWare's default IPX communication frame type?

○ a. Ethernet_802.3

○ b. Ethernet_802.2

○ c. Ethernet_II

○ d. Ethernet_SNAP

Question 76

What type of objects can be created in an Organization object? [Choose the two best answers]

❑ a. [Root]

❑ b. Country

❑ c. Organization

❑ d. Organizational Unit

❑ e. Leaf

Question 77

NetWare 5 requires you to use the **LOAD** command to load an NLM.

○ a. True

○ b. False

Answer Key

1. c, d	21. a, b, d	41. c	61. a
2. c	22. e	42. a	62. a, c
3. b	23. b, c	43. b	63. a, c, d
4. a, b, c, d	24. b	44. c, d	64. a, b
5. d	25. d	45. c	65. b, c, d
6. d	26. b	46. d	66. a
7. a, b, c	27. c	47. a, b, c	67. c, d
8. e	28. a	48. a	68. c
9. b	29. c	49. a	69. a
10. a	30. a, b	50. b	70. a, c, d
11. c	31. b	51. e	71. b
12. c	32. b	52. d	72. d
13. b, c, d	33. a, c, d	53. a	73. b
14. a	34. b, c	54. b	74. c
15. a, c, d	35. b	55. a, c, d	75. b
16. c	36. b	56. b, c, e	76. d, e
17. e	37. b, h	57. c	77. b
18. d	38. a, b, c, d, f	58. a, c, d	
19. a, e	39. b	59. d	
20. a, b, d	40. b	60. a	

Question 1

The correct answers are c and d. Although NetWare servers do multitask, the operating system is not preemptive. They also don't have workstation capabilities. Therefore, answers a and b are incorrect.

Question 2

The correct answer is c. Repairing PCs is a hardware problem and is not typically assigned to a network administrator. The other options are all true of a NetWare administrator's duties. Therefore, answers a, b, and d are incorrect.

Question 3

The correct answer is b. NDS is necessary even when you run NetWare as a standalone server. In the NDS design, no resource on a NetWare 5 network can be accessed except through NDS; all NetWare 5 servers on a given multiserver network contain NDS, and they all have access to any part of the NDS tree. Therefore answers a, c, and d are incorrect.

Question 4

Answers a, b, c, and d are all correct because they are false. The [Root] object does not have definable properties and values; objects must be named with 64 characters or fewer; Country and Organizational Unit objects are not required objects; and Country objects cannot contain leaf objects.

Question 5

The correct answer is d. A typeful distinguished name must have a leading period and the complete path to—and including—the organization container. It must also include the common name of the leaf object (if there is one) and have the correct typeful name identifiers for all objects. Only answer d contains all of these. Therefore, a, b, and c are incorrect.

Question 6

The correct answer is d. Current context is defined as your current location in the NDS tree relative to the [Root]. The location of the [Root] object is constant; it does not change. Therefore, answer a is incorrect. There's no such thing as a current object. Therefore, answer b is incorrect. And the location of your cursor in NetWare Administrator has no bearing on your current context. Therefore, answer c is incorrect.

Question 7

The correct answers are a, b, and c. Answer a is a typeless distinguished name, and answers b and c have unknown identifiers for their common names. Answer d is the typeful distinguished name for Jjonas and is therefore incorrect.

Question 8

The correct answer is e. The operating system is located in the second section. The components of the workstation, from the network board up, are the LAN driver, the TCP/IP and IPX protocols, the Novell Client software, the operating system, and the application. Therefore, answers a, b, c, and d are incorrect.

Question 9

The correct answer is b. The LAN driver is located in the fifth section. The components of the workstation, from the network board up, are the LAN driver, the TCP/IP and IPX protocols, the Novell Client software, the operating system, and the application. Therefore, answers a, c, d, and e are incorrect.

Question 10

The correct answer is a. The communication protocols (such as IP and IPX) are located in the fourth section. The components of the workstation, from the network board up, are the LAN driver, the TCP/IP and IPX protocols, the Novell Client software, the operating system, and the application. Therefore, answers b, c, d, and e are incorrect.

Question 11

The correct answer is c. The application is located in the first section. The components of the workstation, from the network board up, are the LAN driver, the TCP/IP and IPX protocols, the Novell Client software, the operating system, and the application. Therefore, answers a, b, d, and e are incorrect.

Question 12

The correct answer is c. The User object is the most fundamental object in the NDS database because all resources in the NDS database represent resources that are associated with the User object(s) that access them. Therefore, answers a, b, and d are incorrect.

Question 13

The correct answers are b, c, and d. You can create User objects in three other NetWare utilities in addition to NetWare Administrator—ConsoleOne, NETADMIN, and UIMPORT. Therefore, answer a is incorrect.

Question 14

The correct answer is a, true. You can run the ConsoleOne utility from a workstation if you have Java loaded on it.

Question 15

The correct answers are a, c, and d. Answer b is incorrect because you use the UIMPORT utility, not the Template object, to create multiple users from a database of usernames.

Question 16

The correct answer is c. The Country object is the only one listed that cannot be created in ConsoleOne. Therefore, answers a, b, d, and e are incorrect.

Question 17

The correct answer is e, because the container license is not a valid component of the NetWare licensing system. All the other objects listed are valid components. Therefore, answers a, b, c, and d are incorrect.

Question 18

The correct answer is d. You cannot create a Template object in ConsoleOne. Therefore, answers a, b, and c are incorrect.

Question 19

The correct answers are a and e. IBM and Microsoft do not ship gateways with NetWare 5. Hewlett-Packard, Novell, and Xerox are all valid gateways for NetWare 5. Therefore, answers b, c, and d are incorrect.

Question 20

The correct answers are a, b, and d. A public access printer is not an NDS object. Therefore, answer c is incorrect.

Question 21

The correct answers are a, b, and d. The NDPS Manager does not affect printer maintenance. Therefore, answer c is incorrect.

Question 22

The correct answer is e. There is no such object as an NDPS printer queue. Therefore, a, b, c, and d are incorrect.

Question 23

The correct answers are b and c. CD-ROMs and disk drives are not components of the NetWare file system. The five components that make up the NetWare file system are servers, volumes, directories, subdirectories, and files. Therefore, answers a, d, e, and f are incorrect.

Question 24

The correct answer is b. You use the **MAP** command to map a drive letter that is recognized by every version of DOS and Windows. Answer a is incorrect because Windows Explorer is unnecessary. Answer c is incorrect because the IPX protocol is unrelated and cannot be bound to the application interface. The **CAPTURE** command is used elsewhere in NetWare. Therefore, answer d is incorrect.

Question 25

The correct answer is d. Deleted files are saved in the DELETED.SAV directory at the root of the volume where the directory existed. Answer a is incorrect because the recycle bin does not contain files deleted from NetWare volumes. The files are still recoverable and they are not in the parent directory of the deleted directory. Therefore, answers b and c are incorrect.

Question 26

The correct answer is b. NetWare Administrator can be used to restrict volume space. FILER, FLAG, and Windows Explorer do not allow you to restrict volume space usage for a directory. Therefore, answers a, c, and d are incorrect.

Question 27

The correct answer is c. You need both the Read (R) and File Scan (F) rights to execute an application. Therefore, answers a and b are not the "best" answers and are incorrect. Write (W) and Access Control (A) are not the minimum rights necessary to execute an application. Therefore, d and e are incorrect.

Question 28

The correct answer is a. Although answer b is true, it's not the best answer. Therefore, answer b is incorrect. The statements in answers c and d are not true and are therefore incorrect.

Question 29

The correct answer is c. Inheritance allows a User object to receive rights in a directory that has no trustees listed in its ACL. Explicitly assigned trustee rights obviously contain trustees. Therefore, answer a is incorrect. "Trustee security" is meaningless in this context. Therefore, answer b is incorrect. Trusteeship does not adequately describe indirectly acquired rights. Therefore, answer d is incorrect.

Question 30

The correct answers are a and b. Supervisor rights to the file and directory system are passed on by virtue of having Supervisor rights to a Server object. No file and directory rights are passed on to another object by being a trustee or a creator of a Volume object. Therefore, answers c and d are incorrect.

Question 31

The correct answer is b. Minimal file and directory rights should be granted at the higher levels, and rights should be added only when and where they are necessary. This is the most secure model. Therefore, answers a, c, and d are incorrect.

Question 32

The correct answer is b. The container login script is the most commonly used login script for mapping network drives. The profile login script should only be used for commands that cannot be handled with a container login script. Therefore, answer a is incorrect. The default login script maps search drives, and the user login script should be used only when absolutely necessary. Therefore, answers c and d are incorrect.

Question 33

The correct answers are a, c, and d. There's no login directory on the Profile object. Therefore, answer b is incorrect.

Question 34

The correct answers are b and c. The container login script executes first, followed by the profile, and then the user login scripts. If there's no user login script, the default script executes. The default will not execute if there is a user login script. Therefore, answers a and d are incorrect.

Question 35

The correct answer is b. Note the commands are not case sensitive, so any combination of upper- and lowercase is okay. The syntax in answer a is for the wrong physical name. Therefore, answer a is incorrect. The last two answers are using spaces before the colon. Therefore, answers c and d are incorrect.

Question 36

The correct answer is b, false. If a user login script exists, the default login script does not execute at all.

Question 37

The correct answers are b and h. The Add/Remove Self and Compare rights are property rights. The object rights are Supervisor, Browse, Create, Delete, Inheritable, and Rename. Therefore, answers a, c, d, e, f, and g are incorrect. Use the mnemonic "Some Bob Cats Danced In (the) Rain" to remember the object rights.

Question 38

The correct answers are a, b, c, d, and f. The user's home directory automatically receives RWCEMFA (Read, Write, Create, Erase, Modify, File Scan, and Access Control) rights when NetWare Administrator creates a user's home directory when the User object is created. The Supervisor right must be assigned. Therefore, answer e is incorrect.

Question 39

The correct answer is b, false. In NDS security, an Inherited Rights Filter (IRF) can block the Supervisor right, whereas file-system security cannot.

Question 40

The correct answer is b. The property rights assigned under the Selected Properties option always take precedence to those rights assigned through the All Properties option. Therefore, answers a, c, and d are incorrect.

Question 41

The correct answer is c. Both a and b must be true for her to inherit the Create right. If an IRF is blocking the Create right or the Inheritable right is turned off, she will not inherit the Create right. Therefore, answers a, b, and d are incorrect.

Question 42

The correct answer is a. Application Launcher supports application load balancing, which does not include server load balancing, or making another copy of an application when the original application becomes unavailable. Therefore, answers b, c, and d are incorrect.

Question 43

The correct answer is b, false. An AXT file is not used to configure Template objects.

Question 44

The correct answers are c and d. Partitioning requirements and licensing costs are not affected by Application Launcher. Therefore, answers a and b are incorrect.

Question 45

The correct answer is c. NAL.EXE uses the # symbol to execute consecutively; it does not use command-line switches to execute, and it uses the @ symbol only to execute concurrently. Therefore, answers a, b, and d are incorrect.

Question 46

The correct answer is d. DOS is not supported by Application Launcher. Therefore, answers a, b, and c are incorrect.

Question 47

The correct answers are a, b, and c. SnAppShot takes before and after pictures (but not during an installation); "application text files" is meaningless in this context; and NetWare Administrator is used to create Application objects. SnAppShot is used to create Application Template objects. Therefore, answer d is incorrect.

Question 48

The correct answer is a. Many features in NetWare Administrator provide access to other objects. Alias objects are designed to avoid access to other objects through navigation, and they do not provide access to objects in other trees. Therefore, answers b, c, and d are incorrect.

Question 49

The correct answer is a, true. The recommended maximum number of levels in an NDS tree is six.

Question 50

The correct answer is b. There's no such thing as a login script object, and there's no Login Properties dialog box. Therefore, answers a and d are incorrect. If you put the **CONTEXT** command in a login script, it will usually be user, group, profile, or container specific. Therefore, answer c is incorrect.

Question 51

The correct answer is e. You cannot set the context in the default login script.

Question 52

The correct answer is d. The ability to set global or current contexts does not simplify the login process, nor does the ability to change contexts. Therefore, answers a, b, and c are incorrect.

Question 53

The correct answer is a. Enhanced structural integrity is not a benefit of NDS tree design. Therefore, answers b, c, and d are incorrect.

Question 54

The correct answer is b. A Volume Map object, Directory Access object, and a Directory object map are not valid objects. Therefore, answers a, c, and d are incorrect.

Question 55

The correct answers are a, c, and d. Application objects are used to provide location-independent access to applications on other networks. Therefore, answer b is incorrect.

Question 56

The correct answers are b, c, and e. The three instances that would force you to update the workstation information in the NDS tree are when you add, remove, or move workstations; when you replace a network board in a workstation; and when workstations do not appear in the NDS tree. Workstation NDS objects are user independent. Therefore, changing the users that operate the workstations will not change the Workstation NDS objects. Therefore, answer a is incorrect. The NDS information is stored in a database and does not need to be rebuilt or updated after a server reboot. Therefore, answer d is incorrect.

Question 57

The correct answer is c. You cannot manage the users by associating the Policy Package to the workstations. Associating users directly with the Policy Package will be burdensome because you have to manage the users individually, and using a Template object will not work. Therefore, answers a, b, and d are incorrect.

Question 58

The correct answers are a, c, and d. Network boards are internal to a PC or server, whereas a PCMCIA card is plugged in externally. Therefore, answer b is incorrect.

Question 59

The correct answer is d. Read carefully: There's no such thing as a Novell Intranet Access Server; however, there is a Novell Internet Access Server. Therefore, answer d is incorrect.

Question 60

The correct answer is a, true. There are numerous classes of leaf objects.

Question 61

The correct answer is a, true. The Country object is not a required object.

Question 62

The correct answers are a and c. The [Root] object cannot be replicated nor renamed. It's part of the NDS tree when the NDS is installed, so you do not create it, and it can only be named [Root]. Therefore, answers b and d are incorrect.

Question 63

The correct answers are a, c, and d. An Organization object cannot contain itself, nor can it contain [Root] or Country objects. Organization objects may contain only Organizational Unit objects or leaf objects. Therefore, answers b and e are incorrect.

Question 64

The correct answers are a and b. The user must log into the network to activate the registration agent, and the NetWare Client software must have the Z.E.N.works component installed on the workstation. The workstation registration process is platform-independent and works with all Windows platforms. Therefore, answer c is incorrect. There is no registration account. Therefore, answer d is incorrect.

Question 65

The correct answers are b, c, and d. Workstation Policy Packages can be associated with container, Workstation, and Workstation Group objects. Container Policy Packages can be associated with only container objects. Therefore, answer a is incorrect. User Policy Packages can be associated with container, User, and User Group objects. Therefore, answers e, f, and g are incorrect.

Question 66

The correct answer is a, yes. You can use the Application Launcher or a login script to automate the registration process. Therefore, answer b is incorrect.

Question 67

The correct answers are c and d. You will not find the Remote Control Policy in the Container Policy Package. And there is no such thing as a Template Policy Package. The Remote Control Policy is found in both the User and the Workstation Policies. Therefore, answers a and b are incorrect.

Question 68

The correct answer is c. Users will only be able to send a trouble ticket (via email) if two criteria are met. First, you must have a messaging infrastructure in place. Second, you must enable the Allow User To Send Trouble Ticket option in the Configuration page of the Help Desk policy. Therefore, answers a, b, and d are incorrect.

Question 69

The correct answer is a. If the user denies you access to remotely control his or her workstation, you cannot override it; the user's choice is final. Neither the administrator, the NetWare operating system, nor the help desk rules can ultimately determine whether you can remotely control a workstation. Therefore, answers b, c, and d are incorrect.

Question 70

The correct answers are a, c, and d. The four buttons are Mail, Call, Info, and Help. The other options don't appear in the Help Requester application. Therefore, answer b, e, and f are incorrect.

Question 71

The correct answer is b. The Help Desk Policy is found in only the User Policy Package, because only users (not workstations) have access to the Help Requester Application. Therefore, answers a, c, and d are incorrect.

Question 72

The correct answer is d. You cannot load EXE files from the NetWare console. Therefore, answers a and c are incorrect. There's no such console as JCONSOLE. Therefore, answer b is incorrect.

Question 73

The correct answer is b. The default directory for the NetWare 5 server is \NWSERVER, and the executable is SERVER.EXE. Therefore, answers a, c, and d are incorrect.

Question 74

The correct answer is c. The frame type that is specified by the installation wizard when you configure IP for NetWare is Ethernet_II. Therefore, answers a, b, and d are incorrect.

Question 75

The correct answer is b. The frame type that is specified for IPX by the installation wizard is Ethernet_802.2. Therefore, answers a, c, and d are incorrect.

Question 76

The correct answers are d and e. Organization objects may contain only Organizational Unit or leaf objects. Therefore, answers a, b, and c are incorrect.

Question 77

The correct answer is b, false. NetWare 5 no longer requires you to use the LOAD command to load an NLM. You can now type in the name of the NLM, and NetWare will load it.

Glossary

access control list (ACL)—A list of objects (trustees) that have been granted or denied rights to perform operations on a particular object. Also called the Object Trustees property and the Object Trustees (ACL) property.

Access Control right—A file-system right that allows users to changes to files, directories, and trustee assignments.

American Standard Code for Information Interchange (ASCII)—The 8-bit character system that is standard for transferring data between systems.

Application object—The fundamental NDS object employed by Application Launcher to efficiently and seamlessly deploy applications to users at workstations in the NDS tree.

Application Object Template (AOT) file—A file created using the SnAppShot utility to record the differences in a workstation before and after an application is installed. The AOT is subsequently used to create an Application object. The Application object is then triggered to deploy the application into a user's desktop environment.

Application Object Text Template (AXT) file—The manually editable version of the binary AOT file used by Application Launcher to produce Application objects. Because it's a text file, it's more flexible than the AOT file, but it's slower when used to create Application objects.

architecture—The logical design of a system.

Asynchronous Transfer Mode (ATM)—A high-speed data transmission protocol characterized by its ability to provide dynamic allocation of bandwidth using a fixed-size packet. An ATM packet is called a cell.

AUTOEXEC.NCF—A Novell server boot file.

Automatic Client Upgrade (ACU)—A utility that allows you to upgrade Novell Client for Windows NT software automatically. It contains the NWDETECT, NWSTAMP, and NWLOG applications.

Berkeley Internet Name Daemon (BIND)—Originally created by the University of California at Berkeley, it's a DNS server widely used by Internet Service Providers (ISPs) and hosts.

bindery—The flat database used in NetWare 3.x and earlier to contain User, Group, and Print objects. An NDS container can emulate a 3.x bindery, allowing the creation and management of Bindery objects for backward compatibility.

block suballocation—The process that allows partially filled disk data blocks to be segmented in 512 byte segments to recover the empty space. These empty subblocks can then store smaller files as needed.

Bootstrap Protocol (BOOTP)—This protocol gives a network node the ability to request IP address configuration. Unlike DHCP this is a one-time configuration.

Broker object—An NDS object created when you install Novell Distributed Print Services (NDPS). It provides three basic NDPS services: the Service Registry Service (SRS), Event Notification Service (ENS), and Resource Management Service (RMS). It's also called the NDPS Broker and NDPS Broker object.

Btrieve—One of the first database programs created for networks. It was purchased by Novell and used in NetWare 2.x, 3.x, 4.x, and 5. Btrieve is still widely used by networks around the world.

catalog—A flat-file database that holds information gathered from the NDS database.

Certificate Authority (CA)—A cryptographic verification form used to identify a person or other entity, such as a corporation.

Common Gateway Interface (CGI)—Server-side scripts that interact with input from a user, usually via a Web browser.

common name—The actual name you assign to an NDS leaf object (as opposed to an object's distinguished name).

Console Manager—The graphical Java applet that can run on the server console and on a Windows workstation that has the Java Runtime Environment (JRE) installed.

ConsoleOne—The NetWare management utility that uses a Java GUI environment to allow you to perform basic administrative functions on NDS objects, access the file system, and edit NetWare configuration files in a Java text editor.

container object—An NDS object that can contain or hold other objects, in contrast to leaf objects, which cannot.

context—An object's location in the NDS directory structure.

controlled access printer—A printer that can be used only by NDS-authenticated users with sufficient permissions. Controlled access printers have corresponding NDS objects. Contrast with public access printers, which have no security and no corresponding NDS objects.

Country objects—Objects that can exist only between the [Root] object and an Organization object. The Country object is usually used to designate a country as a valid NDS container object for wide area networks (WANs) that employ a geographical NDS design. It can only have a valid two-letter international country code as its name, such as US.

current context—An object's current position in the NDS directory structure.

digital persona—How a user is represented on a network.

Directory services—Another way to refer to NDS.

Domain Name Server (DNS)—Machines that convert domain names (for example, zyxyx.com) to IP addresses, using databases of hostnames and IP addresses.

Domain Name System (DNS)—A naming service utilized by the Internet that translates hostnames into IP addresses.

drive mapping—A drive association, created using a workstation-based map utility (such as the Novell **MAP** command) that associates a drive letter with a directory or sub-directory on a hard drive. The drive letter association provides a way for the operating system to access files that reside on the hard drives of completely different operating systems.

Dynamic Host Configuration Protocol (DHCP)—A protocol that assigns dynamic, or temporary, IP configuration to workstations.

Dynamic Link Library (DLL) files—Files that are libraries of executable code linked to applications when the applications are run, rather than being compiled with a program's executable. The files may be shared by several applications because they are linked dynamically and exist as independent files on the hard drive.

effective rights—The rights you actually have in a given location in NDS or the NetWare file system. They are determined by adding all rights you have received by whatever means and subtracting all rights that have been revoked by the IRF or blocked by explicit assignments.

Ethernet—A network communications protocol characterized by its unique encapsulation of data (packet type), network board design, supported topology, and media type.

Ethernet cards—Network boards that provide Ethernet services for computers.

Event Notification Services (ENS)—A procedure that creates specific messages assigned by a network manager regarding any printer function, such as print queue or other actions.

Fiber Distributed Data Interface (FDDI)—A network communications protocol characterized mainly by its use of fiber media for data transmission.

File Transfer Protocol (FTP)—A TCP/IP protocol used to transfer data between remote machines.

FILER—A utility used to manage NetWare volumes and files.

forced run—An Application Launcher feature that allows you to enforce the loading of programs, files, patches, and utilities on a user's workstation when he or she logs in. No user intervention is allowed; therefore, a user cannot prevent the running of the installation.

Group object—An NDS object designed to represent groups of users in the NDS tree and to the NetWare operating system. Changes made to a Group object are passed on to all members of the group automatically.

GroupWise—An email, scheduling, and workgroup product developed by Novell that uses NDS to store configuration information.

Help Requester—A NetWare client side program used to aid and support a user on the network. It allows end users to access help resources.

Hierarchical Storage Management (HSM)—A data storage system that manages the movement of files between more expensive but faster media, such as hard drives, to less expensive but slower media, such as tapes, based on frequency of access. The process is generally transparent to the user.

hostname—The recognizable DNS name of a machine on a TCP/IP network.

Hot Plug PCI—A hardware specification that allows "hot swapping" of PCI cards so a machine doesn't have to be shut down when a new card is put in or removed.

HP printer gateway—One of several gateways for NDPS services to legacy printers. The HP printer gateway was developed by Hewlett-Packard specifically for its own printers. Other gateways include the Xerox gateway and the Novell gateway, the latter of which is generic and may be used with any brand printer.

Hypertext Markup Language (HTML)—The page description language used on the Web.

Hypertext Transfer Protocol (HTTP)—The standard set of rules that define how Web servers communicate with Web clients, or browsers.

Inheritable object property—A property that is enabled by default and allows object rights in the NDS tree to flow down the tree or be inherited by subordinate containers and the objects in them.

Inheritable property right—A property that is enabled by default and allows property rights in the NDS tree to flow down the tree or be inherited by subordinate containers and the objects in them.

Internetwork Packet Exchange (IPX)—Modeled after Xerox Corporation's Internetwork Packet protocol, XNS, this is the NetWare protocol that operates at the Network layer of the OSI model. IPX is sometimes used to include the entire protocol suite.

Internetwork Packet Exchange/Sequences Packet Exchange (IPX/SPX)— The native protocol stack for NetWare networks. SPX provides reliable connections and operates on the Transport layer, relying on IPX for lower level network functions.

IPX/IP gateway—Provides gateway or translation services between an IP-only network and IPX clients without an IP stack of their own through a Winsock interface. Functionality is limited to certain applications, such as Web clients, email, and FTP.

Java—Sun Microsystems' cross-platform programming language.

Java applets—Programs written in Java that run within a Java-compatible browser.

Java bean—A small piece of Java code written to perform a very specific function.

Java classes—Full-blown applications that are written in Java.

Java Virtual Machine (JVM)—A virtual, or non-physical, computer that executes Java code. The JVM provides hardware and operating system independence for Java applications.

jukebox—A system of multiple drives set up on a mechanism that swaps media when others are needed, just like the music jukeboxes popular in the 1950s.

kernel—The base of most operating systems. The kernel provides just the core functions deemed critical for the operating system. Further functionality is added by additional program modules.

LAN driver—A file containing software code that provides a communication link between the operating system and the network board.

leaf objects—A class of NDS objects that represent actual resources in the NDS tree and do not contain other NDS objects.

License Certificate object—An NDS leaf object that contains information about the software publisher, product, and its version. It also designates the number of licenses the certificate has, the number of licenses in use, and the number of licenses available.

Line Printer Daemon (LPD)—A standard for print services on TCP/IP networks, and is analogous to Rprinter in the NetWare world.

location independent—Access to a network resource that is not based on the resource's location. A resource can be moved and it will not affect the way it is accessed by the end user.

login script—A set of instructions that the network client executes during the login process.

MAPI-compliant—A term used to describe items that are compliant with Microsoft's Windows Messaging Application Programming Interface (MAPI). These items have increased ease of communication with Microsoft message services.

Media Access Control (MAC) address—The unique address hard coded into a network board that distinguishes it from all other network boards.

Message (MSG) files—Files that contain system or error messages.

multiprocessor—More than one CPU on an individual machine. Multiprocessor systems come in several architectures, including symmetric multiprocessing (SMP) and asymmetric multiprocessing.

multitasking—The ability to handle several tasks, generally giving the impression of simultaneous execution. Multitasking is managed either by time slicing execution between processes, multiple processors, or a combination of the two.

multithreading—The ability to run multiple threads within a program or computation.

native IP—Novell's term for its implementation of NCP and other high-level NetWare protocols over TCP/IP without use of an IPX stub.

NDIR—A NetWare utility somewhat like the **DIR** command in DOS, only more powerful.

NDPS Broker object—*See* Broker object.

NDPS Manager object—An NDS object that is a repository for NDPS Printer Agents. You must first create an NDPS manager in NDS before you can create Printer Agents that reside on file servers.

NDS object—Any object in the NDS tree. NDS objects can be divided into the subtypes [Root], container, and leaf.

NDS tree—The entire hierarchical NetWare Directory Services database of objects. If you have access to more than one tree, you must be authenticated to each tree to gain access to its resources.

NETADMIN—The text-based counterpart of NetWare Administrator. NETADMIN is a utility that is run from a DOS window or DOS workstation that enables you to manage the NDS tree and its objects without a GUI interface.

NetWare Administrator—NetWare's graphical utility for managing NDS databases. Also called NWAdmin, although it's not a trademarked term.

NetWare file system—NetWare's system of storing, manipulating, securing, retrieving, and otherwise managing files on disk drives connected to NetWare servers.

NetWare Loadable Module (NLM)—One of several types of NetWare server executables; the other types include DSK, CDM, HAM, LAN, NAM, and DLLs. Each executable has a specific function, with the NLM being the most general form.

Network Time Protocol (NTP)—An Internet standard for providing time synchronization. This protocol enhancement for TCP uses authoritative time servers to provide network time information through a hierarchy of time servers. NTP is similar, but not identical, to the timesync protocol for NetWare 4, which is still provided for NetWare 5 IPX servers.

Novell Directory Services (NDS)—Novell's directory service that stores information on the network resources and regulates their access.

Novell Distributed Print Services (NDPS)—A service that provides administrators the ability to control printing through NDS. It also provides bi-directional communications between control points, management applications and workstations, and network printers.

Novell gateway—*See* Novell printer gateway.

Novell IP gateway—*See* IPX/IP gateway.

Novell Licensing Services (NLS)—A service introduced with NetWare 4.11. NLS manages licensed applications, such as NetWare 5, in the NDS database.

Novell printer gateway—The means through which NDPS communicates with non-NDPS printers that do not have a proprietary gateway written for them.

Novell Storage Services (NSS)—An enhanced file system that overcomes many of the limitations of the traditional NetWare file system.

object classes—General types of objects in the NDS tree differentiated by their schema. Organization and Country are two different classes of objects. Each object class has a different set of properties that designate its purpose. The set of properties defines the object class.

Object Trustees property—The property of an object that lists the trustees of an object in its ACL. Also called the Object Trustees (ACL) property and simply ACL.

Open Systems Interconnection (OSI) reference model—The standard model for network protocols. It contains the following layers: Physical, Data Link, Network, Transport, Session, Presentation, and Application. Often called simply the OSI model.

optical drives—A drive that uses a laser to store information on media optically, instead of a magnetic head. Optical drives are generally removable, and have the advantages of being stable and long lasting. Technically, CD and DVD are optical drives, although the term is usually reserved for high-speed read/writable drives.

Organization objects—The class of container object that contains the subordinate objects that represent the resources of a specific organization in the NDS tree.

Point-to-Point Protocol (PPP)—A protocol developed by the Internet Engineering Task Force (IETF) to provide a more comprehensive dial-up alternative to the Serial Line Internet Protocol (SLIP).

Policy Package—NDS objects that allow you to create and maintain Workstation objects in the NDS tree. These policies are grouped into packages according to the types of objects (such as container, User, and Workstation objects) that the policies can be associated with.

Port Handler—A component of NDPS that provides communication between the Print Device Subsystem and the printer.

preemptive multitasking—An operating-system feature that allows the CPU to control when applications may execute. Preemptive multitasking provides some protection from poorly behaved applications but is characterized by higher processing overhead.

print queue—The temporary storage location (logical and/or physical) for documents sent to the printer but are waiting to be printed.

Printer Agent—The component of NDPS that provides the functionality that used to be provided by the print server, print queue, and printer. This entity must be created before an actual NDPS printer can be created in NDS.

Printer object—An object on the NDS structure symbolizing a physical printer.

processes—In the NetWare operating system, the number of simultaneous processes or threads that may execute. Each process takes a small amount of RAM for thread stack space and other storage locations, which is offset by the greater efficiency under heavy load. The number of processes is controlled by admin configurable settings accessed on the command line or the Servman and Monitor utilities.

Profile object—An NDS object that contains a common login script that executes for a set of users (assigned to the object) that exist in different containers or for a subset of users within a container.

public access printer—NDPS printers that are accessible to anyone on the network. Public access printers have no NDS objects or security.

Redundant Array of Independent Disks (RAID)—Multiple drives linked together via hardware or software, used to increase reliability. There are six recognized levels of RAID, with additional levels being developed. The exact features are highly dependent on the RAID level used.

remote control—A client mode of communication that allows a remote workstation to do all the processing, with the local machine merely transmitting screen updates and input, such as keyboard and mouse control.

remote control agent—The service that enables remote control of a workstation.

replica ring—The group of servers that stores copies of an NDS partition.

Resource Management Service (RMS)—A regulated system that provides centrally located resources to the rest of the network. Resources include drivers, printer definition files, fonts, banners, and so on.

Routing Information Protocol (RIP)—A protocol that allows routers to communicate and inform each other of routes to available networks. RIP is available on TCP/IP and IPX, but has generally been superceded by the Interior Gateway Protocol (IGP) and Open Shortest Path First (OSPF) on TCP/IP, and the NetWare Link Services Protocol (NLSP) on IPX.

Secure Socket Layer (SSL)—A standard for the secure exchange of data transmitted via public key encryption.

Semantic Agent layer—The NSS layer that stores modules loaded into the system.

Sequenced Packet Exchange (SPX)—In the IPX/SPX protocol suite, this protocol provides reliable data transfer between nodes, and is roughly equivalent to the TCP protocol. SPX is characterized by a connection setup, ensuring data receipt and session termination.

Server object—An object that is created automatically whenever you install NDS on a server. It represents the physical server as an object in the NDS tree.

Service Advertising Protocol (SAP)—A protocol used by IPX to broadcast information on available services. SAP is characterized by limited scalability countered by easy configuration.

Service Registry Service (SRS)—A broker system that gives public printers the ability to broadcast their information over the network.

SLP Directory Agent—An agent that builds a table of services from SAP and NDS for use by IP clients, as well as to advertise IP services to IPX clients.

SnAppShot—A Z.E.N.works application that takes a before and after scan to discover changes that an application install makes to a workstation. These changes are then made into an AOT file that is used to create Application objects in the NDS tree.

spooler—A temporary file location on a hard drive or in RAM, usually used for output, such as printing. Spool is an abbreviation for Simultaneous Peripheral Operation On Line. There is little practical distinction between a spooler and print queue.

STARTUP.NCF—A boot file for the NetWare server.

Storage Management Services (SMS)—Novell's suite of services that allow information on NetWare volumes to be archived and retrieved. Typically, SMS is used to send data to and retrieve data from a tape drive.

suballoaction—The means by which Novell maximizes both performance and available storage. NetWare volumes use suballocation to break down unused portions of larger blocks (that contain a segment of data but leave an unused and otherwise wasted piece of disk space) into smaller 512K blocks; therefore, data can be written to the smaller blocks.

subnet mask—The 32-bit number that separates an IP address into node and network components.

Supervisor object right—The right that allows you to perform any and all actions on an object. This right can be blocked by the IRF.

Supervisor right—The unrestricted right to perform any operation on any file or directory for which the right is granted. This right cannot be blocked by the IRF.

SYS volume—The mandatory name of the first volume on a NetWare file server.

Template object—This leaf object creates a "boiler plate" of information. This template is then used to create users. The Template object can contain information such as home directory paths, email accounts, and group memberships, along with many other properties.

threads—A logical program component that allows multitasking, and may run separately from other modules on a system. Also referred to as an *executable object*. Typically, a single program consists of many modules that create, run, and destroy operation threads as needed.

topology—The physical layout of a network. Examples are star, ring, and bus.

Transaction Tracking System (TTS)—A system that prevents corruption of data through tracking logical transactions from start to finish. TTS is the embedded tracking system in NetWare servers, and is used for basic system integrity in NDS and other Btrieve functions.

Transmission Control Protocol/Internet Protocol (TCP/IP)—Created by the Advanced Research Projects Agency (ARPA), the transmission protocol suite that is the standard used for Internet communications.

trustee—Objects with the rights to access certain network resources. A trustee is defined as an object in the access control list (ACL) that has access to an object. There are five different objects that can be designated as a trustee: Users, Groups, Organizational Roles, Parent containers, and [Public].

typeful naming—Used in distinguished naming of NDS objects where the object class is referred to before naming the object, such as CN=DOUGB.OU=CALGARY.O=ACME. Generally, you use typeful naming when typeless naming does not work properly. This can occur when you have Country objects in your tree.

typeless naming—Used in distinguished naming of NDS objects where the object class is not referred to and the syntax of the distinguished name is trusted to identify the object correctly, such as DOUGB.CALGARY.ACME.

Unicode—Standardized by the Unicode Consortium, a 16-bit code that is fixed-width and provides a single character to represent over 65,000 symbols (including letters and graphical symbols).

Uniform Resource Locator (URL)—An addressing system used to locate files on a network or the Internet. (for example, www.zyxyx.com).

Unix— An interactive time-sharing operating system developed in 1969 by a hacker to play game. This system developed into the most widely used computer operating system in the world, and it ultimately supported the birth of the Internet.

User Datagram Protocol (UDP) packet—An Internet transmission protocol that uses IP, but without the tracking of the data package as with TCP.

User object—An NDS object representing an individual user containing personal information and access privileges.

Video Electronics Standards Association (VESA)—A group committed to the standardization of VGA monitors.

Video Graphics Adapter (VGA)—The minimum standard for modern monitors. VGA displays at up to 640 by 480 pixels at 16 colors. Super VGA adheres to no one standard, but expands on the number of pixels, colors, or both.

virtual memory—A method of emulating physical memory with drive space.

VREPAIR—A NetWare utility used on traditional NetWare volumes to fix volume problems and remove namespace entries from the FAT and Directory Entry Table (DET).

Workstation Import Policy—A set of rules for naming Workstation objects and specifying they are created.

Workstation objects—NDS Objects that represent workstations attached to your network and enable you to manage them efficiently.

X Windows—A graphical environment commonly seen on Unix and Linux. ConsoleOne is an X Windows environment.

Xerox gateways—Proprietary gateways provided for non-NDPS printers in the NetWare

Xerox Network Services (XNS)—The basis of IPX. It utilizes a different encapsulation format than Ethernet.

Z.E.N.works (Zero Effort Networks)—A group of utilities for administrators, used to increase the ease of most network management tasks by making them centrally available.

Index

CORIOLIS HELP CENTER

Here at The Coriolis Group, we strive to provide the finest customer service in the technical education industry. We're committed to helping you reach your certification goals by assisting you in the following areas.

Talk to the Authors

We'd like to hear from you! Please refer to the "How to Use This Book" section in the "Introduction" of every Exam Cram guide for our authors' individual email addresses.

Web Page Information

The Certification Insider Press Web page provides a host of valuable information that's only a click away. For information in the following areas, please visit us at:

www.coriolis.com/cip/default.cfm

- Titles and other products
- Book content updates
- Roadmap to Certification Success guide
- New Adaptive Testing changes
- New Exam Cram Live! seminars
- New Certified Crammer Society details
- Sample chapters and tables of contents
- Manuscript solicitation
- Special programs and events

Contact Us by Email

Important addresses you may use to reach us at The Coriolis Group.

eci@coriolis.com

To subscribe to our FREE, bi-monthly on-line newsletter, *Exam Cram Insider*. Keep up to date with the certification scene. Included in each *Insider* are certification articles, program updates, new exam information, hints and tips, sample chapters, and more.

techsupport@coriolis.com

For technical questions and problems with CD-ROMs. Products broken, battered, or blown-up? Just need some installation advice? Contact us here.

ccs@coriolis.com

To obtain membership information for the *Certified Crammer Society*, an exclusive club for the certified professional. Get in on members-only discounts, special information, expert advice, contests, cool prizes, and free stuff for the certified professional. Membership is FREE. Contact us and get enrolled today!

cipq@coriolis.com

For book content questions and feedback about our titles, drop us a line. This is the good, the bad, and the questions address. Our customers are the best judges of our products. Let us know what you like, what we could do better, or what question you may have about any content. Testimonials are always welcome here, and if you send us a story about how an Exam Cram guide has helped you ace a test, we'll give you an official Certification Insider Press T-shirt.

custserv@coriolis.com

For solutions to problems concerning an order for any of our products. Our staff will promptly and courteously address the problem. Taking the exams is difficult enough. We want to make acquiring our study guides as easy as possible.

Book Orders & Shipping Information

orders@coriolis.com

To place an order by email or to check on the status of an order already placed.

coriolis.com/bookstore/default.cfm

To place an order through our online bookstore.

1.800.410.0192

To place an order by phone or to check on an order already placed.

CERTIFIED CRAMMER SOCIETY

PHI SLAMMA CRAMMA

A breed apart, a cut above the rest—a true professional. Highly skilled and superbly trained, certified IT professionals are unquestionably the world's most elite computer experts. In an effort to appropriately recognize this privileged crowd, The Coriolis Group is proud to introduce the Certified Crammer Society. If you are a certified IT professional, it is our pleasure to invite you to become a Certified Crammer Society member.

Membership is free to all certified professionals and benefits include a membership kit that contains your official membership card and official Certified Crammer Society blue denim ball cap emblazoned with the Certified Crammer Society crest— proudly displaying the Crammer motto "Phi Slamma Cramma"—and featuring a genuine leather bill. The kit also includes your password to the Certified Crammers-Only Web site containing monthly discreet messages designed to provide you with advance notification about certification testing information, special book excerpts, and inside industry news not found anywhere else; monthly Crammers-Only discounts on selected Coriolis titles; *Ask the Series Editor* Q and A column; cool contests with great prizes; and more.

GUIDELINES FOR MEMBERSHIP

Registration is free to professionals certified in Microsoft, A+, or Oracle DBA. Coming soon: Sun Java, Novell, and Cisco. Send or email your contact information and proof of your certification (test scores, membership card, or official letter) to:

Certified Crammer Society Membership Chairperson
THE CORIOLIS GROUP, LLC
14455 North Hayden Road, Suite 220, Scottsdale, Arizona 85260-6949
Fax: 480.483.0193 • Email: ccs@coriolis.com

APPLICATION

Name:

Address:

Society Alias:

Choose a secret code name to correspond with us and other Crammer Society members. Please use no more than eight characters.

Email: